THE MEANINGS OF DEATH IN RABBINIC JUDAISM

There are many books devoted to explicating Jewish laws and customs relating to death and mourning and a wealth of studies addressing the significance of death-practices around the world. However, never before has there been a study of the death and mourning practices of the founders of Judaism – the rabbis of late antiquity. *The Meanings of Death in Rabbinic Judaism* fills that gap.

The author examines Rabbinic Judaism's earliest canonical texts – the Mishnah, the Tosefta, the Midrashim and the Talmud of the Land of Israel. He outlines the rituals described in these texts, from preparation for death to reburial of bones and the end of mourning. David Kraemer explores the relationships between the texts and interprets the rituals to uncover the beliefs which informed their foundation. He discusses the material evidence preserved in the largest Jewish burial complex in late antiquity – the catacombs at Beth Shearim. Finally, the author offers an interpretation of the rabbis' interpretations of death rituals – those recorded in the Babylonian Talmud.

The Meanings of Death in Rabbinic Judaism provides a comprehensive and illuminating introduction to the formation, practice and significance of death rituals in Rabbinic Judaism.

David Kraemer is Professor of Talmud and Rabbinics at the Jewish Theological Seminary of America in New York.

THE MEANINGS OF DEATH IN RABBINIC JUDAISM

David Kraemer

London and New York

First published 2000
by Routledge
11 New Fetter Lane, London EC4P 4EE

Simultaneously published in the USA and Canada
by Routledge
29 West 35th Street, New York, NY 10001

Routledge is an imprint of the Taylor & Francis Group

© 2000 David Kraemer

The right of David Kraemer to be identified as the Author of this
Work has been asserted by him in accordance with the Copyright,
Designs and Patents Act 1988

Typeset in Garamond by Keystroke, Jacaranda Lodge, Wolverhampton
Printed and bound in Great Britain by Biddles Ltd, Guildford and King's Lynn

British Library Cataloguing in Publication Data
A catalogue record for this book is available from the British Library

Library of Congress Cataloging in Publication Data
Kraemer, David Charles,
The meanings of death in Rabbinic Judaism / David Kraemer.
p.   cm.
Includes bibliographical references and index.
1. Death – Religious aspects – Judaism. 2. Death in rabbinical
literature. 3. Jewish mourning customs – History. I. Title.
BM635.4.K73 1999
296.4'45'09015 – dc21   99–20720

ISBN 0–415–21183–2 (hbk)
ISBN 0–415–21184–0 (pbk)

CONTENTS

CONTENTS

ILLUSTRATIONS

PREFACE AND
ACKNOWLEDGMENTS

Despite possible appearances to the contrary, this book is not the second in a series that began with my earlier *Responses to Suffering in Classical Rabbinic Literature* (Oxford, 1995). This work did not emerge from that earlier research, nor are the two books connected in their fundamental questions. In truth, the present project took shape when I began to notice that the Talmud's death-related rituals are often distinctly different from the rituals I knew from contemporary observant Jewish communities. As I discovered more and more such examples, my curiosity was piqued, and I wanted to know as much as I could about the shape and meanings of ancient practice. I went searching for the book that would answer my questions and quickly found that it did not exist. I had no choice, therefore, but to write the book myself.

This has been a project of several years' duration and, as is the nature of such projects, many people have contributed to my work. In particular, students in two classes at the Jewish Theological Seminary – one an under-graduate Honors Seminar and one a Doctoral Research Seminar – undertook exploration of death-practices in particular rabbinic documents, and their findings often served as the foundations for my own more expansive research. They also had an important part in testing my interpretations and suggesting alternatives. I also benefited immensely from the generosity of Isaiah Gafni, who undertook to shepherd me through tombs at Beth Shearim and shared his considerable wisdom both at the tombs and during our long ride back-and-forth from Jerusalem. I know few people who would share their time so kindly under difficult circumstances.

The plates in Chapter 5 are reprinted with the permission of the Israel Exploration Society (Plates 5.2–11) and the Israel Antiquities Authority (Plate 5.1). I thank both organizations for sharing their resources. I am also grateful to the Abbell Research Fund at The Jewish Theological Seminary for making it possible for me to visit Beth Shearim and come to appreciate the phenomenon there first-hand.

GLOSSARY

Amora A rabbinic sage of the period during which the gemara was produced, from the third to the sixth centuries.

baraita A rabbinic teaching said to be from the period of the Mishnah (first two centuries) which was not, however, included in the Mishnah.

Bavli The Babylonian Talmud, completed by rabbinic sages in Babylonia probably in the mid-sixth century.

gemara Rabbinic commentary on the Mishnah. The Mishnah and gemara together comprise the Talmud.

geonic Pertaining to the period of the *geonim*. The geonim were the heads of the academies in Babylonia (Iraq) in the centuries following the publication of the Talmud.

halakha (pl. **halakhot**) Rabbinic law.

lulav A palm branch tied to myrtle and willow branches, used for ritual purposes during the autumn festival of Sukkot.

Mekhilta The midrash halakha on the book of Exodus.

midrash A rabbinic exposition of scripture.

midrash halakha An early (tannaitic) midrash on one of the predominantly legal books of the Torah (excluding Genesis).

minyan Quorum of ten men required for Jewish public prayers.

Mishnah The earliest rabbinic composition, containing laws and customs pertaining to most areas of Jewish life. Formulated by Rabbi Judah the Patriarch in Palestine in *c*.200 CE.

mitzvah (pl. **mitzvot**) From the biblical root, "to command." A commandment, originating in the Torah or rabbinic interpretation, incumbent upon Jews.

onen A person who has lost a close relative, during the period after death but before burial of the deceased.

Order The Mishnah is organized into six broad subject categories, called "orders."

Rabbah Literally "great" or "expanded." Designation of standard midrashim on biblical books.

Shema The biblical passage from Deuteronomy 6, beginning with the

words "Hear [*shema*], O Israel," that is to be recited by a Jew twice each
day – morning and evening.

shiva Literally, "seven." The seven-day period of most intense mourning,
beginning immediately after burial and continuing until the morning of
the seventh day following burial.

shloshim Literally, "thirty." The period of diminished mourning, following
shiva, which comes to an end on the thirtieth day after burial.

shofar The ram's horn which was blown on Rosh Hashana (the Jewish New
Year), during the service in the Jerusalem Temple, and on other special
occasions.

Sifri The midrash halakha on the books of Numbers and Deuteronomy.

sugya (pl. **sugyot**) A sustained Talmudic argument; the Talmud's primary
"rhetorical unit."

Talmud The Mishnah together with its commentary, the gemara.

tanna A rabbinic sage of the period of the Mishnah (first two centuries CE).

tannaitic Of or pertaining to the period during which the tannaim
flourished.

tefillin Black leather straps that are worn by Jewish men, on one of their
arms and on their head, during prayer. In antiquity, tefillin were worn all
day.

Tosefta A collection of baraitot, many commenting upon or supplementing
Mishnaic teachings, that is organized according to the same orders and
tractates as the Mishnah.

Tractate A book of Mishnaic law, addressing a single area of the law.

Yerushalmi The Talmud produced by the rabbis in Palestine, completed in
the early to mid-fifth century.

yeshiva Traditional rabbinic academy.

ABBREVIATIONS

A.Z.	Avodah Zarah
b.	Bavli
B.B.	Baba Batra
Ber.	Berakhot
B.R.	Bereishit (= Genesis) Rabbah
Deut.	Deuteronomy
Ex.	Exodus
Gen.	Genesis
Ket.	Ketubot
Kil.	Kilaim
Lev.	Leviticus
L.R.	Leviticus Rabbah
m.	Mishnah
Meg.	Megillah
M.Q.	Mo'ed Qatan
Ned.	Nedarim
Num.	Numbers
Ohal.	Ohalot
Pes.	Pesaḥim
Prov.	Proverbs
R.H.	Rosh Hashana
San.	Sanhedrin
Shab.	Shabbat
Sheq.	Sheqalim
Suk.	Sukkah
t.	Tosefta
Taan.	Ta'anit
y.	Talmud Yerushalmi
Yev.	Yevamot

1

THE PRESENCE OF DEATH

Introduction

Death is a universal human experience, an unavoidable fact of every life. But the ways death is experienced differ significantly, even radically, from one place and time to another. This, too, is a fact, but one we often forget.

In modern Western societies death is largely hidden from common experience. This is, first, because death before advanced age is today far less common than it once was. Infant and child mortality is relatively low. Sudden, unexpected death occurs with relative infrequency. Instead, those who are fatally ill are hospitalized. Death, therefore, most often occurs in hospitals, seldom at home. This is true even of deaths of the elderly. Furthermore, death is deemed an acute and even unnatural condition, to be fought as long as possible, often by any means possible. Thus, the intensive care ward, with its limited hours and access, is the arena of death. Those who incline toward death are most often hidden from the view of all but their closest relatives and a few select medical professionals.

The cloistering of death in our society extends beyond death itself. Those who pass away are immediately stored in special places, usually the mortuaries of hospitals and funeral homes. There they remain until the funeral. And funerals, too, take place in specialized, private locations. Memorial services are personal affairs, rarely open to a broader public. Funeral processions may be seen only in transit; we identify them by the line of cars with headlights on in broad daylight. Cemeteries are usually distant from people's homes, and only family and close friends generally attend the burial itself. From the decline toward death to interment, our society isolates death from common experience.

This was not so in the ancient world, where death was ever-present. In the world that will concern us in this book, that of Jews in the Roman and Persian empires, early death was shockingly common. Women often died in childbirth, babies when they were born. Scholars now believe that fewer than half of all children survived their fifth birthdays (van der Horst 1991: 75). And though those who lived past this milestone were relatively more likely to

1

live out their natural years, premature death at all ages, from any variety of causes, was far more frequent than it is today.

The evidence of Jews in the Roman age powerfully supports this picture. As evidenced by Jewish epitaphs from the entire Roman world, the life expectancy of Jews during this period was 28.4 years. Even though the epitaphs represent only a minute proportion of the Jewish population from these centuries, there is no reason to believe that this number is significantly skewed in one direction or the other (van der Horst 1991: ch. 5). Life expectancy was, from a modern perspective, shockingly low.

Jewish testimony from this period sheds light on the ancient experience of death in another way as well. The Jewish literary record suggests that Jews expected their lives to exceed their "life expectancy" by several decades. Psalm 90 – difficult to date but certainly more ancient than the period which concerns us here – suggests that "the days of our years are seventy, or if by great strength eighty years" (v. 10). An addition to Mishnah tractate Avot, at the end of chapter 5,[1] affirms these numbers, remarking that "at sixty, one is elderly; at seventy, one has white hair; at eighty, one has achieved special strength; at ninety, one is bent over; at one hundred, one is as though dead". And a Talmudic tradition attributed to Rabbah, of the late second and early third centuries, remarks that "if one dies between his fiftieth and sixtieth year, this is a death of 'excision'" (*karet* = spiritual death, death at the hand of heaven). Excision was a serious punishment, directed by the Torah against those who sinned in particularly grievous ways. Thus, to say that such a death is a "death of excision" is to declare it unusual and especially lamentable. For this reason, when R. Yosef reached his sixtieth birthday, he celebrated, saying "I have emerged from [the danger of] excision!" Death at fifty-to-sixty was still thought an early death. Death at seventy was a death in old age, death at eighty (= "special strength") a "kiss of God." R. Ḥisda, according to the Talmudic record, lived ninety-two years (all b. Mo'ed Qatan 28a).

How are we to understand this literary record, one which so contradicts the inscriptional evidence? The rabbinic testimonies remind us that "life expectancy" is only a statistical, not an experienced, reality. Life expectancy tells us not of the progress of aging *but of the presence of death*. In other words, *the lower the life expectancy statistic the more common is death in infancy and youth*. So the statistical reality supports what we have already suggested: that *death in ancient Jewish society – as in Roman society in general – was ever-present*. Inevitably, therefore, death-practices were also central presences in this society – lived expressions of some of the society's most fundamental beliefs.

Death was a constant presence in common experience not only because of high mortality rates but because, when people died, they tended to do so at home. Or, if they did not actually die at home, they were nevertheless laid there until the funeral. Furthermore, both in Roman society in general and in Jewish society in particular, transport to the grave was a public affair. In fact, the rituals of funerals assured that the population would be aware of the goings-on.[2] People commonly experienced death and saw those who had deceased. None of this was hidden. Death was ever-present.

Because of the presence of death, and because of its unknown and even frightening qualities, one of the first tasks of religion was (and is) to make sense of death. Peter Berger expresses the need in this way:

> The confrontation with death . . . constitutes what is probably the most important marginal situation . . . Death radically puts in question the taken-for-granted, "business-as-usual" attitude in which one exists in everyday life. Here, everything in the daytime world of existence is massively threatened with "irreality" . . . Insofar as the knowledge of death cannot be avoided in any society, legitimations of the reality of the social world *in the face of death* are decisive requirements in any society. The importance of religions in such legitimations is obvious.
>
> (Berger 1967: 43–4)

Religions make sense of life by making sense of death. This struggle with the meaning of death is central to the purpose of any religious community, from the mists of antiquity until the present day.

Commentaries on the meaning of death are preserved in a community's texts and rituals. Sometimes these commentaries are explicit, although, in the realm of ritual at least, they are more often implied. Either way, through careful interpretation of its teachings and practices relating to death, we may discover some of the most fundamental beliefs of any religion. Moreover, since, as Metcalf and Huntington write, "the moment of death is related not only to the process of afterlife, but also to the process of living, aging, and producing progeny," we cannot but admit that "life becomes transparent against the background of death" (Metcalf and Huntington 1972: 108, 25). If we understand a religious community's beliefs concerning death, we will gain a far better understanding of its valuation of life.

The Focus of This Book

In this book, I explore the death-practices and beliefs of the "inventors" of Judaism – the rabbis of the first several centuries of the common era. My interest in these visionary religious leaders is a function of their pivotal place in the history of Judaism. It was they who, on the foundation of traditions inherited from Jewish communities of the late Second Temple period, defined the forms of what would be known simply as "Judaism" from late antiquity until the modern era. Though the Judaism of the rabbis would exhibit important continuities with the Judaisms of Jewish communities before them, it would also be different in significant and distinctive ways. One familiar with "Biblical Religion" or the religion of the Maccabees, for example, would have a hard time recognizing many of the particular expressions of rabbinic Judaism. One familiar with the religion of the Talmud, however, would have no problem recognizing it as the same "species" (though perhaps a different "breed") of Judaism as that practiced by Maimonides in the twelfth century. To state matters as simply as possible, to understand Judaism, one must understand the religion of the classical rabbis.[3] It is for this reason that I focus my inquiry on their world.

Previous scholarship on the rituals and practices of rabbinic Jewish tradition is extremely meager, and the limited work which has been done is flawed in methodological and other respects. To be sure, one will have no problem finding books on the *halakhot* (accepted Jewish laws and customs) of death and mourning. But these offer only instruction in latter-day Jewish practice, mostly Orthodox. Their authors are uninterested in earlier Jewish practices or in the development of present customs. In fact, for the most part they seem not to know that Jewish practices relating to death even *have* a history beyond their initial record in the canonical "oral Torah."

In a more scholarly vein, Nisan Rubin has written (in Hebrew) on Jewish death-practices during the rabbinic period, mostly as reflected in the literature of the rabbis but with reference to archaeological finds.[4] A doctoral dissertation, written by Byron McCane under the direction of Eric Meyers, surveys archaeological reports to detail Jewish and Christian burial customs in Palestine during the first several centuries of the common era, using contemporary religious writings to illumine the beliefs of these respective communities (McCane 1992). There are also scattered articles, including a particularly important piece by Saul Lieberman on rabbinic beliefs regarding the afterlife (Lieberman 1965). Recent books by Simcha Paull Raphael and Neil Gillman describe the history of the same topic, including chapters on the rabbinic period (Raphael 1994 and Gillman 1997). Finally, archaeological studies of ancient Jewish burial sites are voluminous, and many include refer-ence to contemporary rabbinic opinions.[5] But none of these studies addresses the literature of the rabbis except to illumine the "reality on the ground," and all are, like the literary scholarship on which they depend, incomplete and methodologically flawed, as I will explain below. A comprehensive study, informed by recent developments in rabbinic scholarship and related fields, has not, until now, been written.

How To write such a history: questions of method

Evidence for classical rabbinic practices and beliefs is almost exclusively the literature produced by the rabbis themselves. But this literature obviously cannot be interpreted in a vacuum. How we understand what the rabbis did or did not do, did or did not believe, will in part be a function of what others around them did and believed.

In fact, there is considerable evidence, of various sorts, for the world in which the rabbis lived. For the earliest years of this period we have other literatures, including the New Testament, the writings of Josephus and various apocryphal works. As importantly, death-practices leave an enduring material record. Burial is typically done in or under the ground, which itself endures and, in addition, tends to protect what is contained in it. Bodies or bones may be laid to rest in coffins or sarcophagi constructed from durable materials. Monuments and grave markers are manufactured from similarly durable substance. The graves, sarcophagi and markers are often inscribed, meaning that beliefs relating to the dead are not only symbolized in the means of burial itself, but are also expressed in written words. Of all ancient religious and social practices, death customs leave perhaps the richest permanent record.

Though we preserve substantial evidence concerning death-practices from this period, the task of interpretation is not easy, and earlier writers have tripped over a variety of obstacles along the interpretive road. The literature is subject to (at least) the same interpretive difficulties as any literature, particularly from an ancient, foreign culture. The bulk of the literary record is, as I said, rabbinic, and, in recent decades, scholars have only *begun* to appreciate the challenges of interpreting this literature for historical purposes. To begin with, there is a tradition of reading the Talmud and other rabbinic works that extends back for 1500 years and more. This tradition is tied strongly to the traditions of practice from the same centuries, centuries during which rabbinic authorities exercised hegemony over most common Jewish practice. But, historians have now come to realize, the rabbis were, from the years following the destruction of the Jerusalem Temple in CE 70 to the end of late antiquity, a small, elite group, controlling the practices of relatively few. This means that, contrary to the practice of many historians (including *virtually all* who have written on Jewish death-practices during this age), we may *not* assume that the rabbinic record represents common Jewish practice. So, if we discover burial practices that might be illuminated by rabbinic teachings, we should not assume a necessary or immediate connection. It is our obligation to consider alternative explanations of the same practices as well. By the same token, if we discover practices which seem to contradict rabbinic prescriptions, we should not conclude that these practices are heterodox. We do not know whether rabbinic teachings reflect *any* lived reality (as I shall explain below), let alone that of Jews beyond rabbinic circles.

Even when we recognize that rabbinic documents speak only for an elite group of religious masters and their disciples, we still have barely begun to overcome the obstacles which confront the interpreter of this literature. The more primary question, perhaps, is that of the relationship between the written record we preserve and the "original" teachings on which the record is based. Rabbinic tradition claims of itself that it was oral, passed from master to disciple by word of mouth. If we admit the fundamental orality of the society in which this tradition was produced – as we indeed must[6] – then we must ask about the reliability of transmission in oral cultures. Those who have studied such cultures notice a great degree of fluidity in the repetition of traditions. This is true even of recitations of the same person from one repetition to the next, even when the speaker claims that he has repeated the tradition or story in a form that is identical with the previous recitation.[7] Where training (memorization) begins early and traditions are chanted or sung, success is greater, but even such repeaters "make changes . . . of which they are unaware" (Ong 1982: 63). The many variations in "the same" rabbinic teachings from one record to another are evidence of the reality just described. It is in the nature of an oral tradition that teachings change from one recitation to the next, mostly unnoticed.

The unsensed changes that typify all oral traditions are often a function of the habits, assumptions, beliefs and prejudices of the context in which any given tradition is repeated. Again, examples in the rabbinic corpus are abundant. I cite just one: When we compare the responses of R. Yohanan and his colleagues to suffering as recorded in the Babylonian Talmud (Berakhot 5a) to those preserved in Midrash Song of Songs Rabbah (2, 35), we find that, in the former version, sufferings are rejected whereas in the latter acceptance of suffering is recommended. These and other differences in these teachings conform completely to approaches to suffering which unmistakably typify the Babylonian and Palestinian rabbinic traditions (Kraemer 1995). The rabbinic repeaters may not have been aware of the changes they were introducing into their teachings, but change them they did, under the inexorable pressures of the settings in which they were living.

The next problem with the rabbinic evidence, as we preserve it, lies in the difference between the *forms* of its original expression and the form of the later record. The formulation of a "literature" in an oral-literate society like that of the rabbis is extremely complex. On the one hand, there can be no question of the centrality and importance of written documents in ancient Judaism. Scripture – the Torah and the rest of the Hebrew Bible – was authoritative throughout Israel, and the study of these books was clearly a central act of rabbinic piety. On the other hand, because of the scarcity of written scrolls and widespread illiteracy, the experience of these books of most ancient Jews, including rabbis, was oral; they would *listen* to the scroll as it was read by a designated reader. In such a society, there is not, as has typically but wrongly been assumed, a unidirectional model for how literatures are produced (the false models are these: either oral production is later recorded in writing or written composition may be memorized by selected readers or disciples). Rather, there is always a complex interplay between orality and literacy, what Susan Niditch, following Ruth Finnegan, has characterized as a "continuum" between one mode and the other (Niditch 1996). So a teaching, originally spoken by the master, might be recorded for recollection by a disciple. The disciple might then recite the teaching based upon his abbreviated mnemonic record, changing or expanding the teaching in unknown and unsensed ways.[8] As we noted earlier, oral teachings might be similarly changed. Crucially, "the writing down may preserve a snapshot or moment in what continues as a lively oral tradition. The writing down of material need not necessarily signal the end of the production of oral versions of such works" (Niditch 1996: 118–19). In such a society, any writing down is a "snapshot" of the developing life of a tradition. In the rabbinic context, the version recorded in the Palestinian Talmud may be one "snapshot," the different version recorded in the Babylonian Talmud another. Neither may be "original," though the version in the Palestinian Talmud is indisputably earlier (more on this below).

Still another difficulty with the extant rabbinic evidence lies in the fact that teachings that were once given oral expression, by and before living, authoritative masters of the tradition, are now (more or less) "frozen" in writing. Oral and written expressions differ in significant ways, and if "the medium is the message" then the reduction of oral rabbinic teachings to the written form will change them radically. I can barely improve on Martin Jaffee's articulation of the consequences of this change in form:

> the passage of a literary work from exclusively oral to written/oral transmission is profoundly transformative. What was once present as direct address and shaped inevitably to suit the needs of the moment as these took shape in the interaction of speaker and audience is now deprived of the fluid form which constitutes its social reality. A tradition, once reformulated and changed with each performance, is now stabilized and objectified in a form which exerts a powerful control over future performances or readings. What was formerly "authored" at each recitation must now be reproduced "as it is written."
>
> (Jaffee 1992: 66)[9]

I would modify Jaffee's description only slightly, insisting that unofficial writings were surely part of the earliest life of rabbinic teachings and noting that what we now preserve, even if memorized by some students of the tradition with imprecision, is effectively frozen in writing. But the point, and the consequences, are the same.[10] As Walter Ong writes, "Written words are isolated from the fuller context in which spoken words come into being. Spoken words are always modifications of a total situation which is more than verbal . . . In oral speech, a word must have one or another intonation or tone of voice – lively, excited, quiet, incensed, resigned, or whatever." Context, tone, audience, and the like all affect the meaning of a communication. But when words are written, removing the eyes, the brow, the hand movement, and the tone of voice, then the force of the words will be thrown into doubt, their meaning subject to differing interpretation. As Ong points out, one need only consider the hours an actor spends determining how best to utter the written words of a script (and the drastically different interpretations of how to utter and perform the same words) to appreciate how radically a transformation of medium affects the message (Ong 1982: 101–2).

The writing of oral teachings shifts context in more than one way. In whatever document rabbinic traditions find their written home, the choice of a precise context for quotation is unlikely to be that of the "original" speaker or later repeater. It is, instead, ultimately the decision of the "author" or "redactor" of the document. If we admit that all meaning is contextual, then the choice of a context for written record transforms earlier meanings perhaps significantly. And once a teaching has found a written home, its earlier oral contexts – and therefore meanings – can never be fully recovered.

For purposes of the study of rabbinic history, and for the purposes of this book, the consequence of this understanding of the production of the literature is this: *Presumptively*, the "original" or earliest forms of any given teaching or tradition are unavailable to us. We simply have no way of knowing whether we have recovered such an early tradition. If a teaching is attributed to Rav or Samuel, of the mid-third century, we have no way of knowing the form of the original teaching nor the changes which affected it in the course of preservation and transmission from the third to the sixth century, when it was finally recorded in the Babylonian Talmud. All we can know with relative surety, because it is all we actually preserve, is the "snapshot" of the teaching at the time of its preservation in the final document. (Of course, written documents also suffer the imprecisions of copying, scribal misreadings, and changes imposed by overzealous interpreters. It is always necessary to compare the versions of different manuscripts.) The only history we can write with confidence is the history of these "snapshots," that is, the history of the traditions of completed rabbinic documents in the order of their composition.[11]

Accordingly, the chapters of this book, beginning with Chapter 3, follow the chronological development of the works of classical rabbinic Judaism.[12] The Mishnah was undoubtedly the first of the rabbinic classics to be formulated in (more-or-less) the form we preserve, in *c.*200 CE. This work defines the basic norms of rabbinic practice while imagining correct Jewish conduct in a restored world, with the Jerusalem Temple rebuilt. During the next century or so, the rabbinic community produced an expansion of and commentary on the Mishnah, known as the Tosefta ("additions"), as well as a variety of scripture-commentaries (midrashim; sing.: midrash) which justified rabbinic practice by reference to the Torah. Then, in the fifth century, the Palestinian Jewish community enjoyed a wave of literary creativity, producing a large commentary on significant sections of the Mishnah – the Palestinian Talmud (henceforth: the Yerushalmi) – and major narrative midrashim on the books of Genesis and Leviticus (as well as several smaller midrashic works). Finally, in the sixth century, the Babylonian rabbinic community composed what many consider the crown of classical rabbinism, the Babylonian Talmud, known as the Bavli or, simply, *the* Talmud.

Above, I wrote that, when using rabbinic sources to write history, we must presume that original teachings are unavailable and must therefore restrict ourselves to the evidence of the canonical record. By speaking of presumption, I meant to leave open the possibility that more precise histories, based upon verifications of datings from sources outside the rabbinic record, might sometimes be written. In fact, when I approached the work of this book, I had hoped that a history of death-practices might permit such greater precision. My hope was based on the recognition that burial customs leave extensive remains of the actual practices of ancient Jews. If the archaeological evidence could (or could not) be correlated with the literary record, this might serve as a verification or falsification of the chronological claims of the rabbinic tradition.[13]

I am now of the opinion, however, that what I had hoped for cannot be accomplished, for two reasons. First, in reviewing the classical rabbinic record from its earliest to its latest stages, I found a surprising continuity both in practice and, particularly, in belief. This does not mean that there are no significant changes or developments between the Mishnah and the Talmud. Indeed, there is a far more complete record of recommended rabbinic death-practices in later documents than in earlier ones: imprecise or unclear directions are clarified, basic instructions are supplemented or filled in. But we have no way of knowing whether the later record is *different* or merely more complete. And without clear developments and differences, it is impossible to correlate changes in the literary record with changes on and under the ground. Second, in view of the analysis of oral transmission and repetition outlined above, I came to appreciate that, even if death-practices did change, *and even if practices recorded in a later document reflect earlier practices*, this does not mean that a given tradition – in the form we now preserve – can be dated to an earlier time. It is equally as reasonable to suppose that a particular tradition originated in an earlier period – and thus partially portrays an earlier practice – and was then transmitted *and transformed* from one generation to the next. Only the archaeological record itself permits more definitive dating, and this only with a minimalist interpretation. We should not naively assume that possibly later rabbinic interpretations or enhancements accurately reflect an earlier practice.[14]

This same analysis explains why I do not, in this book, use the well-known rabbinic tractate on death-practices known as *Semaḥot* or *Evel Rabbati*. *Semaḥot* is one of the so-called "minor tractates," generally assumed by scholars to be geonic in origin (eighth century or later). Three tannaitic traditions from something called *Evel Rabbati* are quoted in the Talmud, but two of these do not appear in the extant minor tractate by that name and the third appears only in a modified form. In fact, there is no clear quotation of this tractate until the Middle Ages. D. Zlotnick suggests a date of the late third century for *Semaḥot*, but he does so without proof and with prejudice; he merely assumes that if the tractate cannot be proved later, we must believe its attribution of teachings to sages of the second and early third centuries (Zlotnick 1966: 1–9). But he fails to account for the possibility of pseudonymous attribution, or perhaps the better possibility that the tractate is an anthology of and elaboration upon earlier rabbinic traditions, written and oral. Eric Meyers' argument that archaeological realia support Zlotnick's dating (Meyers 1975: 39–40) fails on the grounds outlined above: there is no doubt that some of the practices described in tractate *Semaḥot* were common in the third century (and were no longer practiced after the mid-fourth), but this hardly serves to date the relevant traditions in their present form, let alone the tractate as a whole. The authors of a medieval tractate could just as easily quote from Talmudic and other earlier traditions, intentionally anachronizing in order to give record to what they deem "ideal" Jewish practice in the best of all worlds.[15]

For a history of rabbinic death-practices in late antiquity, we must thus rely exclusively on the works listed earlier, supplemented, of course, by the record of archaeology. But even on the foundation of this greater certitude, we are left with significant interpretive challenges. For example, are the teachings of a given rabbinic work prescriptive or descriptive? Some have argued that certain classical rabbinic documents, at least, portray idealized or otherwise theoretical versions of Jewish practice, and this possibility cannot be dismissed (Neusner 1981: 41, 235–6). This means that we cannot even assume a relationship between "official" rabbinic teachings and actual rabbinic practice. Certainly, the evidence of the burial caves at Beth Shearim (see Chapter 5) suggests such a gap, reinforcing the caution just stated. Yet few who have written about rabbinic beliefs and practices (in this and other areas) have even known to ask these questions.

If such difficulties confront the interpreter of the literature, this will obviously affect interpretations of the contemporaneous archaeological evidence. Again, if the rabbis were only a small, elite group in ancient Judaism – as we now realize – then we cannot assume any relationship between the remains we seek to interpret and the opinions recorded in rabbinic sources. Yet Israeli and other Jewish archaeologists, who have dominated the study of the archaeology of the Land of Israel, have all assumed that burial-in-reality may be illuminated by the Mishnah, the Talmud and other contemporary rabbinic writings, without asking about the relationship between the people who produced these writings and the people buried at the excavated sites. They have, furthermore, assumed that the various rabbinic writings represent what is essentially a single religious tradition, ignoring the possibility of significant differences of opinion or changes from one century to another. They have, finally, been insensitive to the many problems with the literature-as-history outlined above. These, in my opinion, are fatal assumptions and insensitivities, leading to many unjustified and unjustifiable conclusions.

In the chapters that follow, I have made other choices. First, although I have read and sought to interpret both the literary and the material records, I have assumed no necessary connection between them. In this matter, I have assumed an agnostic position, noting similarities and differences and leaving the question of the relationship between rabbinic teachings and Jewish practice to the end. When reading the literature, I have not assumed that the rabbinic record is a unified corpus. Instead, as I said earlier, I have read the rabbinic writings in the chronological sequence of their composition, asking what each says that the previous one did not. Where the tradition is continuous, I have taken note of the same. But I have been equally attentive to differences between one rabbinic tradition and the next.

In my reading of both the literature and the archaeological remains, I have learned much from the interpretations of anthropologists who have devoted their scholarly lives to studying death-practices.[16] I have noted, in particular, their interpretations of practices similar or identical to ancient Jewish or rabbinic practices (such as the reburial of bones at some period following death). Crucially, in considering such possible interpretations, I have tried to assume nothing about what Jews from this period could or could not have believed. Many modern Jewish interpreters have wanted to believe that their ancestors were, like themselves, relatively "rational." They have consequently dismissed more "mystical" or "irrational" explanations.[17] As a consequence of these preferences they have, in my opinion, also mistranslated and misinterpreted. I have tried to avoid these pitfalls.

All interpretation is circular. No one interpretation is definitive. I have often, therefore, considered multiple interpretations of the phenomena of death. There is no need to insist on one or the other when multiple interpretations are offered. Symbols such as those employed in death-practice are multi-vocalic, that is, they may mean different things to different people at the same time. Still, certain interpretations may be preferred. I have assumed that the more evidence explained by a particular interpretation, the more plausible the interpretation. I will not hesitate, therefore, to defend certain interpretations above others. But I also admit that alternatives will often be reasonable.

The relationship between practice and belief

I conclude this chapter by relating a personal discovery, one which sensitized me to the full symbolic quality of death rituals and to the inevitable connection between rituals and beliefs.

I had been studying ancient rabbinic teachings concerning funerals and mourning customs. I had discovered, as you will see in later chapters, that before interment the survivor was not yet a mourner. He was not yet ready to mourn, in large part because he, like everyone else, was supposed to concern himself with the needs and honor of the deceased. Since the deceased was

11

believed to know everything that was going on around her, it was crucial that the survivor not yet turn to other matters, not even to the business of addressing his grief. This would indicate to the deceased that those still living cared little about her. Their inattention would be tantamount to insult, an expression of lack of concern.

During this period, I attended the funeral of the mother of a friend, an Orthodox funeral for a member of an Orthodox rabbinic family. As I entered the funeral home, I witnessed the following scene: those arriving for the funeral were standing in line to enter a small side-parlor where the family was assembled. There the visitors were sharing expressions of sorrow and comfort with members of the family of the deceased, who were standing around the perimeter of the room in a kind of receiving line. When visitors were finished offering condolences, they went into the large adjacent room where the funeral would actually take place. The deceased was laid in her coffin in the front of the long room. A yeshiva student was reciting psalms by the side of the coffin. Everyone else was speaking quietly. The tone in the room was subdued, but there was an unmistakable "hum." The talking stopped only when the family entered for the funeral to begin.

I was stunned by the difference between the Talmudic funeral and the modern Orthodox funeral. How could the family accept expressions of sorrow and comfort — how could those attending offer such expressions — when the survivors were not yet even mourners? How could the survivors and the visitors assemble in a side room, ignoring the deceased? How could the large crowd of visitors sit talking, oblivious to the deceased who was lying in front of them? From the perspective of Talmudic tradition, all of this would be considered offensive. What was the meaning of this flagrant disregard of Talmudic (and later halakhic) prescriptions?

As I sat struggling with these questions, the answer to all of them became clear to me. Modern people (who may be distinguished from people living in modernity, not all of whom are "modern" in their attitudes and beliefs) do not believe that those who have died know what is going on around them. They do not believe that the deceased are sentient and therefore have actual physical needs. Why not speak in the presence of the dead, then? What harm can quiet talking possibly do? Of course, in the belief of moderns, it is the survivors who have needs (emotional), not the deceased. Attention must therefore turn to them, to the family, in order to begin the job of providing comfort. Without knowledge or feeling, those who have passed away have no need of anyone's attention, not even that of their close family. Whatever is needed for the funeral will be taken care of by professionals. Freed from any responsibility, unconcerned for what the deceased might be thinking or feeling (the assumed answer is: nothing), survivors may begin the process of mourning.

What I discovered, in other words, is that there is an inevitable relationship between beliefs and practices. If we believe that the dead are conscious, our practices will reflect that belief. But if we cease to believe in such a reality, our practices will change to reflect the same shift – even when our tradition would direct us to do otherwise.

It is this nexus of practice and belief that concerns me most. In the chapters that follow I examine classical Jewish death customs to discover, as much as possible, classical Jewish beliefs. There are not a few surprises in the texts and practices of antiquity. Practices and beliefs have changed significantly, and our memories are very short. As we rediscover the beliefs of those who lived before us, we will be challenged to consider and reconsider what we today believe.

2

JEWISH DEATH CUSTOMS
BEFORE THE RABBIS

As in all matters of human social practice, no generation originates its own death customs, in their multifarious details. There are always traditions concerning death, and subsequent generations will learn those traditions, finding their customs and understandings profoundly influenced by those who came before. At the same time, there is always the possibility of change. What a prior generation believed may be implausible to a later generation. As conditions change, so too will beliefs, and as beliefs change, so too, inevitably, will practice.

Therefore, if we hope to understand the death-practices and beliefs of Jews – particularly rabbinic Jews – from the second through the sixth centuries of the common era, we must first learn what we can of the customs and beliefs of Jews of prior centuries. We may find continuities, traditions of practice and belief that will shed light on those of the rabbis who inherited them. We may find modifications or ruptures of tradition, allowing comparison of earlier and later, demanding that we ask why Jews began to observe death differently. But, whatever we find, our understanding will be enhanced. We thus begin by searching out the documents and material evidence of earlier centuries. On this basis, we will, in subsequent chapters, proceed to examine and interpret the evidence of the rabbis themselves.[1]

Sometime around 200 BCE,[2] a Jewish author in Judea wrote of a hero by the name of Tobit who was distinguished by his immense piety. To highlight Tobit's piety, the author described his devotion to "acts of charity," the most notable of which (that is, those the author chose to single out) are feeding the hungry, clothing the naked and burying the dead. As the narrative develops, Tobit's devotion to burying the dead, even in the face of possible danger, becomes his signature act of piety.

Descriptions of Tobit's involvement with the dead, together with stories of his preparation for his own death, reveal several important details of Jewish death-practice as this author knows it. In chapter 2, we learn that, after contact with the dead, Tobit washes himself, presumably to remove the impurity of contact (though, according to biblical law, mere washing would have no power to accomplish this). Verse 5 of the same chapter describes

Tobit, the dead as yet unburied, eating his food "in sorrow." Is this merely a general description of his frame of mind or is it reference to a specific ritual, a manner of eating that is appropriate for the person who eats while his dead lies before him (literally or figuratively)? Unfortunately, the narrative is insufficiently specific. But the suggestion of such a ritual posture must be noted.

Other details: in good biblical fashion, Tobit prepares for his end by blessing his son and issuing a variety of directives – from sage advice to requests concerning his disposition after death (see chapters 4 and 14). The author suggests that it is appropriate for husband and wife to be buried together (14:12), and it may be appropriate for survivors to "feed" the deceased, at least the righteous deceased, leaving bread at their tombs (see 4:17).[3]

Joshua Ben Sira, probably a contemporary of the author of Tobit,[4] adds to our record and our understanding. According to Ben Sira, the body of the deceased should be laid out, there to be wept and wailed over. In chapter 38 (vv. 16–23) of his book, Ben Sira directs us to cry in abundance, because our weeping must be worthy of the departed; he or she will be honored by our show of sorrow. But earlier, in chapter 22 (vv. 11–12), he remarks that there is a limit – our weeping for the dead should be less than our weeping for a fool because the deceased, at least, "is at rest." It is unclear whether these sentiments, certainly in tension with one another, are actually contradictory.

But, comparing Ben Sira's two brief excursuses on death and mourning, we discover another detail that surely falls victim to contradiction. In chapter 22, Ben Sira suggests that mourning should last for seven days. If we disregard the rabbinic equation of part of a day with a whole – thus making the rabbinic *shiva* (= "seven") effectively six days – this will be parallel to later Jewish practice. But in chapter 38, the sage directs that mourning should last for only one or two days and then the mourner should be comforted, because "grief may result in death." There will be no coming back, he says in verse 21, and there is thus no purpose to be served by extended grieving. Just as the deceased is at rest, so too should remembrance of the deceased rest.

Is there a difference between grieving and the ritual mourning period? If so, then there need be no contradiction here. But the sense of these directives is surely at odds. Seven days may define a custom or ritual requirement, but the beliefs of the author, at least, seem to demand less. If death is an irreversible step, a permanent rest from which there is no turning back, then extended grieving makes little sense. As the progress of the life-changes of the deceased comes to an end, so too should the emotional and, perhaps, ritual responses of the survivor. Let the dead be buried, Ben Sira says, agreeing with the author of Tobit. Then let him rest in peace. Let there be wailing appropriate to the honor of the deceased; let others in the community mourn with those who cry (7:34), then be silent.

But if the deceased is to be left in peace – if, as Ben Sira appears to believe, death is radically distinguished from life – then there is no reason to leave provisions for the dead. In this respect, these two contemporaries disagree (the author of Tobit, as we saw, deems it appropriate to leave food with the deceased). A Hellenistic Jewish author, living perhaps before these authors,[5] agrees with the writer of Tobit that the dead must be visited and, if not fed, then at least left with gifts (Letter of Jeremiah, v. 27). This was, in fact, a common Jewish practice in later antiquity, as the archaeological record demonstrates. It is also attested as a popular, if perhaps condemned, custom in the biblical record (see Deut. 26:14). Thus, Ben Sira may well represent a restricted and perhaps elitist opinion. For others, while there might not yet be hope of return from death (the first clear expression of this belief will wait until Daniel, written several decades later), there is still belief in certain important continuities between life and death.

The Letter of Jeremiah also knows that some howl and shout at a "funeral banquet" (v. 32). Ben Sira, who, as we saw, emphasizes the importance of loud emotional expressions, believes them appropriate in the presence of the deceased, perhaps before and certainly during the funeral. The author of the Letter thus refers to a different custom, the details of which we may only surmise. Rabbinic tradition later knows of special meals with particular customs in the home of a mourner. For the rabbis, these meals will be occasions for the recitation of defined blessings. For the author of the Letter, the funeral banquet seems to be an occasion for ritual expression of grief.

The next available Jewish records follow a fundamental change in Jewish experience and belief. The Jewish war with the Syrian-Hellenistic king, Antiochus Epiphanes, was extremely bitter for Jews in Judea. The hardships and persecutions of the war were experienced as unparalleled; the situation was, from a religious perspective, intolerable. If the life of the Jew living during this period was so difficult – if God's justice was, to the naked eye, so completely absent – then loss of hope was a real danger. Against this conclusion, some (soon many) Jews began to assert that death was not the final stage of life. "Daniel," in the last chapter of his book,[6] and (several decades later) the writer of 2 Maccabees[7] (in chapter 7) both expressed their confidence that death would be followed by resurrection. For the righteous, at least, death would be followed by a new life in the flesh.

However we understand the relationship of belief and practice, there is no question that along with these developments in belief came different attitudes and practices in the face of death. So, following initial burial of his brother Jonathan at Baskama, where he was killed in battle, Simon directs that Jonathan's bones be reburied "in Modein, the city of his ancestors" (1 Macc. 23–5). At that time, the Maccabees narrative tells us,

> all Israel bewailed him with great lamentation, and mourned for him
> many days. And Simon built a monument over the tomb of his father

and his brothers; he made it high . . . with polished stone at the front and back. He also erected seven pyramids . . . erecting about them great columns, and on the columns he put suits of armor for a permanent memorial, and . . . he carved ships, so that they could be seen by all who sail the sea.

(vv. 26–9)

Some of what is reported here may be explained by the grand aspirations of the Maccabees: triumphant warriors, soon to be High Priests and kings, merit extravagant tombs. Undoubtedly, such tombs will be quite unlike the tombs of common people. But other parts of this narrative do not bespeak a uniquely royal perspective. For example, the demand for reburial, long after the death itself (the text speaks of the reburial of *bones*, following what was necessarily an extended period of decomposition of the flesh), suggests that the final rest of the deceased does not come immediately. What happens to the deceased, even to his bones, matters for a long time. It appears, therefore, that death is viewed as an extended process. Surely the mourning for Jonathan is described as lasting for many days, ignoring, if you will, Ben Sira's advice. Perhaps an extended period of dying or transformation in death is mirrored in the extended period of mourning. Undeniably, the attitude which undergirds this narrative is distant from that expressed in earlier Jewish texts.

Another detail is of considerable interest. What is the purpose of the ships carved on the tomb? The writer seems to suggest that the ships were to be seen by those who sailed the sea, but Modein is sufficiently distant from the coast as to make a literal reading of this explanation preposterous. For this reason, recent commentators have proposed that the ship inscriptions are a monument to (hoped-for) naval victories and perhaps a warning to potential naval invaders (Goldstein 1976: 475). However we understand the author's explanation, we must recall that it is only that – a later explanation or interpretation of an earlier symbolic ornament, reflecting the author's understanding but not necessarily that of those who built the tomb (which, the author comments, "remains to this day"). We may thus imagine other possible understandings of these ships.

I press for an open approach to interpreting this symbolism because, centuries later, Jewish tombs at Beth Shearim will be decorated by drawings and carvings of sailing ships.[8] The insides of burial caves could surely not be seen from the sea, and a Jewish settlement beyond the ridge of the Carmel, away from the coast, is unlikely to have been populated by many seafarers. So it is conceivable that we witness here a common ancient Jewish motif – a tradition extending over many centuries – relating to death. What could be the meaning of this motif? A brief suggestion will suffice here. Ships, we know, symbolize journeys, and death has been viewed as a journey in innumerable cultures (Toynbee 1971: 38). Indeed, it has been viewed as a journey on a ship or ferry, over a river that separates the world of the living and the world of the dead. At the time of the composition of Maccabees, death had already come to be understood as an extended process or journey leading to a new world. What better than a ship to represent this belief?

Judith, roughly contemporary with Maccabees (Moore 1985: 67), offers a picture of a different kind of hero, a common woman whose actions are said to exemplify the highest in piety. The narrative introduces Judith (in chapter 8) following the death of her husband Menasseh. After Menasseh is buried with his ancestors "in the field between Dothan and Balamon" (most of the places mentioned in Judith are fictional), Judith remains a widow for three years and four months. For the duration of her widowhood, Judith removes herself to a tent on the roof of her house, wears sackcloth and "widow's clothing," and fasts all days but the sabbath and the day before, the New Moon and the day before, and festivals (vv. 5–6).

The practices attributed to Judith are meant to illustrate her unusual piety. Thus, it would be an error to conclude that what is described here was common – or even that it was practiced by the pious few. What we may be sure of is that, in the imagination of the present author at least, such practices would be praiseworthy expressions of mourning in the best of Jewish worlds. Thus, ideally, a woman would mourn for her husband for an extended period, perhaps until she married again. She would, presumably along with other mourners, wear sackcloth and possibly other special clothing. And she would, with the exception of festive days and days of preparation, fast.

In biblical and post-biblical Jewish practice, fasting is primarily an expression of self-affliction intended to effect atonement. But it is little associated with mourning, and later (that is, rabbinic) Jewish sources preserve scant reference to such an association. Still, it is essential to recognize that the standard connotations of fasting are perfectly appropriate to the context of mourning. Death is widely viewed as punishment, and it may be understood to be as much punishment of the survivor who loses a loved one as it is of the one lost. Thus, the mourner may view herself as a sinner (which she certainly is) and may fast to atone for her sins.

But it would also be a mistake to restrict our understanding of fasting to this connotation alone. Fasting was also seen, quite simply, as an act of piety or holiness. There is no doubt that fasting was far more widely practiced among Jews of these centuries than the rabbinic record would have us believe. For example, Hellenistic authors report that Jews fasted on their special holy day, the sabbath (Stern 1976, vol. 1: 302, 337, 444, 524). Such reports are simply too widespread for this to be a confusion with the Day of Atonement, as some scholars have suggested.[9] Moreover, though neither the sabbath nor the mourning period are suitable occasions for fasting in rabbinic tradition, rabbinic literature does include reference to both practices. Thus, we may properly see Judith's fasting as a pious manifestation of her grieving, representing what other Jews may not do but ideally should.

Nothing in 2 Maccabees adds to our picture of death-practices from this period. But it does contribute an important insight for our understanding of these practices. In the latter part of chapter 14, the author relates how Judas (= Judah Maccabee) undertook the responsibility to bury certain fellow Jews who had been killed in battle. As he did so, he discovered that they were carrying "sacred tokens of the idols of Jamnia" under their tunics (v. 40), and he came to understand that this sin was the cause of their deaths. In response, Judah and his men prayed on behalf of the fallen, asking that their sins be forgiven. "He also took up a collection of two thousand drachmas of silver, and sent it to Jerusalem to provide for a sin offering" (v. 43). The author then goes on to explain:

> In doing this he acted very well and honorably, taking account of the resurrection. For if he were not expecting that those who had fallen would rise again, it would have been superfluous and foolish to pray for the dead. But if he was looking to the splendid reward that is laid up for those who fall asleep in godliness, it was a holy and pious thought. Therefore he made atonement for the dead, so that they might be delivered from their sin.
>
> (vv. 43–5)

Point well taken. Our actions and customs concerning the dead must have a purpose. And no purpose would be served by extended prayer or acts of atonement on their behalf if we did not anticipate their resurrection or some other meaningful afterlife. It is as though the present author is responding to Ben Sira while confirming that he is in principle correct: Yes, he would admit, if death is the final rest, then grief should be brief and ritual remembrances limited. But death is not the final rest, this author believes. Those whose sin has been forgiven will be resurrected. It is therefore necessary and appropriate to pray on behalf of deceased sinners (that is, virtually everybody) and, if possible, to engage in acts that will assure their complete atonement. But, whatever the underlying belief, the activity of ritual will reflect it. This is the crucial point the author of 2 Maccabees wants to make here.

From this same period, give or take a century, comes the so-called Temple Scroll of Qumran.[10] This rewritten Torah has much to say about Temple and purity, as its modern name would suggest. But it records surprisingly few laws concerning the practices of death. In column 48, it emphasizes the importance of appropriate burial, insisting that the purity of cities be protected by setting apart areas for burial outside of settled territories. On the next column, it adds that, when the body has been removed from the house, the house and everything in it must be cleansed, evidently to restore them to purity. This remarkable document speaks for a group that is extremely concerned with maintaining purity, so it is difficult to say whether other Jews would follow the same strictures. Still, we have seen several mentions of burial in fields *outside* of cities, and Tobit washed himself after coming into contact with the dead. Jews from these centuries were broadly concerned with purity. These laws of the Temple Scroll were therefore probably not the practices of a sect alone.[11]

The record of Jewish practice in the first century CE is more complete, though still sketchy. Most of the literary testimony comes from the latter part of the century – from the pens of Josephus and the authors of Matthew, John, Luke and Acts. But the Gospel of Mark, believed to have been written closer to mid-century, before the destruction of the Jerusalem Temple, also preserves important details. According to Mark (15:46, repeated at Matthew 27:59ff.), following death (and following the granting of permission to afford him honorable treatment), Jesus's body was wrapped in clean linen cloth and he was laid in a tomb "hewn in the rock." Then a large stone was rolled in front of the entrance to seal it. Finally, on the third day, the two Marys returned to visit the deceased. Written later in the century, Luke (23:56) adds that the women "prepared spices and ointments" with which they intended to treat the body on the third day. The author of John agrees that spices were used, but thinks that they were wrapped in the linen cloths, "according to the burial custom of the Jews" (19:39).

Before commenting on this sequence of practices, it is necessary to recall a prior step, spoken of in Acts 9. There we read the story of a disciple named Tabitha, Dorcas in Greek. The story, ultimately about Tabitha's miraculous restoration to life, relates that, when she died, she was washed and laid in the room upstairs (v. 37). No reason is given for either step, but both are paralleled in later rabbinic tradition. Explanations offered in this later tradition want us to believe that the laying of the body upstairs was intended to keep it cool, to delay decomposition. Washing is nowhere explicitly explained even in rabbinic literature, so interpretation will have to await a fuller context.

These testimonies speak only of the preparation and burial of the dead. Because Jesus was, in the eyes of the authorities, an executed criminal, there was no possibility of a proper funeral. Fortunately, Josephus, a contemporary of these early Christian writers, turns his attention to the funeral as such. Defending Jewish faith and practice against its attackers, Josephus writes:

> The pious rites which it provides for the dead do not consist of costly obsequies or the erection of conspicuous monuments. The funeral ceremony is to be undertaken by the nearest relatives, and all who pass while the burial is proceeding must join the procession and share the mourning of the family. After the funeral, the house and its inmates must be purified . . .
>
> (Against Apion, II, (26) 205)[12]

If we synthesize the accounts of Josephus and those of the Gospel authors (though, of course, we cannot be sure that they would have done so), the picture we have of first-century practices looks something like this: the deceased is washed and laid in a cool place. In preparation for burial, he is dressed in simple linen garments, which may contain spices and incense. The funeral itself is the responsibility of the family, though others in the community will join in accompanying the deceased to the grave. The body is laid in the grave and a large stone rolled in front of the entrance to the tomb. Returning home, survivors purify the house and everything in it. On the third day, they visit the tomb, possibly bringing spices and ointments for treatment of the deceased.

The visit on the third day after burial (which itself should take place on the day of death) is of particular interest. The third day is distinguished, by implication but nonetheless clearly, from the fourth day in John 11 – the story of Lazarus. This story emphasizes that Jesus arrives at the tomb of Lazarus on the fourth day following his death. Because Lazarus has been dead for four days, there is an immense stench which issues from the tomb when it is opened. Nevertheless, Jesus prays to God and then calls to Lazarus to come out of the tomb. Thereupon, miraculously, Lazarus steps forth.

The key to this story is the *miraculous* revival of Lazarus. It is miraculous because, on the fourth day following death, the stench of death gives indisputable evidence that the individual is dead and decaying. Before this, though, it is not certain that what looks like death is indeed that. For this reason, it appears, survivors visit the deceased on the third day: to anoint him with oils (for his comfort), (presumably) to pray on his behalf, perhaps to visit him for the last time before death is absolutely certain, and generally to ascertain his state.

The many burial tombs in the environs of Jerusalem confirm, in important measure, the testimony of the literature. These tombs are, as the Gospel of Mark reported, carved into the rock, creating burial caves of various sizes (McCane 1992: 43). Filling in the silence of contemporary writers, the tombs show that the deceased were mostly laid into body-sized niches (loculi) in the walls of the caves or placed on shelves carved into the sides of the caves (arcosolia), over which were arched ceilings. The deceased could be placed in stone sarcophagi or wooden coffins, or simply laid directly into the burial niche (McCane 1992: 46). Many tombs are constructed of only one chamber, for use by a single family, but others are far more elaborate (McCane 1992: 87–9).[13]

Various personal effects, found at burial sites around Jerusalem from this period, provide evidence that the deceased would be visited and gifts left behind. For example, in a large catacomb south of the Temple Mount, archaeologists have found oil lamps from the late Second Temple period. It is possible, though not likely, that these lamps were left in the belief that the deceased needed light to see by. More likely, the lamps were used by survivors visiting their dead. Small glass jugs (amphora), used for holding liquids, were also found. These may have been used to hold oils for anointing the bodies of the deceased or fragrances to mask the smell of death. In any case, they are again evidence that the dead were visited by the living. Unfortunately, we can only guess when and how often these visits took place (Avni and GreenHut 1994).

Adding significantly to the literary record, the remains of burial tombs also show that secondary burial of the bones of the dead (ossilegium), following decomposition of the flesh, was commonly practiced by Jews during this period. McCane's catalogue of sites shows relatively few exceptions to this rule. Bones may merely have been relocated in charnels. But dignified reburial of the bones in small stone boxes designed for this purpose (ossuaries) was common. In fact, the decorative motifs of these ossuaries have drawn much attention. They are commonly decorated with rosettes or other floral motifs, various geometric designs, representations of ashlar building stones and architectural columns, and menorahs. The meaning of these decorations has been much debated, some claiming that the carvings are *mere* decoration, mundane in every sense, and others arguing that they represent various eschatological beliefs. I lean in the latter direction, for reasons I will explain in Chapter 5. At present, what we may say without hesitation is that death ritual was not completed until long after death, when the bones of the deceased were finally reinterred (for more on the archaeological record, see Chapter 5).

The practice of ossilegium (reburial) has been associated with the belief that death is not a moment but an extended process, a process that is not over until only the bones are left (Metcalf and Huntington 1972: ch. 5). Is this the belief of Palestinian Jews in the first century? We have seen in the literature of this period that the first three days following death were significant, probably because, during this time, it was not even clear that death had occurred ("it may have been a swoon"). So people do not burst into death; they fall into it slowly. And the literature of prior centuries had already recorded the belief that death would be followed by resurrection. Death is not the end, then. It is an extended and possibly progressive state, one that is followed by new life. It is reasonable to suppose, therefore, that reburial as practiced by Jews meant the same thing as it did when practiced by others. Flesh decomposed, death had finally been accomplished. For this reason, the deceased was removed to his or her final resting-place; final, that is, until resurrection itself.

A full picture of death practices would demand much more. But these sources yield a clear outline, at least, of Jewish death-practice in the centuries before the rabbis. As we shall see, despite a variety of differences in detail, the traditions and teachings of the rabbis replicate what we have learned here in significant respects.

3

EARLY RABBINIC
DEATH-PRACTICES

The evidence of the Mishnah

In the late second century, a small group of rabbinic masters and their disciples gathered in the Galilee. Having recovered from the ravages of the war with Rome (133–5 CE), these scholars and religious visionaries sought to redefine Judaism for an unprecedented age. Mere decades following Rome's suppression of the revolt led by Bar Kokhba, these rabbis, like other Jews around them, could no longer imagine that the Temple in Jerusalem would be rebuilt "speedily and in their days," that Jewish autonomy would be recovered through some messianic miracle. Facing a people traumatized by upheaval and loss, the rabbis grappled with fundamental issues of definition and direction.[1]

The document that records the outcome of their collective deliberations is the Mishnah. Produced under the leadership of the Jewish patriarch, Rabbi Judah, this Mishnah was an extraordinary composition – a work which, in six "orders" containing ten times as many tractates, defined the laws, practices and institutions of Judaism in intimidating detail. Part practical guide, part idealized vision, this great rabbinic opus would form the foundation of (rabbinic) Jewish forms for centuries to come.[2]

The Mishnah addressed much, though not all, of Jewish life, public and private. Naturally, it addressed many matters of concern to common Jews: prayers, holidays, and the like. It also built a structure for the administration of justice, beginning with torts, proceeding to laws of property and inheritance, and concluding with regulations of the court, its disposition of capital and civil cases, and procedures relating to judges and witnesses. Matters of more esoteric concern also commanded ample attention. At length, the Mishnah defined the structure of the Jerusalem Temple and its sacrificial service. It left no stone unturned when elaborating the system of ritual impurity – who was impure, at what level, and with what consequences? It expounded on agricultural gifts to the priests, the Levites and the poor. In sum, the Mishnah defined a system, a vision, a religious society in the broadest sense.

But, for reasons that defy discovery, the Mishnah also failed to elaborate systemic visions for crucial elements of Jewish life. Among these omissions were laws and customs relating to death, burial and mourning. Despite the constant presence of these concerns in human experience, and despite the apparently unbreakable nexus between death and religion, nowhere does the Mishnah lay out in detail a comprehensive system for dealing with these things. This is not to say that the Mishnah says nothing about death and mourning. Indeed, one may "cut and paste" scattered Mishnaic teachings concerning death-practices to create a relatively clear picture of the early rabbinic vision. But, if *we* seek to synthesize such a vision, we cannot forget that *the rabbis* did not present it to us complete, in whole cloth. Rather, however they imagined death, its practices and their meanings, they did not see fit to paint the picture on a single, large canvas. For the rabbis who composed the Mishnah, death was evidently not part of the systemic structure.[3]

Still, as I said, we may synthesize a relatively clear picture of death-practices as imagined by rabbis "in the academy."[4] If we take the Mishnah's word, how would its rabbinic authorities have wanted us to prepare and bury our dead and mourn for them after interment?

In the opinion of the rabbis of the Mishnah, death must be prepared for, or at least so in the case of a criminal convicted of a capital crime. Anticipating execution, the convict must, the Mishnah directs, confess his sins (San. 6:2). The Mishnah then adds: anyone who does so has a place in the World to Come.[5]

The convict, a sinner, must atone for his sin. Without atonement, his place in the World to Come is in doubt. This suggests that there will be judgment at some point following death. This judgment will determine who has a place in the future world and who not. Hence the need for the sinner to confess, to seek atonement. If there were no future judgment, no future life, there would be no sense talking about atonement in anticipation of death.

The language of this Mishnah (*"everyone* who confesses") suggests that the recommendation of confession (and therefore atonement) extends beyond the convicted criminal. Another text, in tractate Avot (2:10), is more explicit: "Repent one day before your death" the text demands. Why? Because atonement is contingent on prior repentance. If all persons are sinners – as we indeed are – then all must strive for atonement before the judgment after death. So this teaching, addressed to all Jewish persons (at least), also understands the need for appropriate preparation for death. We may already see that, for the sages of the Mishnah, death is not the end. It is a transition to something else, as yet barely defined.

Death was spoken of, and therefore understood, as "the exit of the soul" (or, overly literally, "the exit of the breath"). The Mishnah (Shab. 23, end) directs that a bystander should not touch the dying person, even to close his or her eyes, before the "exit of the soul" is clearly accomplished. Is this for fear that touching the dying will somehow hasten death? Certainly the Mishnah's warning that one who touches the dying person prematurely "spills blood" supports this interpretation. But we must also entertain the possibility that the Mishnah's prohibition is a reflection of the belief that the eyes are the "windows of the soul." If you close the window, you interfere with the death. Possibly the Mishnah's warning seeks to rationalize a more popularly held belief. We will see evidence of such a rationalizing tendency elsewhere.

Upon witnessing or hearing of the death of a relative, one must tear one's clothes and uncover one's shoulder (M.Q. 3:7), both symbols of grief.[6] The tear represents, on one level, the death itself, which "tears" the loved one from the presence of the living. The violence of the act evokes the violence of the experience and the emotion, the gravity of the loss. Clothes are civilizing elements, symbols of one's entry into society and civilization. The naked body which, in the opinion of ancient Jews (excepting those who had accepted Hellenistic norms), could not be uncovered in public, was rendered socially acceptable – public – by agency of clothing. Rending one's clothes, therefore, removed one from society, declaring that one who had lost a relative was no longer a part of general society.[7]

Immediately following death, the "needs of the dead" must be attended to. These "needs" – nearly identical to Roman practice (Toynbee 1971: 44)[8] – include closing the eyes of the dead, anointing and washing the body, removing the pillow, placing the dead on the sand (= the ground), and tying the jaw in place (Shab. 23:5). What is the purpose, individual or collective, of these various acts? The Mishnah explains the requirement to lay the body on the sand: "so that he may remain" or, according to another version, "be cooled." Reasonably enough, in a warm climate where the dead might quickly begin to decompose, steps would be taken to delay the process. But this does not explain the other practices, nor does it exhaust the possible interpretations of this one. Even the term used to describe these collective customs, "the needs of the dead," cries out for more extended interpretation. The Mishnah's explanation appears to be another "rationalization," much as in the case of the Mishnah's warning concerning closing the eyes of the dying person. What lies behind the rationalization? Consideration of the other steps taken at this time may provide a direction for interpretation.

Washing the dead, a practice maintained in many Jewish communities to this day, has long been called *tohara* – purification. But the term has no precedent in classical rabbinic literature, and its connotation is contrary to the essential qualities of the death context. The Torah (Numbers 19) makes it clear that the dead human body is the most powerful source of ritual impurity, so powerful, in fact, that contact with the dead can make something else a "father of impurity" (see m. Kelim 1:1, 5). It is inconceivable, therefore, that the dead can be purified. What else might washing, in combination with anointing, accomplish or represent?

As we seek an explanation for this practice, we should be aware that it is not only not uniquely Jewish, but it is, in fact, a common human practice, found world-wide.[9] As stated, the custom of the Roman citizens among whom Jews lived also commonly included washing and anointing. Virgil describes preparations for the funeral of Misenus this way:

> first they raise a huge pyre [preparing for the cremation of the dead]
> ... Some heat water, setting cauldrons a-bubbling on the flames, and wash and anoint the cold body.
>
> (Aeneid vi. 215–19)

The author emphasizes that the body is cold. For this reason, it seems, is the water heated – to dispel the cold which the body now experiences. No such explanation is stated or implied for the anointing but, if we posit a similar causation, it will not be difficult to imagine one. Just as the body is cold following death, so too is it increasingly stiff. If cold makes humans – *including the dead* – uncomfortable, so too does stiffness. If we want to insure the comfort of the dead, just as we must fight cold, so too must we fight stiffness. How better to fight this condition than to "oil" (quite literally) the body that is losing its flexibility?

How outrageous would such an explanation be in the Mishnaic context? The Mishnah's discussion of the "needs of the dead" is part of a larger discussion of stringencies and leniencies pertaining to acts that are technically permitted on the sabbath but are still problematic. For example, immediately preceding its discussion of preparations for burial, the Mishnah prohibits one to wait at the boundary of sabbath-settlement in order to be closer to his fields at the sabbath's end – if, that is, his purpose is to collect produce after the sabbath. But if his intent is merely to guard his fields, then he is permitted to wait by the boundary even before the sabbath has ended. In fact, merely standing by the boundary is technically permissible in either case (no prohibited act of labor is involved). The Mishnah's question is which technically permissible acts are prohibited or permitted and for what reasons. In the next ruling, "the business of the bride" and "the business of the dead" (bringing the casket and shroud) are permitted, apparently because of the importance of marriage and burial.

Which brings us to "the needs of the dead." These "needs of the dead" are distinct from the "business of the dead" – the latter involving preparations for the funeral and the former relating directly to the dead. The needs of the dead are apparently considered sufficiently important to warrant some flexibility with respect to acts that would ordinarily be prohibited on the sabbath. Why so? If we suppose that the dead was considered sentient, then the dead would have bona fide needs. And if the dead could experience discomfort, then these needs would include steps to diminish the discomfort. Washing and "oiling" (anointing) would then be called for, even on the sabbath. Admittedly, the Mishnah does not suggest the water should be heated. In fact, it recommends cooling the body to slow the process of decomposition. But, if a body is soiled in death, as is commonly the case, then washing would eliminate the discomfort of soiling. By the same token, if the body is sentient, decomposition would hurt, and slowing the process would postpone such discomfort. Surely, such an interpretation can find considerable support.[10]

The act of placing the dead on the ground, potentially rich in purpose and symbolism, likewise demands extended analysis. True, the Mishnah does, in this detail, carry its interpretation with it ("in order that he wait/be preserved"). But, as remarked earlier, such an explanatory phrase is highly unusual in the Mishnah; more typically the Mishnah merely prescribes a practice without such elaboration. Perhaps, then, the present explanation serves a polemical purpose. Perhaps there was a popular belief relating to this custom that the rabbis wished to argue against. The Mishnah's insistence on a pragmatic purpose may be an attempt to deny a more "mystical" explanation. At the very least, we must insist that such practices potentially carry multiple meanings, and so explanation is not exhausted by the Mishnah's own proposal.

In their discussion of the burial practices of the Mambai people of Indonesia, Peter Metcalf and Richard Huntington propose a connection between death-practices and creation myths. In the particular case considered there, Mother Earth, who gives birth to humanity, is owed a debt – a debt that is paid with the bodies of the dead (Metcalf and Huntington 1972: 106–7). Is such a connection also at work in the present Jewish ritual? Genesis 2:7 relates that "the Lord God formed the person [out of] dirt from the ground and blew into his nostrils the breath of life." Much later, Ecclesiastes states the opinion that, just as all life comes from dirt, so will all life return to dirt (3:20). Placing the dead on the ground may therefore represent the first step of the return of the life to the soil.[11] Saul Lieberman documents the ancient Jewish belief (held by other peoples as well) that no fate was worse than lack of burial – lack of return to the soil (Lieberman 1965: 515–22). If the dead would suffer by distance from the soil, then this practice may also be another "need of the dead" intended to avoid discomfort. This act, like others listed in the Mishnah, addressed or responded to genuine needs of the dead, literally conceived. For this reason were these practices permitted on the sabbath.

Following immediate attentions to the dead, the next step is preparation of the funeral and burial place. The same Mishnah just examined speaks of the need to ready a coffin and a shroud and, according to one version,[12] also requires the hiring of flute-players and female wailers for the procession to the grave. The grave site needs to be dug out or, at the very least, requires final preparation (M.Q. 1:6). Different opinions were recorded concerning the details of the burial structure, but there was fundamental agreement on the nature of burial. Burial – a misleading word in this context – takes place in caves of different sizes and capacities. Within the caves are "loculi" (Heb.: *kokhim*), holes carved straight into the walls which are large enough for a single body. Several kokhim are carved into the wall opposite the entrance and more on each side wall. Several such caves might open onto a central "courtyard," a larger room within the cave structure (B.B. 6:8). These caves must be at least 50 cubits outside of the city, and might be found in what the Mishnah calls "grave neighborhoods" (Ohal. 6:3).[13]

The requirement of distancing burial from the place of settlement invites several explanations. The Mishnah itself (B.B. 2:9) groups this law with similar regulations concerning tanneries and the dumping of animal carcasses, suggesting that offensive smell is the primary concern. But earlier Jews were also accustomed to bury their dead outside of cities, probably motivated by the immensely powerful impurity of the dead. The Qumran *Temple Scroll*, zealously concerned with maintaining the purity of at least the "sanctuary" city, expresses the same demand polemically: "You shall not do as the nations do; they bury their dead everywhere . . . Rather you shall set apart areas in the midst of your land where you shall bury your dead" (cols. 46 and 48; Vermes 1987: 144–5). If for earlier Jews purity was a concern, this must certainly have been a factor for the purity-concerned rabbis who wrote the Mishnah as well.[14] Finally, though there is no direct evidence here, we might speculate that there was fear of the immediate presence of the dead – and of possible consequences for the living – following death.

Crucially, the Mishnah prohibits leaving the dead unburied overnight, except "for his honor," such as to bring a casket and shrouds (San. 6:5). I have already mentioned the ancient fear – Jewish and non-Jewish – of leaving the dead unburied. The Mishnah's prescribed urgency is an unmistakable expression of the same sensibility. I have also proposed that the desire to "return the dead to the earth whence he came" seems to be at work in regulations concerning death rituals. The present prohibition might likewise represent a desire to uphold the normative consequences of the mythical creation narrative. We should also not forget that Deuteronomy (21:23) – along with the Mishnah in which this general burial obligation appears – demands that the executed criminal be buried "on that very day." If the criminal merits such treatment, can the rabbis allow the common person to be treated with any less dignity?

While the dead relative is as yet unburied, or if one is directly involved in the funeral, one is exempt from the obligations of reciting the Shema and donning tefillin (prayer straps) (Ber. 3:1). Presumably, one is also released from the obligation of reciting prayers, which are viewed as a rabbinic and not a scriptural obligation.[15] Why these exemptions? Again, pragmatic and symbolic explanations suggest themselves.

Practically speaking, the demands of preparing a funeral and burial are considerable, particularly since, as we have seen, burial should ideally be done on the same day as death. The importance of burial and the urgency of preparations would have been reason enough to grant release from other obligations. But the Mishnah also tells us that one awaiting the burial of his or her relative may not eat "holy things," excepting the Paschal lamb, in which case one may immerse and then eat (Pes. 8:8). If the Mishnah were speaking of someone who was actually impure by reason of contact with the dead, eating of the Paschal lamb would not have been permitted (see Pes. 9:1). So relation to death, even independent of actual impurity, is contrary to "holiness." One who has been "touched" by death bears the consequences, even if he or she has not actually come into contact with the source of defilement.[16] For this reason also must the close relative of the deceased refrain from holy rites.

The details which the Mishnah records can be reconstructed into a funeral which looks something like this: Functionally, the funeral is a ritual for transporting the dead to the grave. The dead is carried on a bier, and several groups of transporters might be involved in a single funeral (Ber. 3:1). On the way to the grave, the dead male might be placed down in the road, to provide opportunity for the expression of grief. Probably because of the private nature of women in rabbinic society, the Mishnah directs that this ritual not be performed for women (M.Q. 3:8). Still, this does not mean that women should not be mourned publicly; they should be. It is simply deemed inappropriate to place their bodies down in the public thoroughfare.

Depending upon interpretation, the Mishnah may require a quorum (a minyan) for the ritual of transporting the deceased to the grave, called "standing and sitting" (Meg. 4:3). Unfortunately, the reference to "standing and sitting" stands alone, without a context to clarify either the substance of the ritual or when it takes place. Similar isolated references are found later in the Tosefta (Pes. 3:15 and Meg. 3:14) and the Yerushalmi (Meg. 4:4, 75a), leaving us without early interpretive traditions to illuminate the Mishnah's reference. The Bavli will later clearly interpret the "standing and sitting" ritual as a ritual of comfort, to be enacted immediately after burial (see B.B. 100b).[17] But the minor tractate, Soferim, understands "standing and sitting" to speak of a funeral ritual, to be conducted on the way to the burial place.[18] This interpretation, representing Palestinian rabbinic tradition, seems to me the more likely one; in other words, the Babylonian tradition, without direct familiarity with the Palestinian practice, misinterpreted the sources it inherited. If this judgment is correct, then, in the opinion of the Mishnah, not only is the funeral procession to be public, but it is also to be interrupted by numerous "standings" and "sittings," during which time expressions of grief should be enunciated. The interruptions themselves represent the difficulty of saying goodbye to the deceased. The beginning of transport to the next world is undertaken without eagerness.

As in contemporary Roman society, women are seen as central to the public lamentation of the dead, male or female (Toynbee 1971: 45). In the Mishnah's vision, women should cry out, together or responsively, and clap loudly (M.Q. 3:8–9). As we saw earlier, flutes should also be played. In fact, this was viewed as so crucial to the funeral that the Mishnah assures a married woman that her husband will provide, at her funeral, at least two flutes and one "wailer." This latter detail suggests that women who participated in funerals in this capacity were specialists, if not professionals.[19]

The wailing and noise-making of the Mishnah's funeral, known also in many other societies, provides us with important insight concerning the "appropriate" emotional posture one should assume at a funeral.[20] The crying and wailing would, at the very least, give expression to the official sadness of the community in the presence of death. Presumably, the ritualized crying was also meant to evoke genuine feelings of remorse in participants and passers-by. *Ritualized* crying would lead to *spontaneous* crying. The sound of the flute, reminiscent of the wailing human voice, would contribute to setting the same general tone, and clapping could be an expression of anger, of remorse, or of fright. Heard together, the din of the lament would allow few in the neighborhood to escape this public expression of the community's (not merely the individual's) loss.[21]

The Mishnah says nothing about a ritual at the grave itself. From the grave structures described earlier, we know that the dead are to be placed in holes in the sides of caves. The Mishnah assumes that, following insertion, the hole will be covered by a rolling stone (Ohal. 2:4 and 15:8). A board might also be used for the same purpose (Ohal. 15:8). At this point, with the dead in his or her not-so-final resting-place (more on this later), immediate attention turns to surviving relatives. No longer an *onen* – the Mishnaic term for a person between the death and burial of a close relative – one now officially becomes a mourner.

The mourners and those who accompany them "return." (Does this mean "begin to return?" Actually return to their homes? The Mishnah is not clear.) The comforters stand in lines, some on the inside (i.e. closer to the mourners) and some on the outside (Ber. 3:2). There they offer comfort to the mourners (M.Q. 3:7). Mourners addressed by the lines of comforters are described either as "receiving" comfort (Ber. 2:7) or as being comforted (San. 2:1). By speaking of the mourner as "receiving" comfort, the Mishnah may be alluding to a ritual expression of condolences or, to be more precise, to a "blessing of/ for mourners" (which, however, is explicitly distinguished from "comforting of mourners") (M.Q. 3:7). The blessing requires the presence of a minyan (Meg. 4:3) and is therefore considered a community event.

Though the Mishnah preserves no record of a formula for this blessing, it does suggest formulae for offering comfort. The first such formula is preserved in an unexpected context. In the midst of its enumeration of the gates of the Jerusalem Temple and specification of the measures of that Temple, Mishnah Middot (2:2) relates that, under ordinary circumstances, those who entered the Temple Mount would turn to the right and traverse the mount's circumference in a counter-clockwise direction. However, those who had experienced tragedies, including the death of a loved one, would instead tread in a clockwise direction. Because they were "going against the flow," mourners would be recognized in their mourning and the larger population would have the opportunity to offer comfort. And what, according to the Mishnah, were they to say? "May the One who dwells in this House comfort you."

This simple expression is reminiscent of later common formulae for comforting mourners. However, its representation in this Mishnah raises more questions than it answers. The most immediate question is why this is described as a Temple ritual. If there is a historical foundation for the Mishnah's much later description, then we have discovered little concerning general rituals of comfort. If what is offered here is an imagined ideal, then it is even more perplexing that the Temple is given as the stage for performance of the ritual. In either case, the ritual is extremely restricted in its application. Moreover, there is no evidence that the rabbis want to extend its performance beyond the long-since-destroyed walls of the Temple Mount.

The second proposed formula is meant to be expressed to the High Priest who has lost a relative. In the words of Mishnah Sanhedrin, "the people say to him: we are your atonement; and he says to them: may you be blessed from heaven" (San. 2:1). Unlike the ritual described in Middot, this one finds no echo in later practice. Still, we must inquire into the meaning of this required expression of comfort to the priestly mourner. In particular, why should the mourning priest require atonement? What, if anything, is the general relation of mourning and atonement? These questions are especially suggestive because, as we have already observed, death itself is viewed as atonement. The Mishnah, speaking of the impending death of the convicted felon, is explicit in this connection: before execution he is directed to declare "May my death serve as expiation for all of my sins!" (San. 6:2). This parallel suggests (again!) that survivors are somehow touched by death.[22] Is the death of a loved one understood as punishment for one's sin? Does the survivor somehow participate in the death, in however small a measure? It is impossible to say. Still, it seems clear that there is a mysterious relationship between the dead and the survivor.

But even this interpretation is not without its problems. Why is this formula addressed *only* to the priest? Why is there not a similar sense in the formula directed to the common Jew on the Temple Mount? Such limited applications speak against general conclusions. Furthermore, we cannot fail to notice that both formulae of comfort appear in contexts that are not merely restricted but also outmoded. At the time of the Mishnah's composition, the Temple was in ruins and the High Priesthood was no more. Why would the rabbis restrict formulae for comforting mourners to such forgotten contexts? Do they not know of formulae employed by their contemporaries? Or are they suggesting that formulae, as opposed to more spontaneous personal expressions, are inappropriate? This latter proposal, while not impossible, seems contrary to the rabbis' general affection for ritual formulae. Yet the absence of models in contemporary practice would not seem to restrict the rabbis elsewhere. Why would they not formulate appropriate general expressions here? We are probably safest in merely noting that the Mishnaic record concerning these matters is incomplete. If there was a general formula of comfort, the Mishnah does not record it.

Upon return from the burial-place, a post-funeral meal should be provided. Unlike in contemporary Roman custom, this meal is eaten at the home of the mourner, not at the grave itself.[23] It should be brought to the mourner's home in a simple basket and eaten by the mourner on an overturned divan (M.Q. 3:7).

The symbolisms of this ritual are multiple and complex. The meal itself is a life-affirming act. The taking of sustenance, enjoyed only a short period after the interment, distinguishes the survivor from the deceased – although we have to consider the possibility that the dead, too, were imagined as eating. The very name applied to the meal – "the meal of giving health (or strength)" – supports this reading of the ritual's significance. It is notable, moreover, that the Mishnah attaches no restrictions to what may be eaten at the meal. By contrast, Mishnah Ta'anit 4:7 declares that, during the final meal before the fast of the Ninth of Av (the commemoration of the destructions of the Temples), no wine may be drunk nor more than one sort of dish consumed. If the pre-Ninth of Av meal emphasizes mourning for the destructions, the post-funeral meal, by contrast, affirms the return back to life.

At the same time, the post-funeral meal is to be eaten on an overturned couch, suggesting a disruption of normal routine, a failure fully to re-enter the land of the living. Does the overturned couch declare that normal comfort is unavailable to the survivor? Or (as later commentaries will suggest) does it echo the condition of the deceased, whose life has been overturned and who now, quite literally, lies on the ground? Indeed, the survivor's proximity to the ground imitates the dead, suggesting again the commonality of experience. Finally, we may imagine that this proximity brings the living closer to the dead, a position which the survivor will leave slowly as mourning progresses. If, as we will suggest, mourning is a process by which the mourner re-enters the society of the living, it would be reasonable to see him/her as beginning the process in close connection with the world of the dead.

The Mishnah records astoundingly little on mourning as such, and though we may glean scattered details, nothing like a full picture of mourning practices emerges from its many tractates. The Mishnah does clearly indicate that mourners are not permitted to wash (Ber. 2:6). From regulations relating to restrictions on work during the intermediate days of festivals (Sukkot and Passover), we learn that mourners are restricted from working as well (see M.Q. 2:1–2). And the Mishnah's reference to different time periods relating to mourning (seven days and thirty days) suggests that certain enactments (probably prohibitions) pertain to each of these periods. From the text of the Mishnah itself, we have no idea what the other specific practices of these mourning periods might be.

But, even on the basis of these few details, we may venture out on an interpretive limb. At least at the earliest stage of mourning, the mourner sits on the ground (as we saw above). He does not wash. Both acts are, in the context in which the rabbis wrote, distinctly anti-social. In that society, one reclined on a couch to take a formal meal with others. Though few washed frequently, washing was certainly necessary to participate in social contact and the failure to wash, therefore, would distance or separate one from such contact. The same would be the consequence of restricting work which, under ordinary circumstances, involves a range of social contacts. The latter restriction might also symbolize the alienation of the mourner from acts of building or settling the world.

At the same time, the designation of different mourning periods suggests a process which brings one, in progressive fashion, from the state of mourning to a state of normality. The mourner begins by separating him or herself from the society of others. Her or his relationship with the dead diminishes (or, we might prefer, changes) slowly. Somehow, the rituals of these consecutive periods direct the mourner to bid farewell to the dead and rejoin the living.

Before leaving the mourning ritual, it is essential to note that the two restrictions which the Mishnah does explicitly list – on washing and on work – are part of the package of restrictions that are observed in the case of a communal fast. To be more specific, according to Mishnah Ta'anit, chapter 1, ongoing drought necessitates a series of increasingly severe fasts. At the most extreme stage of a drought, the court declares communal fasts which, in addition to beginning in the evening (as opposed to preliminary fasts which are considered "individual" and begin only in the morning of the fast-day), are marked by a series of additional restrictions. These restrictions, formulaic in their repetition, are: no work, no washing, no anointing, no wearing shoes, and no sex (mishnah 6). Furthermore, later in the same tractate, the Mishnah records a dispute concerning the ritual for marking the destruction of the Jerusalem Temple, an occasion of both fasting and mourning. There (4:7) R. Judah requires that Jews commemorating the destruction "overturn the couch/bed," though the sages don't agree. As we have seen, the Mishnah knows this practice as a mourning ritual during the post-funeral meal, and the association with mourning seems a reasonable source for R. Judah's directive to those lamenting the destruction. Thus, though the Mishnah is far from explicit, we may imagine that this practice is already accepted by early rabbinic authorities as a mourning ritual.

The partial overlap of fasting and mourning customs suggests at least a partial theological association as well. If, as the Mishnah proposes, cessation of rain should be understood as a divine rebuke, then we might imagine the loss of a loved one as a sort of divine rebuke, at least in the minds of the rabbinic authors. If we recognize that all suffering is, for these authors, probably God's punishment, then we may readily understand such an interpretation of the suffering caused by the loss of a loved one (Kraemer 1995: ch. 4). Because of the imperfect mishnaic equation of mourning and fasting rituals, at least on the explicit level, we shall have to reserve judgment on the viability of this interpretation until a later time.

The Mishnah tells us nothing about what the deceased is doing at this same time. This is not because he or she is doing nothing – at least not necessarily so. As we have already noted, burial caves in the Land of Israel have yielded an abundance of common objects, mostly what we would call household goods. These include, with varying frequency, eating and drinking vessels, lamps, cooking pots, small bottles and jugs for oils, jewelry and the like.[24] Did some of these vessels serve surviving family members who, like their neighbors elsewhere in the Roman empire, ate meals with the dead during the first year after death (Toynbee 1971: 51)? In all likelihood they did. Did survivors supply their deceased with food for their own support during this same period? If, as we have said, the practice of reburial means that death was viewed as an extended process, it is reasonable to suppose that survivors did indeed undertake the feeding of the dead. While it is possible that the rabbis whose views are recorded in the Mishnah imagined death in ways distinct from common Jews, other evidence suggests that they shared at least some of these common beliefs. Therefore, the Mishnah's silence to the condition of the deceased during this period may not be because there is nothing to say about it. The Mishnah may simply be more interested in what comes at the end of these developments.

Confirming the rabbis' acceptance of popular practice, the Mishnah assumes that, at some point after burial (after the flesh of the deceased has finished decomposing), the bones of the dead will be collected and reinterred.[25] R. Meir and R. Yose dispute the affective nature of this procedure: is it an occasion for joy or mourning (M.Q. 1:5)? Presumably, sadness would be the consequence of the final intimate contact with the deceased. On the other hand, joy would be a product of the recognition that, whatever the status of the deceased in life, the end of the process of decomposition brings the confidence that the sins of the dead have been fully atoned (San. 6:6). Whatever the emotional experience of the ritual of reburial, the one who collects the bones returns, however briefly, to the condition of one who has just lost a loved one; like an *onen*, the bone-collector must immerse before he may partake of certain holy portions (Pes. 8:8).

If mourning is a process then, the present evidence suggests, so too is death. If it takes time to return to the society of the living, it also takes time to arrive at the world of the dead. Jews (as described by these early rabbis) are hardly the only ones to have practiced collection of bones and reburial (ossilegium). On the contrary, this is a common practice, prevalent in many societies around the world at different periods.

In connection with secondary treatment of the dead (that is, final treatment of the bones months after what we call death), Metcalf and Huntington support the following interpretation:

The metaphor is that, where secondary treatment occurs, the fate of the corpse is a model for the fate of the nonmaterial component of the person . . . At least two things follow in terms of ideology. First, that dying is a slow process of transition from one spiritual state to another. Second, the process of spiritual change is disagreeable, in the same way that the decomposition of the corpse is disagreeable . . . also that the recently dead somehow hover near human habitation, whereas the long dead are removed and anonymous.[26]

Based upon the scant explicit evidence of the Mishnah, it is difficult to say how completely this interpretation aligns with the view of the Mishnaic rabbis. Still, there is strong presumptive support of such a reading. As we saw earlier, Mishnah Sanhedrin (6:6) believes that the completion of the decomposition of the flesh represents the culmination of atonement for the dead. Suffering is viewed as a means of effecting atonement, and death, as the most extreme or final suffering, is thus thought a powerful (perhaps the most powerful) force for realizing personal atonement. The later rabbinic record will preserve reference to the "sufferings of the grave" and, though we must admit the danger of "reading in" in the case of this Mishnah, it may nevertheless be true that, in its view, decomposition brings suffering to the dead and the realization of atonement (the flesh finally being gone) represents the end of that suffering. We must also not forget the Mishnaic opinion that the wicked are judged in Gehenna for twelve months (Edduyot 2:10) – presumably the twelve months following death, the same period during which the flesh is decomposing. The evidence, while neither explicit nor abundant, is still strong. It appears likely, then, that death is understood as a process – one which begins with what we moderns would call death and extends until the bones alone are left.

What is apparently the last step in the long process of death is unremarkable and fully expected: the grave should be marked (Sheq. 1:1 and M.Q. 1:2) and a tomb – called *nefesh* (soul) – may be built over it. If the graves of the dead are to be visited, markers will designate the exact places they may be found. If the concern is the ritual impurity of the dead, markers will serve equally as pragmatic a purpose: to direct the individual who wants to preserve his purity where not to tread. Whichever the more immediate purpose, the final "resting-place" is identified.

Does the dead, now without body, still rest at this place? The belief of the Mishnah in this matter is nowhere recorded. However, given what we have surmised about the life of the dead before "collection of the bones," we should not immediately dismiss the possibility that the marker also reminds the survivor where her loved one may be contacted, consulted, and otherwise engaged. The tomb may continue to be the home of the soul. Popular belief, surely, will support such a view.

4

EARLY EXPANSIONS AND COMMENTARIES

The testimony of the Tosefta and Tannaitic Midrashim

The Mishnah's record of teachings relating to death, burial and mourning was clearly deficient. Though, in an unsystematic fashion, the Mishnah included significant details, it would be difficult for even ancient students of the document to reconstruct complete rituals based upon its selective account. In the matter of mourning, in particular, those looking to the Mishnah for direction would find themselves without an adequate foundation.

The condition just described characterized not only laws of death and mourning but other parts of the Mishnah as well. Further, whether relatively complete or incomplete in its exposition of a particular body of law, there was always something that demanded clarification, always details which could be added. Accordingly, some time in the century following the redaction of the Mishnah, other sages undertook to collect other teachings, most relating to the Mishnah in some way, to clarify and supplement the groundwork laid by the Mishnah. This collection was known, appropriately, as the Tosefta ("additions").[1]

At the same time, sages of this period recognized that one of the Mishnah's most significant "gaps" was its general failure to indicate the relationship of its regulations with the laws of the Torah. Probably in response to this condition, they began to assemble teachings – midrashim – that justified rabbinic law on the basis of Torah law, showing how the former derived from the latter. These midrashim were organized as "commentaries" on the legal books of the Torah (excluding Genesis) – hence, they are called halakhic midrashim – and they represent the other side of the rabbinic record from this period (third to early-fourth century) (Neusner 1983; Kraemer 1995: 79–80).

The halakhic midrashim contribute little to our record of rabbinic death and mourning practices. But the Tosefta is an abundant source, and though the Tosefta often repeats the substance of the Mishnah's laws – adding only a detail here and there – in some instances the Tosefta's additions allow us, for the first time, to recreate the ritual as a whole. Again, we can only be certain that we have in these additions the imagination of the study-house. Whether

36

the teachings of the sages reflect the lived reality of other Jews in the same environs we cannot yet judge.

What did the sages of the Tosefta teach that we did not earlier know?

The Tosefta adds several rituals pertaining to the funeral and the house of mourning, supplying "histories" for each. First, any objects which have come into contact with the corpse of a woman require immersion. The Tosefta relates that this practice originated in connection with women who died while menstruating. But because of the "honor of women" this practice was extended to include all women. Similarly, while the deceased is being transported to the place of burial, he or she should be preceded by someone carrying burning incense. Again, as the Tosefta understands it, this practice first pertained only to the funerals of those who died from intestinal illness, the stench of which the incense would presumably mask. But to avoid embarrassing those who died this way, the practice was extended to all funerals. In addition, it was earlier the case (as the Tosefta "remembers" it) that the wealthy would be carried to burial on elaborate beds and the poor on simple biers. But to preserve the dignity of the poor, it became the custom to carry out all dead, whether rich or poor, in a similar fashion (all t. Niddah 9:16).

How are these "developments" and "protections" to be understood? In the case of the enactment protecting the "honor of women," we might well understand that the purpose is indeed to protect the dignity of living women. In a society where the menstrual taboo was a powerful force, distinguishing those who died while menstruating might be the source of embarrassment for other menstruating women. But, in the case of the practice of burning incense, a parallel analysis is impossible. In this instance, the Tosefta explicitly indicates that the goal is to protect the honor of the *dead*. In the other cases, therefore, we must consider the possibility that the women and poor whose honor is being defended are those who have already died. That the honor of the dead (as well as the living) requires protection is clear. And the Mishnah already hinted that the dead continue to sense what is happening in the world they have begun to leave, so they would naturally feel disgrace or pain. The current practices, whatever their origin, seem to respect this perceived reality.

At the same time, the proffered "histories" (= interpretations) of these rituals indicate that death is understood by the rabbinic authors as what we might call "a levelling experience." Whatever distinctions may have divided people in their lives – wealth or poverty, health or sickness, gender – are symbolically erased with the advent of death. That this may not earlier have been recognized (as far as the Tosefta is concerned) is beside the point. The practice currently endorsed by the sages whose opinions are recorded in this document recognizes and upholds equality. Though other considerations (such as righteousness or wickedness) might divide individuals after death, distinctions that living persons experience most frequently are erased when the journey to the other world begins.

Additional or alternative preparations of the dead are described. According to the Mishnah, the deceased was to be placed on the soil "so that he may remain" or, in another version, "so that he may be cooled" (m. Shab. 23:5). The Tosefta evidently prefers the latter version, though, in its record, the cooling is to be accomplished by placing "cooling vessels" and metal vessels on the belly of the deceased (whether this is in place of or in addition to placing the deceased on the ground is not clear). Further, in addition to tying the jaw of the deceased, the Tosefta requires that his or her orifices be stopped up (t. Shab. 17(18):18).[2]

In the Mishnah, steps of the sort described here were called "the needs of the dead." I proposed, in that connection, that this might be taken literally, that is, that the deceased actually has needs – potential discomforts or embarrassments – which these actions are meant to avoid. The Tosefta, however, may seem to call such an interpretation into question. In its larger discussion of vows, the Tosefta indicates that even if a person has taken a vow to derive no benefit from his neighbor, that neighbor may nevertheless provide the needs of his funeral because "there is no benefit for the dead" (t. Ned. 2:7). If this be taken literally, then the authority behind this particular teaching, at least, would not countenance my proposed interpretation. If the dead can derive no benefit or pleasure, then we must suffice with a more "rational" explanation of the present practices.

Yet, the claim that the dead have no benefit may be a mere legal position, an insistence that, for purposes of the law of vows, what one does for the deceased following death does not technically qualify as "benefit." Alternatively, it is possible that the authority behind the teaching in Tosefta Nedarim is doing no more than the teacher behind the Mishnah itself, that is, seeking to rationalize customs that are, at their base, far less rational. In either case, I incline to think that we should not read too much into the Tosefta's denial of benefit enjoyed by the deceased, for the evidence of belief in the sentience of the dead – in both earlier and later rabbinic texts – is too powerful to dismiss.

The Tosefta also notices a custom according to which women sit around the deceased on couches and pillows and cry for the dead (Kelim B.B. 2:8). This is apparently distinct from the practice, described in the Mishnah, of hiring women to wail for the dead during funerals. The custom spoken of here is more intimate, involving "their dead." Still, it is apparently assumed that it is women who will sit and cry in this fashion, not men. This distinction of genders in ritual responses to death is paralleled in other societies and commonly carries important symbolisms.[3] Women, we suppose, are socially accustomed to cry, and their cries – whether personal or professional – appropriately establish the mood by which death should be marked, at least in rabbinic understanding. Does the wailing, beyond expressing raw emotion, also communicate certain fears? Is it meant to drive away evil spirits? The rabbinic record, at this stage, offers no proof of such purposes or associations.

Nevertheless, we know enough about the beliefs of contemporary Jews to surmise that behind this brief rabbinic mention lie precisely such popular views.

We already noted that, according to the Tosefta, steps should be taken at the funeral to mask the odor of the deceased. This might be done with burning incense (as seen above) or by sprinkling perfumes before the bier (t. Sheq. 1:12). Local custom determines whether mourners should walk before or after the bier (t. Pes. 3:15–16). The lament ritual, often incorrectly translated as "eulogy," is defined according to the more literal meaning of the term *hesped*, that is, "*beating* the heart." The Tosefta (M.Q. 2:17) supports this definition by reference to Isaiah 32:12, where the meaning of the related term is indeed clear. The same funeral ritual also includes clapping and "beatifying" (from the Greek *kalos*), the latter defined as the spreading out of the arms.

These details, combined with related details preserved in the Mishnah, make it clear that the funeral was to be a very loud affair. Wailing, clapping and beating, flutes – all accompanied by dramatic movements – would create a spectacle that would be hard to ignore. As noted in the previous chapter, in a world where genuinely loud noises were relatively unusual, such a noisy event would be particularly notable (Metcalf and Huntington 1972: 67). Whether the noise was meant to define the affective quality of the funeral, to evoke response in passers-by, to chase away demons, or all of the above, again we may only speculate. What is certain, though, is that the Tosefta's Jewish funeral, like the Mishnah's before it, shared many of its rituals and sensibilities with "primitive" funerals in other societies distant from Palestine. It would be fair to say, in fact, that this funeral was as much a "human" one as it was a Jewish one – perhaps an indication that, in death, humans are humans and "artificial" distinctions therefore disappear. Again, death is the great leveller.

Concerning the burial itself, the Tosefta records several important additions. What is striking, first of all, is the tolerance of different burial customs. The Tosefta recognizes that the deceased might be buried naked or dressed. He or she might be buried in an ark of stone or wood, on a paved floor or a tablet of marble or on the ground. Once in place, the burial niche may be sealed with one or several stones, or even with a pile of smaller stones (Ahilot 2:3, 3:9–10, and 15:8). All of these variations are recorded essentially without comment, indicating the Tosefta's approval of each. Jews are evidently understood to lay their deceased to rest in a variety of ways, and the teachers behind the text see no reason to insist upon one custom above the other.

Perhaps the most important of its comments relating to burial is the Tosefta's indication of preference for burial in the Land of Israel because "one who is buried in the Land of Israel is as though buried under the altar [of the Temple in Jerusalem]" (A.Z. 4:3). The altar, of course, was the place where the sins of Israel (individual or collective) could be atoned. The assumption behind this teaching is therefore clear: one who dies requires atonement, because he or she will finally be judged. A sinner in life, he or she must remove the stain of sin, and, according to the present teaching, death alone (or, at least, the *beginning* of death) does not accomplish this cleansing.

The expression of this belief occasions no surprise; we already saw the assumed association of death and atonement in the Mishnah. The Tosefta, here and elsewhere, makes this association more explicit. In the final chapter of tractate Yom Hakippurim, for example, death is described as the most effective of the "four stages of atonement" that a sinner can experience (5:8). Other records of the early rabbinic tradition are likewise clear; words preserved in the tannaitic midrash, the Mekhilta, declare, "all those who die are atoned by their death" (*de-shira* 2; Horowitz and Rabin 1970: 126). So the need for atonement and the power of death to effect atonement are much attested. The present teaching merely adds that the *place* of burial may affect the final accounting. It is best to be buried in the Land of Israel because the land itself has the power to effect atonement. What may accomplish the same end for those buried elsewhere (and who, following death, still require atonement) is not yet indicated.

Why does death atone? Traditions commenting on atonement maintain silence on this question. But a related teaching, articulated within the contemporary rabbinic community, aids our analysis. In the early midrash on Numbers (Sifri 112; Horowitz 1966: 121–2), R. Nathan declares, "It is a good sign for a person if he is collected from [= punished] after his death. If he was not lamented or not buried or eaten by a wild animal or if rain fell on him [before he was buried] it is a good sign, for he was collected from after death. . . . " If it is good to be lamented and buried in dignity, why would these events constitute "a good sign?" This can all be understood only if we assume that the deceased, after death, is still sentient and can therefore still suffer. The experiences (and we may now call them experiences) described by R. Nathan would obviously be a source of pain and humiliation (= suffering) for the deceased. As we saw in the previous chapter, Jews of this period believed that suffering effects atonement (Kraemer 1995: 51–101), so a death which involves greater suffering (*after death*) would effect atonement more completely – surely a good sign for the deceased. And, of course, we may now generalize: death, which causes pain, consequently effects atonement. The deceased, who *feels* after death, *knows* after death, and is judged after death, will enjoy the benefits of this atonement, not in this world but in the World to Come.

The Tosefta's traditions pertaining to the return from the cemetery largely parallel what was recorded earlier in the Mishnah. There is, however, one significant addition: like the Mishnah, the Tosefta imagines that two lines of comforters should address the mourners as they leave the grave (t. Ber. 2:11). R. Judah adds, however, that if there is only one line, those who stand on that line may be divided into two categories – those whose purpose is "honor" and those whose purpose is "the mourner." Those whose purpose is to comfort the mourners are engaged in a *mitzvah* – a religious obligation – and are therefore exempt from other such obligations at that same moment. Those who, by their presence, simply mean to honor the mourners (perhaps because they do not know the mourners personally) would be obligated to perform other *mitzvot* should they arise at the time. Evidently, people are known to join funeral processions for different reasons, and the loud crying and noise-making described above may attract individuals who otherwise have no connection to the deceased or to survivors. Still, even in the absence of personal acquaintance, it is appropriate to honor the dead and the living by "accompanying" them on their respective journeys (the more literal trans-lation of the Hebrew word for funeral is "accompaniment").

At this stage, mourning properly begins, and here, as I commented earlier, the Tosefta's contribution to our understanding is significant. Indeed, it is on the basis of the Tosefta's teachings that we can, for the first time, paint a detailed picture of Jewish mourning customs as defined by the rabbis.

The crucial first step is found at t. Ta'anit 1:6, where we learn:

> All those [fasts responding to drought] concerning which it is said "they may [still] eat and drink when it gets dark," they are permitted to work, to wash, to anoint, to wear shoes and to have sex. . . . All those [more stringent fasts] concerning which they said "wearing shoes is prohibited," when he leaves the city he may put shoes on [and] when he arrives [again] at the city he removes them, *and so too do you say with respect to the one who is banned and the mourner.* [emphasis added]

At the very least, this tradition indicates that mourners are not permitted to wear shoes. But we know from the Mishnah that the rabbis also prohibited mourners from washing (m. Ber. 2:6), and there is no reason to believe that the Tosefta would hold a contrary opinion. The Mishnah also knew that mourners are not to involve themselves in work (m. M.Q. 2:1–2). Thus, at least part of the earlier list also pertains to mourners. If anointing is analogous to washing, then this also is denied to mourners. In fact, while it is not *necessary* to interpret the final phrase (highlighted here) as referring to all of the listed prohibitions, it is certainly *reasonable* to do so. Thus, this teaching will be making explicit the partial ritual equation between mourner and faster noted in the prior chapter. In this equation, we have a much fuller list of ritual prohibitions to be observed by the mourner.

This same source suggests a particular interpretation of the status of the mourner. This text is not primarily concerned with mourners but with individuals or communities who are observing fasts in response to drought. Why is fasting the appropriate ritual response to drought? Because the Torah (see Deuteronomy 11, for example) promises that God will provide timely rain as a reward for obedience to divine commands but will withhold rain as a punishment for disobedience. Thus, drought is considered evidence of sin and divine pleasure. As the Mishnah itself expresses it, those who fast on account of drought should conduct themselves as people with whom God is angry (m. Taan. 1:7). If drought is punishment for sin, then the appropriate response to drought is to seek atonement through fasting and repentance. Such fast days are, in effect, mini-Days of Atonement (Yom Kippur). If atonement is effected, rain will soon come.

Before bringing our attention to the mourner, we should note that the mourner appears here not only in the company of the one who fasts but in the company of the "banned one" as well. A person was banned in rabbinic society primarily for refusing to cooperate with or respect rabbinic judges or other communal officials. In other words, one who, in effect, refused to participate as an upstanding member of society was ostracized from that same society. As the Hebrew term for "banned" (*menude*) itself suggests, such an individual was cast outside, now untouchable.

The question which confronts us is obvious: Why are these three categories of individuals – those fasting in response to drought, those banned from society *and mourners* – spoken of in the same breath and marked by the same or similar rituals? Clearly, what is true of one must be assumed to be true, in some measure, of the others. What is it, then, that they have in common?

Is the mourner, like the faster, somehow experiencing punishment? Is the death of a loved one a sign of divine displeasure? We understood this opinion to be hinted at in the Mishnah (see p. 33) and the present more perfect equation powerfully supports such an interpretation. If the mourner suffers by the death of a loved one and if suffering is generally conceived of as punishment from God, then this interpretation is virtually necessary. Without understanding precisely how and in what measures death punishes both the deceased and the survivor, we may now venture with some confidence that this belief is at work here.

How should we understand the association of the mourner with the banned one? We may begin by building on what we have already said: if a person suffers, God must be angry with her. God's anger, certainly, is sufficient reason for others to avoid the one with whom God is angry – to place him or her outside of society. We need merely recall Miriam's exclusion from the camp of Israel when God was angry with her (see Numbers 12) to appreciate the necessity of this connection. At the same time, it is clear that the mourner is removed from common society. As we noted in the previous chapter, the failure to wash and anoint (to remove one's unpleasant bodily odors) and the prohibition of wearing shoes mean that a mourner has been removed from participation in the public realm. He has been "banned" from social intercourse, restricted to the domain of his private sorrow. He therefore must observe the rituals of the "banned one," whose general condition he shares.[4]

This conceptual association of faster, banned one, and mourner strengthens our proposal that the ritual equation suggested in this Tosefta is meant to be complete. We thus have record here of a much fuller description of the rituals of mourning. A mourner is restricted not only from washing and wearing shoes, but also from working and sexual intercourse. Extending the earlier interpretation to these details, we may suggest that work, too, is a social undertaking, generally requiring one to leave one's home and engage cooperatively with others. Furthermore, to work is to participate actively in the settlement of the world (*yishuv ha'olam*). The mourner's separation from the social world will also explain why he may not participate in its settlement and upkeep. It will also explain why he or she may not have sex, though it is a private and not public matter. Sex is essential for the same civilization-building enterprises from which the mourner is separated. This prohibition also, therefore, symbolically carries forward the same essential meaning previously attached to mourning.

I hesitate to add another level of interpretation which might appear quite natural. If we assume that a mourner is meant to be sad (and this will indeed appear natural to us) we might conclude that the prohibition of sex, for example, is meant to deny joy or pleasure and therefore assure sadness. This interpretation appears to me implausible, though, for two reasons. First, it is not clear what connection washing or, in particular, work have with joy. Will the failure to wash or work decrease one's joy? This consequence is surely not an obvious one (remember, people in antiquity bathed far less than we do, often no more than once a week, and *we* surely have no trouble associating the temporary release from work with *increase* in joy). Second, it is not clear that rabbinic mourning rituals (as opposed to the rituals of the funeral) sought to increase sorrow. Later rabbinic texts (see b. Ket. 8b) record a tradition, purported to derive from the same period as the Mishnah and the Tosefta, which recommends that a mourner drink ten cups of wine (but no more!) during a meal – to aid digestion and decrease sorrow. If later teachers can repeat this advice without hesitation, there is no reason to believe that the teachers of the Tosefta would insist otherwise. It is likely, then, that the rituals of the mourner more mark the rupture between the mourner and society – or the condition of the repentant seeking to gain atonement – than they do the presumed sadness of the one who has experienced a loss.

Details recorded elsewhere in the Tosefta further fill in our picture of the mourning ritual and simultaneously support our preferred interpretation of that ritual. Mo'ed Qatan 2:2 indicates that a mourner, during the initial seven-day mourning period but not during the remainder of the thirty days, may neither cut his or her hair nor do laundry. R. Judah adds that cutting finger nails is also prohibited. Pesaḥim 2(3):16 indicates that, except where customary on the sabbath, mourners may also not be greeted ("asked of their peace") by others. Trimmed hair, beards and fingernails are evidence of a concern for one's appearance, anticipating one's presence in the public realm.

The trimmed, ordered appearance also reflects, now visually, the ideally ordered society. On both levels, the chaos and dishevelment of uncut hair, beard and nails separates one from society – a society which expects conformity to standards of order and discipline.[5] Finally, and most obviously, the prohibition of greeting means that the simplest, most basic social exchange is denied the mourner. For reasons we have already proposed and perhaps others, the mourner is, practically and symbolically, estranged from the society of the living.

One last, crucial mourning ritual is introduced in the Tosefta as well. At Mo'ed Qatan 2:9, we learn that couches and beds in the home of the mourner are overturned (though they should be restored to their normal positions on the sabbath).[6] We saw such a custom in the Mishnah in connection with the first meal in the house of the mourner. However, there was no hint in that context that this practice should extend beyond this particular meal. Here we discover that, in the opinion of the Tosefta, at least, the ritual symbol appropriately marks the entire first week of mourning. Despite its apparently limited application in the Mishnah's vision, we had occasion, in the previous chapter, to venture interpretations of this striking practice (see p. 32). We here return to evaluate those interpretations, now with recognition of the more general presence of this symbol.

To recall our earlier proposals briefly, overturning the couches or beds would require that mourners sit or sleep on the ground, in proximity to their beloved deceased. This is evidence of the "echoing" or "mirroring" (noticed already in the Mishnah) of the experience of the dead and those who survive her.[7] The survivor – the mourner – participates, in limited measure, in the experience of the dead. Seeing, now, that this is true for the entire first week – not just at the first meal – such an interpretation gains considerable plausibility. At the same time, as we noted, later interpretations will suggest that the overturned bed symbolically mimics the overturned life of the dead, to serve as a constant reminder to the mourner. While explicit expression of this meaning will not be found in the Tosefta or contemporary rabbinic writings, such an interpretation of this ritual remains reasonable. The overturned couch or bed, its visual shock and the discomfort it causes, will be everywhere in the house of the mourner. Not only is the public realm unavailable to the mourner, so too is the normal, comfortable private realm.

As we learned in the Mishnah (M.Q. 3:7; see above, p. 30), the rabbis prescribe a "blessing for mourners." The teachers of the Tosefta elaborate the meaning of this obscure Mishnaic reference. In their words:

A place where they were accustomed to say the blessing for mourners three [that is, three distinct blessings], they say three; two, they say two; one, they say one. A place where they were accustomed to say the blessing for mourners three, he includes the first in "the resurrection of the dead" and concludes it [saying] "Who brings the dead to life." [He includes] the second in "the comforting of mourners" and concludes it [saying] "He comforts His people and His city." [He includes] the third in "doer of mercy" and he requires no concluding [formula].

(t. Ber. 3:23–4)

Saul Lieberman understands the present directive to be speaking of a special "blessing after the meal" in the house of mourning, although, in his reconstruction, these or similar blessings were also to be included in the Prayer (the Amidah) in the synagogue (Lieberman 1955: 49–52). However we understand the context of this recitation, the substance of the recitation now becomes far more clear.

First, to observe the obvious: The Tosefta allows that there are different customs for reciting the mourner's blessings, the range of such blessings being somewhere between one and three. If three are recited, the first praises God who returns the dead to life, the second God who comforts God's people, and the third praises those who engage in acts of loving-kindness, such as burying the dead and comforting mourners. The triad of foci is obviously appropriate to the occasion: we speak of the dead, the mourner and the comforter. We declare that the dead will be returned to life. This belief will presumably be a source of comfort to the mourner, whose comforting will symbolize the comforting of the people as a whole. The neighbor who undertakes the obligation of comforting, imitating God who also comforts mourners, is likewise to be praised.

Notably, such an addition to the blessing after meals is likewise prescribed for the table where a wedding is celebrated. The ritual parallel suggests a commonality of experience and therefore of symbolic marking. Without too much fancy, we may suggest the following interpretation: Death, like marriage, is a significant "life-transition." Rabbinic tradition equates a newly married individual with a new-born baby. The deceased, too, is born into a new life. Moreover, the new "birth" of the newly-wed is presumed to be accompanied by an erasure of his or her account of sins. Death, too, atones for sins, ultimately leaving the deceased pure for the next judgment. Such transitions demand ritualized inscriptions of experience and meaning, precisely as the teachers of the Tosefta prescribe.[8]

Concerning the experience of the deceased after death, neither the Tosefta nor other contemporary tannaitic documents say much, though the few recorded traditions contribute important insights. The midrash relates (Sifri Deut. 307; Finkelstein 1969: 345–6) that when a person departs this world his deeds detail themselves in front of him and say, "Have you not done such-and-such [a sinful act] on such-and-such a day?" He is asked to affirm the accusation and "sign on the dotted line." At that point, the accused (= the deceased) declares that the judgment is just and says "I have been well judged." The judgment, described as a proper court procedure, is deemed complete, and the deceased is presumably prepared to face his final fate.

Particularly noteworthy, in this vision, is the assertion that the deceased declares his final judgment to be just. The Hebrew phrase (*hu' mazdiq et haddin*) is the very same phrase used later to describe the ritualized response of those who hear of the death of a loved one. Admittedly, the phrase itself cannot be documented at this stage. But the Mishnah, at Ber. 9:2, prescribes that, upon hearing a bad report (such as, we may assume, of the death of a loved one), one must recite a blessing which speaks of God as "the Judge of Truth." Moreover, the Tosefta (Ber. 6:3) explicitly speaks of the bad news as "a judgment of retribution." It is clear, therefore, that bad news was to be greeted with an affirmation of the true judgment of God. If we assume – not unreasonably – that such a ritualized "declaring the judgment just" was indeed required of those who witnessed a death, then we may see this judgment ritual, assigned here to the deceased, as another example of the "echoing" or "mirroring" noted earlier. As the survivor justifies God's judgment, so too does the deceased. The experience of one mirrors the experience of the other. Living and dead have both been touched by death in profound ways.

Apparently, the bones of the dead are to be collected and reburied, for there are reputed to have been "societies" of individuals responsible for reburial who were active in Jerusalem (t. Meg. 3:17). There is no direct indication of when this should occur. But the Tosefta records a vision of judgment after death which may help us understand both the practice of reburial and the belief which underlies it.

The image is startling:

> The sinners of Israel and the sinners of the nations descend, in their bodies, to Gehinnom, and they are judged there for twelve months. After twelve months, their souls are consumed and their bodies burned,[9] and Gehinnom discharges it and they become dust. Then the wind blows them and they are scattered beneath the soles of the righteous.
>
> (Sanhedrin 13:4)

The next teaching makes it clear that these sinners are lucky. At least they leave Gehinnom after a year. Certain more wicked individuals are said to be judged there forever!

Whatever we make of the details of this grisly scenario, it is clear that, in the vision preserved in this tradition, the year following death is a period of extended judgment for sinners. When the year is finished, the body has been transformed to dust and judgment is complete. Or, to put it in other words, death is complete. The immediate "task" of death has been accomplished and the last remains of the dead (the bones) may therefore finally be transported to their last resting-place. We have no way of knowing whether, for the teachers of the Tosefta, this is generally an occasion for joy or for further sorrow. But we do know that, in their understanding, the process is now complete.

5

JEWISH DEATH-PRACTICES IN REALITY

The Catacombs at Beth Shearim

While, in their houses of study, the rabbis assembled teachings instructing Jews how to prepare, bury and mourn their dead, in the world outside the study-house, Jews of all classes and religious inclinations were actually *doing* these things. Though, of course, many of their death rituals – laments, recitations, customs of approaching or leaving burial, and the like – would leave no physical remains, important parts of the death ritual are durable, leaving for posterity the most significant record of any ancient practice. On the basis of these remains – burial caves, sarcophagi, ossuaries, inscriptions, decorative art work, and burial paraphernalia – we may reconstruct both ancient practices and (perhaps more tentatively) beliefs. What, then, do we learn from the material remains of Jewish burial practice? What do we discover about the customs and beliefs of common Jews? And what, finally, can we say about the relationship between the rabbis' imaginations and the living realities of contemporary Palestinian Jews?

The earliest rabbinic record, as we saw, assumes its (more or less) final form in the last years of the second century, more than a hundred years after the destruction of the Second Temple in Jerusalem. But to understand this record, we cannot ignore the earlier practice which would, for the teachers of the Mishnah, have constituted "tradition." We will, after all, want to know the relationship of second- and third-century Jews, whether in the Mishnah or in the mountains and valleys of the Galilee, to their inherited tradition. We must, therefore, first turn our attentions to the environs of Jerusalem before the first war with Rome. There, in the walls of the deep valleys surrounding the city, Jews hewed caves in which to bury their dead. When we search these caves, what do we find?

Most of the burial caves from this period are modest affairs, intended for use by a single family.[1] The entrances are small and provide access only by bending or crouching. Inside, these caves are composed of a single room whose walls are roughly hewn, and their ceilings are so low that pits must be dug in the floor for visitors to stand erect. In the walls, we find either "benches" for the laying out of the dead or *kokhim*, holes dug straight into the walls, the purpose of which we will discuss shortly.

Some tombs are more elaborate, although, with the exception of royal tombs, they are never grand. Several rooms may be connected, each with places for perhaps six or eight deceased. Doorways are carved to replicate common architectural motifs, the walls more finely finished. On occasion, ceilings are decorated with rosettes and other designs (Ritmeyer and Ritmeyer 1994: 22–35). These decorative elements, when they appear, do not stand alone. They often find echo on the small stone ossuaries almost always found in these tombs, on which more elaborate decorations are also common.

The walls and floors bear evidence of a single predominant burial custom. The holes dug into the walls, though of a size appropriate for the placement of a single body, are not used for this purpose. Rather, into these *kokhim* are inserted the aforementioned ossuaries, boxes for the placement of the bones after the flesh of the deceased has decayed. Pits in the floor might also be used for a less elegant re-placement of the bones, for what immediate reasons we can only guess.

The ossuaries are almost always decorated, sometimes elaborately so (Rahmani 1994). The most common feature is rosettes, usually two on a side, often framed by other decorative motifs. On occasion, we find ossuaries carved to appear as though they are built with ashlar stones, similar to the Herodian stones that defined the retaining wall of the Jerusalem Temple (Rahmani 1994: #34). We also find several carved with columns and gates (Rahmani 1994: #160, #175). On one, we discover a pair of columned structures – a column on each side, together supporting an arch. Sprouting from the side of each arch, and separating the two arched structures, are palm branches. The spaces between the columns and under the arches are empty; rosettes are found only on the ossuary's lid (Rahmani 1994: #160).

How are we to understand these and other ornamental features? Are these "mere" decorations, intended to recall the structures and decorations found outside the tomb, in the world of the living? Or do these decorations represent some mysterious symbolic vocabulary, commenting on the fate of the deceased when he or she has come to the state of final rest?

The last described ossuary (see Plate 5.1), marked with palm branches, tempts us to view such decorations as symbolic statements. Palm branches are the central element of the *lulav*, the primary ritual symbol of the great Sukkot pilgrimage festival. *Lulavim* are a popular decorative element in Jewish art from these centuries, where they often appear in combination with menorahs and shofars (more on this later). One of the central themes of the Sukkot celebration in this period is redemption, and the common combination just described has generally been interpreted (reasonably so) as a symbol of hoped-for redemption. This modest element invites us, therefore, to seek a symbolic vocabulary.

On the other hand, rosettes, the most common ossuary decoration, are stubbornly mute. Rosettes were employed for decoration in Herod's Temple in Jerusalem, and they are found on the ceilings of tombs as well (Ritmeyer

Plate 5.1 Jewish ossuary from Jerusalem tomb, Shemuel Hanavi St

and Ritmeyer 1994: 33). But are they meant to recall the Temple itself, with its redemptive promise? Or are they the eyes of the soul, or an eye to the future world? Unfortunately, little can be said with confidence. Because these are often elaborate decorations, adorning stone boxes for the bones of the deceased, my inclination is to believe that there must be some symbolic quality. But even if this is so – and, as I said, we can't be sure – we haven't the tools to decipher what the message of the symbols might be.[2]

Whatever the meaning of the ossuary decorations, the practice of ossilegium (collecting the bones) itself is surely an expression of underlying beliefs. The state of the body and its treatment subsequent to death symbolize the simultaneous condition of the soul (Hertz 1960; Metcalf and Huntington 1972: 97). In view of the widespread contemporary evidence concerning belief in afterlife, final judgment and ultimate resurrection, it is reasonable to interpret ossilegium as a ritual expression of popular belief. In Rahmani's words: "The ritual of *ossilegium* was intended to reassure the survivors that their relatives 'rested from judgment', cleansed from sin and entitled to resurrection" (Rahmani 1994: 28). Appreciating that ossilegium symbolizes and enacts a *process*, one which evidently comes to an end when the flesh of the deceased has finished decaying from the bones, we may go even a step further: the practice of collecting the bones and depositing them in a final resting-place – often an elaborately carved stone chest – may be understood to express the belief that death is viewed as an extended process, with death being complete only when the flesh is fully decayed and the bones alone remain.

Ossilegium was most common in the environs of Jerusalem before the destruction of the Temple, and so has been described as a "Jerusalemite custom." But not all of those buried in the caves surrounding Jerusalem were residents of Jerusalem, and we have no difficulty understanding why Jerusalem would be the most desirable of burial sites for Jews of whatever locale. Jerusalem, the home of the Holy Temple, will be the center of the hoped-for final redemption and resurrection. Those who wish to participate in this resurrection, immediately and without difficulty, would therefore want to be buried in the hills and valleys surrounding the sacred city. The very manner of their burial – in addition to the locale – expresses this hope. The concentration of this practice around Jerusalem may, therefore, be less evidence of local custom than of powerful hopes for ultimate personal redemption.

In fact, the practice of ossilegium was brought to the Galilee by Jews who, following the defeat of Bar Kokhba, could no longer make their homes in Judah. In the north, Jews would continue this burial practice, by the side of other practices, until at least the mid-fourth century. But as we turn our attentions north, to the very centuries during which the Mishnah, the Tosefta and the tannaitic midrashim were composed, ossilegium will command far less interest. Now, in the third and fourth centuries, we see burial elaborated in unexpected and sometimes astounding ways. The meaning is in the details; we must, therefore, review the evidence slowly.

The center for burial of Jews in the north during the third and fourth centuries was *Beth Shearim*, "the House of Gates [to the next world?]."[3] In the slopes of Beth Shearim there are at least twenty-six catacombs of varying sizes.[4] In them are laid the remains of Jews not only from the Galilee, but from such places as Beirut, Palmyra, and even as far away as Nehardea (Babylonia) (Avi-Yonah 1975, vol. 1: 234). To those who have never before visited these caves, their scope and variety comes as a shock.

The first catacomb on the southern end of the Beth Shearim hill is entered through a long, narrow hallway, descending into the ground between high walls. On either side, at various heights in the wall, are entrances to caves of different sizes, each with several rooms of modest size. Clearly, these particular burial halls were intended for private family visits only.

Entering one hall, we find shelves (arcosolia) carved into the walls of the man-made cave, each with one or more depressions for the laying out of the deceased. Most of these depressions have stone pillows carved at one end, so that the sleep of the dead may resemble the sleep of the living. Caves occupied by Jewish forces resisting the Roman armies at the time of Bar Kokhba have similarly carved depressions with a "pillow" at one end.[5] The resemblance of these burial shelves (arcosolia) to sleeping places of those still alive – at least those who slept in caves – means that the "metaphor" between the sleep of the living and the dead is more than *mere* metaphor. Because they sleep under the same conditions, we must assume that their state of being was believed to be similar as well. What this might imply about common understandings of the condition of the dead we will consider below.

In one wall, we find an arcosolium labelled as belonging to a Jew named Jacob. The deceased is laid directly into the burial place, without a coffin or other enclosure. The walls are incised with graffiti. There seem to be representations of rays of light, and then what is clearly a ship. The ship has no sails or oars; there is no indication of water beneath it. Above the same arcosolium is first a horse, then another horse together with two bulls (Mazar 1973: 52). Horses, we will discover, are quite common in the Beth Shearim caves. What is the meaning of these various figures? To answer this question, we shall first have to collect more evidence. We should note, though, that such figures are common in contemporary non-Jewish art in the same part of the world.

In a nearby room, we find an incised human figure. The face is skull-like, looking much like the "face of death" of later centuries (see Plate 5.2).[6] The arms are extended by the sides of the body, as though positioned for flying. It is difficult to escape the conclusion that the figure is intended to represent the soul of the dead. Other human figures found elsewhere in the catacombs – those with wings – will reinforce this conclusion.

One hall that extends off from the main hallway is a handsome family tomb (Mazar 1973: 75–8). The walls are smoothly dressed and decorated with various motifs, particularly circles and rosettes. In the first room of this hall, we find an incised drawing, painted over in red. The drawing is composed of a lion, a palm tree, a gate and, behind the gate, a man (Plate 5.3) (Mazar 1973: pl. IX, #4). If this were clearly a biblical story, we would be forced to associate it with Daniel in the lion's den. But there is no den here, and no reason to assume any connection to the biblical story. Instead, we may probably take the lion as symbolic of the violent power of death (such lions are common in contemporary Roman funerary art), and the gate as expressing the wish for protection therefrom.

A short distance further up on the same wall is another ship, again without passengers and again without a means of propulsion. This, we may venture, is probably the ship that will transport the deceased from this world to the world of the dead. But more important than the precise interpretation of the particular figure is this: it is already evident that we are in the presence of a particular death symbolism. The pictures are saying in simple figures what it would take many more words to say.

Over the arch leading from this room to the next someone has inscribed the words (in Greek): "Shalom! Judah, have courage, most beloved little Judah." Precisely these wishes, for peace and for courage, are common in such inscriptions. What does it mean to wish the deceased peace, to encourage him

Plate 5.2 Graffito on the vault of Beth Shearim, catacomb 1, Hall C, room I,
arcosolium 1

to be strong? Only if death is believed to be an ordeal of which one is
conscious does such an expression have any meaning at all. Only if death is a
life beyond, one between this life and life in a World to Come, does the cluster
of symbols already witnessed here find a reasonable explanation.

On the passage to the next room in this complex, we find drawings of a
menorah, a lulav, and what is probably a shofar. By the side of this drawing is
a Greek inscription, identifying this as a "place of peace." On a wall nearby
is carved a large menorah in high relief, framed by two carved columns of
similarly large size (Mazar 1973: pl. X, #2). On the arch of the passage, above

53

Plate 5.3 Drawings on wall of Beth Shearim, catacomb 1, Hall G, room I, arcosolium 2

one of the columns, are painted two winged figures, one full-sized. Lest we had any question of the beliefs generating the artwork of this catacomb, the present combination leaves little room for doubt.

The menorah, lulav and shofar are, as noted earlier, a popular combination in Jewish art of this period. All have strong associations with the Jerusalem Temple, now in ruins. The menorah, of course, stood at the Temple, and was one of the Temple's most distinguishable figures. As I commented previously, the lulav was the central symbol of Sukkot, and the primary theater for the enactment of the lulav ritual was the Temple. The blowing of shofars (or at least horns) accompanied the sacrificial offerings on special occasions (see Num. 10:10). The shofar is also the symbol of the New Year festival, which, as all festivals, was celebrated most grandly at the Temple. And the shofar would sound at the Temple to announce the arrival of the Jubilee.

Of course, the shofar would one day announce the coming of the Messiah. And it represents also the ram from which it was taken – the ram offered on the altar, the ram that took the place of Isaac on the altar that Abraham had built. Thus the shofar has profound redemptive connotations.

54

The same is true of the lulav. The ritual of pilgrimage, approaching and circumambulating the altar with lulav in hand, was also a prayer for redemption: it was the time to cry "Hosanna! *Hosha' na!* God, save us, we beseech you!" The "deliverance" of the present day, with God's abundant mercy visibly evident in the recent harvest, foreshadowed the deliverance of the future. The Temple was dedicated on Sukkot (see 1 Kings 8:2); it was rededicated (Ezra 4:1–6) and rededicated again (2 Macc. 1:18) in association with the same festival. It would thus be rededicated a final time in connection with the same redemptive pilgrimage – now a last messianic pilgrimage.

Of course, the Temple symbolism itself can be understood, in the late second or early third century, to have redemptive meaning. As we said, the Temple now stood in ruins. It was not a living reality but a hoped-for future reality. To render the symbols of the Temple in "high relief," therefore, was to declare that the hope for restoration was prominent, a central feature of contemporary sensibilities.

What is the connection of all this to death? Even without additional evidence, it seems reasonable to see in this symbolic commentary an expression of the hope that death will conclude in redemption, that the individual, now deceased, will be resurrected to life in a World to Come. At death, a person sleeps, laid to rest for the foreseeable future. His or her soul leaves the flesh behind, "flies" away, and journeys ("on a ship") to the world beyond. Hopefully, this sleep of death will be peaceful. But, peaceful or disturbed, the deceased should "take courage," for death, too, will be left behind.

On the wall of a room leading off the same central hallway, just below an arcosolium, we discover an inscribed drawing of a man leading a horse (Plate 5.4a) (Mazar 1973: 98–101, and pls. XIV–XV). He is dressed in a Roman tunic, holding a weapon (it looks like a club) in front of him. Crucially, the weapon is at ease; there appears to be no need for defense or aggression. The horse, too, is at ease; only two legs are visible, so the animal, seen from the side, must be standing still. Both man and horse face a series of nine concentric circles. The composition suggests anticipation of entering into the unknown.

Further into the room, carved in high relief by the side of an arched door leading to the next room, we meet the same man again (Plate 5.4b). This time he is riding the horse, grabbing the horse's mane (or bridle) with one hand, holding the other hand aloft with sword drawn. The horse, all four legs seen clearly, is moving forward. Horse and rider seem to be involved in battle, though the enemy is nowhere to be seen.

Slightly higher on the same wall are other drawings and graffiti. There is a menorah and an identification: the name Judah. But, more crucially, there is also (again) a drawing of concentric circles, this time with the word *shalom* ("peace") clearly inscribed in the center. "Shalom" is the state of rest in death, the repose at the end of the journey. Does "shalom" lie in the center of circles,

Plate 5.4a–b Wall graffiti and relief in Beth Shearim, catacomb 1, Hall K, room I

at the end of mysterious hallways through which one journeys from this world to the next? If this is true in the belief of those who left their mark on this burial hall – who with their artwork created a three-dimensional commentary on the state of death – then we may return to interpret the combination of imagery we have already seen here.

Death, evidently, is viewed as a journey (as the ships already encountered elsewhere likewise suggest) that is also a battle. The deceased, the warrior, must face it with courage, for the precise steps to peace are unknown. But the warrior will ultimately be able to dismount from his horse and lower his weapons. Lying in repose, he may look forward to peace. Peace, *shalom*, awaits at the end of the journey.

In another hall in the same complex, we find two similar paintings that deserve our attention. The paintings are found on stones which seal adjacent burial holes (*kokhim*); the burial holes are low to the ground, beneath a burial shelf. The paintings, in the common red paint of Beth Shearim, both represent similar structures (Plates 5.5a and b). In both cases, a building of some sort is flanked by two menorahs. The buildings are crowned with gabled roofs, each with pronounced acroteria (raised architectural extensions, looking like "horns") projecting from each side. Hanging from the inside of each roof is a lamp, perhaps an "eternal lamp." In the center of each structure is a smaller structure, apparently an ark. In one of the two paintings, we clearly see scrolls inside the ark; in the other, the door is closed, so we can only guess what is imagined to be inside. Decorative elements are different in each painting, but the similarities are far more striking than the differences (Mazar 1973: 110–12).

Can we be more precise in interpreting what these paintings are meant to represent? The combination of elements is reminiscent of nothing more than the ark and tabernacle of the desert and Jerusalem Temple. Exodus 25–7 records the instructions for the construction of the ark, the menorah, the tabernacle, the altar and the eternal light, in that order. Missing in these paintings is only the altar. But the so-called "acroteria," horns on the corners of the building, are similar to horns which in fact distinguished ancient Israelite altars (Shanks 1975: 1, 8), and it is possible that an allusion to the horns of the altar is intended here. Alternatively, the acroteria may recall similar architectural elements on the corners of roofs of classical pagan temples, well-known images in the ancient world. Crucially, although the motif of "ark flanked by menorahs" is quite common in Jewish art of this period (the mosaic floor of the Beth Shean synagogue provides a good example), none shows arks housed in larger structures, and the acroteria, too, are relatively unusual. Thus, these pictures clearly do more than borrow a stereotyped symbolic vocabulary. Whether ancient Jewish or pagan temple, there can be little doubt that the present artists meant to represent space of a very special sort: holy space, temple space, a mysterious, atoning space.

Plate 5.5a–b Paintings on wall of Beth Shearim, catacomb 1, Hall M, room I

Could these paintings instead be depictions of synagogues? The argument in favor of such an interpretation builds on the presence in one of the "arks" of a scroll, apparently a Torah scroll, and the depiction in both of an "eternal light." But it is by no means clear whether eternal lights were yet part of synagogue decoration, and such an interpretation offers no explanation of the two huge menorahs flanking the "synagogue" on each side. Of course, the Torah scroll was also placed in the ancient ark (see Deut. 31:26), so a "scroll-in-ark" figure by no means requires us to understand this as a synagogue. Furthermore, as far as we know, synagogues of this period were not crowned with acroteria. One of the two former interpretations therefore seems more likely. Or perhaps we should combine both former readings: we can easily understand how the artists might have imagined ancient Jewish Temple architecture according to forms (Roman) with which they were more familiar.

Be that as it may, these paintings are more important than we might first imagine. We will discover later that the gabled roof with acroteria at all sides is a prominent feature of burial at Beth Shearim. If there is any hint of the meaning of these features, such as provided by these paintings, we must give it ample attention. We shall return to the present discussion below, therefore, when we confront an abundance of cases employing this decorative feature in the most unexpected of places.

Another catacomb, slightly further south on the same hill, is particularly rich in its decorations and symbols. Below one burial-shelf, for example, we find pictures of a goblet, a shofar, a vessel of some sort, a menorah, and an ark with double doors and acroteria (Mazar 1973: 160). Again, Temple symbolism is prominent. In another room we discover an incised picture of a skull and skeleton – a macabre image of death. In the doorway on the other side of the same room, there is a menorah and, by its side, a person with arms extended. Further on are pictures of what appear to be "butterflies," probably meant to represent the souls of the deceased, flying, perhaps, to the next world (Mazar 1973: pl. XXVI). We could go on.

But all of this will pale next to a tomb in the next adjacent catacomb, a tomb we can only describe as a "shrine to the deceased" (Goodenough 1953: 93–6). This is a complex space, one that is difficult to describe. As you approach the far end of this burial cave (walking straight towards the back from the entrance), you see, on the hallway arch on your left side, an incised menorah with rosettes flanking it on each side. Entering the back room, a painting of a rosette stares down at you from the center of the ceiling. It is connected by a band-like decoration to another rosette, further in and above the "shrine" itself. Squiggles decorate one rosette and the band, as they will also the burial niche in the rear wall (Plate 5.6).

Stepping forward, you approach a space defined by two large earth blocks on either side, with a step and short "hallway" in the middle. The blocks do not reach to the ceiling; instead, they form shelves which flank the entrance to the central burial space. The front face of each earth block is incised with similar symbolic carvings. Each has four columns supporting an arched roof. Above the right curve of the arch, in both cases, is a lion. But, beyond this, there are important differences.

The carving on the left (Plate 5.7a) shows seven steps approaching closed doors. Above the doors is a conch shell. Between the columns to the right is a lulav. Are these doors the doors to the ark? The closed doors of the Temple? The doors of a more mysterious temple, closed to all but the dead? We can only speculate.

The parallel carving on the right (Plate 5.7b) has a menorah in the interior space instead of doors. Between the columns to the right there is again a lulav; between the left columns is a human figure. The space below the central arch, where the conch appears in the corresponding carving to the left, is here blank. Again, the symbolism is obscure to those of us who view it from a chronological distance: this certainly represents an imposing structure, perhaps the Jerusalem Temple. But more we cannot say with any confidence.

Plate 5.7a
Carving in
Beth
Shearim,
catacomb 4,
Hall A,
room I

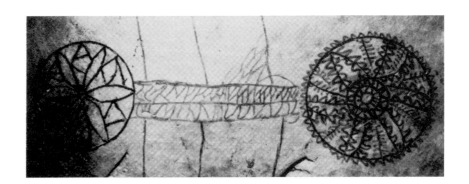

Plate 5.6
Ceiling
painting in
Beth
Shearim,
catacomb 4,
Hall A,
room I

Plate 5.8
"Shelf" or
"step" in
Beth
Shearim,
catacomb 4,
Hall A,
room I

Plate 5.7b
Carving in
Beth
Shearim,
catacomb 4,
Hall A,
room I

As we walk forward into the hallway-like space between the large earth blocks (ascending a single step), we discover that a space is carved on the top of each block for the laying out of one deceased person. These spaces are covered by slabs to protect the deceased from being disturbed. Immediately to the front – that is, in the back-most part of this hall – there is an arched burial shelf stretching back into the wall. Carved in the wall below this shelf, we find what appears to be a pedestal, tapered toward the bottom and broadening toward the top (Plate 5.8). Above it, also carved into the wall, is an arched depression; above the arch is another lion, his body angling down, with face directed toward the top of the pedestal. The pedestal is too high (approximately 2½ feet) to be a step to the very high burial shelf (nearly 5 feet) above it. It looks, instead, to be some sort of altar, appropriate for the presentation of incense or some ritual libation. This is, of course, pure speculation, but no practical purpose can reasonably be assigned to the same feature.

The burial space above the pedestal and beneath the arch contains spaces for two bodies, side by side. Each space has a pillow. The back wall and ceiling of the arched space are painted with bands, zig-zags, and other complex designs. Whether these are "mere" decorations or symbolic paintings we don't know. In any case, they are mysterious and striking.

Crucially, the room is not large. Including the space of what I have called the earth blocks, the room is only approximately 12 feet by 9 feet, a modest size living room in modern terms. The ceiling is approximately 8 feet high. This is, in other words, a family burial room, for Jews from Palmyra (an inscription makes this clear), evidently of considerable means. As we try to make sense of this room, therefore, we must ask what this assemblage of features could mean for such a family.

The concern for detail and elaboration seen in this room is unique. The decorative features, combining Temple imagery and mysterious paintings, are not casually chosen. They make an unmistakable impression. Is this a family shrine, designed for some sort of worship in the presence of the deceased? This is a reasonable explanation – at least as good as any other explanation of the same phenomenon. Is this the worship space of a mystery cult, or a cult of the dead? These explanations, too, cannot be dismissed. Whatever the best explanation, this is designed as a "living" space, a space for the living and the deceased to be in close communion. More of its mysteries, unfortunately, we shall never be in a position to explain.

Leaving this catacomb, we walk north around the hill. There we find the entrances to a considerable number of catacombs of varying sizes. Entering one, we discover a relatively large central passage (18 feet by 11 feet, with a 9-foot ceiling), beyond which there is another central room of slightly smaller dimensions (Avigad 1973: 21–5). Neither of these rooms has any burial spaces in them. Instead, they serve for passage to adjacent burial rooms and, being lined with carved stone benches, it is clearly assumed that they will be used for waiting and possibly assembly. Notably, there are only twenty graves in this entire hall. There is, in other words, a considerable amount of space dedicated to the graves of a small number of individuals. We cannot avoid the conclusion that these deceased were to be visited with some regularity; there is no other reasonable explanation for the size of the rooms and the features intended to provide comfort to visitors.[7]

In this and nearby halls there are a number of inscriptions that shed light on the beliefs of the visitors. On one archway we read: "[May] I [the deceased] attain [happiness]" (Avigad 1973: 22). In an adjacent hall: "Be of good courage . . . no one is immortal" (literally translated: "without death") (Avigad 1973: 26). In the next catacomb: "This is the resting-place of Judan son of Levi, may he forever be in peace . . . " (Avigad 1973: 30), and then, a curse: "Whosoever shall change the place of this one [resting here], God who resurrects the dead shall judge [him]" (Avigad 1973: 36). Lest we had any doubt, these and similar inscriptions make it clear that the Jews who buried their dead here believed in the survival of the soul, a future judgment, and the final resurrection of the dead.[8] The less explicit evidence of these same caves may thus be interpreted in light of these fundamental beliefs.

Progressing to the next catacomb, we face the unexpected, a structure that is different from anything we have seen before (Avigad 1973: 42–63). To begin with, the external architecture of this tomb is monumental. Leading to the entrance is a large courtyard, approximately 50 by 20 feet in dimension. The entranceway is composed of three arches, beautifully finished (Plate 5.9). The large central doors are not serviceable in a regular way; common entrance is through the smaller left door, the central doors being available only for the occasional entrance of the coffins of the deceased. In addition, there is, on the hill directly above the entrance to this tomb, a large open-air theater or assembly space, in which people sit facing the courtyard just described.

These monumental features would lead us to expect something grand inside as well. But when we enter this cave, what we find is extremely modest: rooms of relatively generous size containing, however, only a few unadorned graves (with one significant exception), mostly for the secondary burial of bones. Pit-graves in the floors are placed, obviously with purpose, next to certain wall-graves (arcosolia). Some of the wall-graves are marked to identify their "residents": one belongs to someone named "Rabbi Shimeon," another to "Rabbi Gamaliel," a third to someone called "Anina the Little."

In the rearmost room, against the back wall, is a grave carved for the resting of two bodies side-by-side. The grave is surrounded by a stone wall, indicating that it contained the remains of important people, but it is otherwise unmarked. This is clearly the most important grave of the hall, the purpose for everything around it. The question is, simply, who is buried here?

Talmudic tradition has it that Rabbi Judah the Patriarch, the redactor of the Mishnah, is buried at Beth Shearim. Notably, R. Judah's sons were named Shimeon and Gamaliel. According to a tradition recorded in the Babylonian

Plate 5.9 Entrance to Beth Shearim, catacomb 14

Talmud (Ketubot 103a–b), before his death, R. Judah directed: "Don't eulogize me in the cities, and arrange an assembly (*yeshiva*) after thirty days. Shimeon, my son, is [or, "shall be"?] Sage, Gamaliel, my son, [shall be] Patriarch, [and] Ḥanina b. Ḥama shall sit at the head." The coincidence of the Talmudic record with what is found in (and above!) this burial chamber at Beth Shearim is stunning. The names painted on the wall of the chamber are precisely those of R. Judah's two sons and his close associate (Ḥanina = Anina). The structure on the hill above the chamber is clearly intended for a

64

gathering of some sort, perhaps the same sort that R. Judah asks for following his death. The combination of these coincidences and the special quality of the tomb's entrance and overall structure makes the likelihood that this is R. Judah's burial-place a high one. So too does the presence of the unique floor grave, surrounded by a stone wall, found in the rear of this cave. So too will other phenomena buried beneath the same hill. If this is indeed the tomb of one of the "forefathers" of the rabbinic movement, then the light this site sheds on the rabbinic literary record will be particularly noteworthy.

The surprise of this tomb pales by comparison to the shock of entering a nearby catacomb, the entrance to which is a mere 100 feet to the north-east on the same hill.[9] Nothing we have seen genuinely prepares us for this catacomb and its contents. By way of introduction, suffice it to say that this complex is far larger than anything else in Beth Shearim. But there is much more than size to surprise us here.

This catacomb, too, is fronted by a huge monumental courtyard, this one even larger than the other and surrounded by substantial walls. Again, the entrance is defined by three large arches and, again, there is an open-air assembly place on the hill above the entrance. But this is where the similarity between this catacomb and the prior tomb ends.

As you enter this catacomb, on the wall in front of you, you find, written in Greek, graffiti which declares: "May you be comforted holy fathers, no one is immortal." On the ceiling to the left is written, "Good luck in your resurrection." These are just two of many writings in this catacomb which express the idea that there is some sensation ("comfort") after death, and that after death comes resurrection.

The space of this catacomb is huge, the largest, in fact in the entire ancient world! The catacomb is comprised of no fewer than twenty-eight rooms. The main hall leading back from the entrance extends a distance of 150 feet. A long hall to the left extends even further! The rooms themselves are of an equally grand scale. One room is 22 feet wide. Another is nearly 25 by 28 feet, with 16-foot ceilings. Still another is 36 by 22 feet, with 13½-foot ceilings. When you step into these spaces, you are immediately sure that they are not private spaces. No person would take the trouble to carve out such large rooms from the belly of a hillside if facilitating family visits alone were his intent. Rather, this is clearly a space for public visits, a space for people to *spend time*. At least 200 people are laid to rest here; this is a city for the living and the dead.

All known forms of Jewish burial typical to the third and fourth centuries are in evidence in this complex: there are arcosolia, burial niches (*kokhim*) and graves sunk in the floor. There are both primary and secondary burials. But we also discover something that is, to this point, unknown in a Jewish context: the most common way to lay the deceased to rest in this complex is in *huge stone sarcophagi*. At least 124 such sarcophagi are found in the rooms and hallways of this catacomb.

The sarcophagi are strikingly rich in their ornamentation. Lions are carved on several, sometimes made to appear frightening or threatening, on a couple of occasions even posed for attack. As in contemporary pagan burials employing the same images, these animals appear to represent the violence of death itself, death being a power which devours its victim the way a lion consumes its less powerful target.

One sarcophagus has a carved human face on one end, framed by a garland hanging beneath it (Plate 5.10). This may be a simple mask, or it may be a representation of Hercules (similar such Hercules figures are found elsewhere in the Roman world). One way or the other, there is no avoiding the fact that this carving transgresses the presumed Jewish prohibition against picturing the human form. In the same vein, several sarcophagi are decorated with

Plate 5.10 Beth Shearim, catacomb 20, sarcophagus #84

scenes of the battle of the Amazons. One is carved with winged figures, clearly the mythical nikae. If there is a prohibition against employing pagan mythical motifs, the people who have left their loved ones in this cave seem not to have heeded it. The imprint of the Roman world is everywhere. Even what looks to be a Roman imperial eagle is found on several sarcophagi.

Many other sarcophagi are decorated with (potentially) less controversial motifs. Not unexpectedly, we find rosettes, menorahs, and geometric designs. We find a variety of animals, wreaths, columns, gates and other innocuous figures. Clearly, part of the intent of those who carved the sarcophagi (or commissioned their carving) is to decorate and beautify these containers for the deceased. But the variety and abundance of mythical motifs suggests that there is more than mere decoration to much of this decoration.

One of the most striking elements of the sarcophagi is their covers. Virtually every cover in the entire catacomb shares the same basic design: it is gabled length-wise at the center and the corners are all carved with acroteria (raised projections). We earlier discovered paintings which featured buildings (the Temple?) with gabled roofs and acroteria. To those few earlier examples we may now add over a hundred. This is, therefore, the most common of all decorative features in these many catacombs. What is the meaning of this symbol (or is it a symbol at all?) to the Jews for whom Beth Shearim provides an eternal resting-place?

To understand the phenomenon in Beth Shearim, we have to compare it to its sister phenomenon elsewhere in the Roman world. Gabled lids with acroteria are, in fact, quite common in contemporary Roman tombs. St Peter's necropolis in Rome preserves fine examples, as do tombs in the Danube region.[10] There is little doubt that these covers are intended to recreate, and therefore represent, the same architectural features commonly found on the façades of Roman temples.[11] Notably, both on the burial lids and on the temples, the acroteria are very elaborate affairs. On the temples, they may actually be statues of one sort or another, similar to the winged Victories represented on the corners of the Temple façade in the Dura-Europos synagogue painting. On the Roman sarcophagi, though such prominent features may be absent, the acroteria are still carved with various designs or representations, intricate and always ornate.

But at Beth Shearim the acroteria are almost without exception blank – uncarved and unelaborated (Avigad 1973: pls. XXXIV–XXXVII). Now, it is true that the sarcophagi are themselves often uncarved. But the blank stare of the acroteria persists also on the carved sarcophagi, even when other parts of the same lid are carved or inscribed (Avigad 1973: pls. XL–XLI). And even the very few acroteria which are decorated remain extremely simple, none approaching what is typical on contemporary Roman equivalents (see Avigad 1973: pls. XLIII and XLIV). This is all particularly noticeable because these same sarcophagi, when carved, are otherwise indistinguishable from the Roman examples. How are we to explain this strange and striking contrast?

We might propose that these lids are a kind of standard manufacture and that the Jews who used them for burial simply did not have time to carve them. But they obviously did have time, when they chose, to carve the sarcophagi themselves and even other parts of the lids, so such an explanation is insupportable.

Given the striking avoidance of carving the acroteria, we might guess that the same population had religious scruples about shaping such raised projections, perhaps because of the prohibition of "idolatry." But such a proposal would obviously be naive; some of these sarcophagi are rich with pagan carvings, all of which would fall under the same prohibition. There may indeed be some religious or ideological explanation behind what we find here, but this cannot be it.

As I mentioned earlier in this chapter, the acroteria on the lids of these sarcophagi resemble nothing more than the horns of ancient Israelite (and Canaanite!) altars. But direct awareness of this similarity on the part of those who built the sarcophagi is virtually impossible; such altars already lay beneath centuries of accumulated soil and debris.[12] Still, the similarity remains suggestive. As we saw earlier, the Torah commands that the altar of the Tabernacle (later to be Temple) be surrounded on all four corners by "horns." The text does not specify what these horns should look like, so the reader must use his or her imagination. Could it be that the lids of these sarcophagi preserve this community's interpretation of the Torah's command? True, what we see here in Beth Shearim does not correspond to rabbinic interpretation as recorded in the Mishnah (see Middot ch. 3). But it is possible that, either through tradition or by force of sheer imagination, the manufacturers of the sarcophagi arrived at a more accurate interpretation. Are these lids meant to represent the altar?

Why, given the chronological distance between ancient altars and Beth Shearim burials, do I insist that we consider such a possibility seriously? We have seen, beginning in the Mishnah and continuing in the Tosefta, the belief that death is an atoning force. In the ancient Tabernacle and Temple, the altar was the site of acts of expiation and therefore the place where atonement was effected. If death atones as service at the altar atones, the association we have posited is a perfectly natural one. But there is more. As we saw in the previous chapter, the Tosefta, composed at approximately the same time these burials took place, teaches explicitly: "Anyone who is buried in the Land of Israel is as though *buried beneath the altar*" (A.Z. 4:3). We should not be surprised, then, to find this belief symbolized in the act of burial itself. Are the individuals interred in these sarcophagi symbolically "buried beneath the altar," as represented by the horns (acroteria) on the lids? Surely, this interpretation explains this strange phenomenon as well as any other.

Admittedly, there is no way to be sure of this explanation. But even if the acroteria "merely" copy (poorly) the Roman model, we have here a rough representation of a Temple. Assuming that Jews envisioned *their* Temple according to the model of temples they saw around them, we may conclude that what is represented in the features of these lids is *the* Temple, now in ruins in Jerusalem. And since the Temple was the home of the altar, the place where Israel atoned for her sins, Temple symbolism too is an appropriate commentary on the meaning of death. One way or the other, we return to the same meanings. In this important detail, at least, the texts and the lived rituals speak for the same beliefs.

Who were the people laid to rest beneath these altar-like structures, in what are otherwise common Roman sarcophagi? Several of those buried in this catacomb are identified as rabbis or relatives of rabbis. For example, inscribed on one sarcophagus we read (in Hebrew): "This is the coffin of Rabbi Hillel the son of Rabbi Levi, *who made this cave*" (emphasis added). Nearby, in the same room, another is labelled (on the lid) with these words: "This is the coffin of Lady Megah, the wife of Rabbi Joshua the son of Levi, Shalom" (Avigad 1957: 207–9). Notably, with the exception of the graffiti on the entrance-way, written in Greek (probably by later visitors), all of the inscriptions in this catacomb are in Hebrew. This is in marked contrast with inscriptions in all of the other catacombs in this hillside (with the exception of the adjacent rabbinic cave), which are predominantly in Greek or Aramaic – not in Hebrew. Avigad argues that the abundance of Hebrew inscriptions in this cave is evidence of the fact that its population derives from rabbinic circles (Avigad 1957: 250). This would also explain why such a large number of people are buried in the same catacomb, one that virtually "hugs" the neighboring cave which, we have observed, appears to house the family of Rabbi Judah the Patriarch. These people want to find their resting-place in the vicinity of this great man (or, at least, some great man – that is beyond question). What we appear to have in this catacomb, then, is the lived expression of rabbinic beliefs. Consequently, we should not be surprised to have found a significant reinforcement here of the opinions preserved in rabbinic documents. The culture is perhaps more Roman than those same documents would have led us to anticipate. But the common system of beliefs concerning death is unmistakable.

Indeed, if we step back and reflect upon all of what we have seen at Beth Shearim, we will recognize that the texts and practices of the rabbis, on the one hand, and the practices of the more varied Jewish community represented here, on the other, bespeak a set of common assumptions regarding death. Death is a transition, the beginning of a journey. The dead retain an awareness of their surroundings, making it appropriate to visit them in their graves. Death will apparently atone for their sins, purifying them for the life to come. Following purification, the first experiences of death will give way to an eternal rest, to peace in the world of the deceased.

As I said, the only prominent reality of Beth Shearim for which the early rabbinic texts will not have prepared us is the profoundly *Roman* quality of the Jewish burial practice. But even here there is more accord than we might first realize. According to Toynbee's description, common Roman death-practices included the following steps: When death was soon expected, *close friends and relatives would gather around the dying person*. They would offer comfort and support, and express their own grief. When death occurred, the closest relative would give the deceased a last kiss and *close his or her eyes. The body would be set on the ground, there to be washed, anointed and dressed* in a toga. *Professional female mourners would be hired to participate in the funeral. They would appear with dishevelled hair, raise their hands, beat their breasts and cry out. Women would also play on the double-pipe. Burials would take place outside of cities (the corpse being a source of impurity)*. It was essential that a small amount of soil be thrown on the corpse. Relatives and friends would then call upon the dead by name for the last time (Toynbee 1971: 43–50).

Those familiar with later Jewish funeral practices will see most of these Roman customs as foreign. But anyone who has studied the burial-law preserved in the Mishnah will immediately recognize Roman practice as virtually identical to that of ancient rabbinic Jews (I have emphasized those parts of the Roman practice that are identical with what is prescribed in the Mishnah). Though the preferred iconography may be different, the rituals themselves are extremely similar. Rabbinic death-practice, like broader Jewish death-practice, is Roman practice with mostly slight modifications (the one major difference is the Roman custom of cremation, evidently unthinkable in rabbinic and other Jewish circles).

Ritual practice expresses belief, and if there is similarity in practice there must also be similarity in belief. Toynbee describes the beliefs of others in the Roman empire this way:

> among the great majority of people of the Roman age . . . there persisted and prevailed the conviction that some kind of conscious existence is in store for the soul after death and that the dead and living can affect one another mutually.
>
> (Toynbee 1971: 34)

> a person's conduct and deeds in this world had some bearing on his or her destiny hereafter . . . all men must expect a reckoning and judgment after death.
>
> (Toynbee 1971: 36)

There is more, but these examples will suffice. What we see in general Roman belief is in fact identical with what we have discovered in Jewish – including rabbinic – belief of the same period. With minor variations, a single belief system pervades this world, one which sees death as merely another stage in a continuing life-cycle. Jews translate the particulars into their own terms, but the changes brought about by the translations are mostly insignificant. The entire culture constructs and supports a united set of opinions, a unity in which Jews participate wholeheartedly. Given the unanimity with which these opinions are evidently held, it is hard to imagine Jews doing otherwise. Until the mid-fourth century, at least, the documents (mostly) reflect real life; real life gives concrete expression to the documents. Together, these voices express the Jewish view that after death the fate of the Jew is essentially identical to that of the rest of humankind. Death is death, a universal human experience.

6

JEWISH DEATH-PRACTICES IN EARLY BYZANTINE PALESTINE

The Yerushalmi and Aggadic Midrashim

One century passed, then part of another. The world in which the Jews of Palestine lived underwent radical upheaval and transformation: the former pagan empire became Christian, the Temple in Jerusalem remained in ruins (after a serious attempt under the reign of the emperor Julian to rebuild it), the recognized political leadership of the Jewish community in Palestine was abolished (Neusner 1983: 3–26). But the one literate Jewish group whose record survived late antiquity, the rabbis, did not see fit to capture their teachings from this tumultuous period in a contemporary record. Instead, they taught what they taught, requiring their students to preserve their teachings in memory, allowing these teachings to be transformed by the new experiences and imperfect memories of the transmitters.

Only once the world was different, the older systems displaced, did the body of rabbinic teachings finally find documentary record. In the fifth century, the rabbis of the Galilee finally fixed their teachings in more static contexts, carefully formulated for repetition, study and (presumably) subsequent elaboration. The major documents to emerge from this period – the Palestinian Talmud (the Yerushalmi), Genesis Rabbah and Leviticus Rabbah (along with several more minor midrashim) – capture a massive quantity of details relating to rabbinic Jewish practice and belief. Not surprisingly, we may recover from these works far more relating to death and mourning than from all of the earlier rabbinic record.

Death

How do the rabbis of Palestine, preserving an old world but confronting a new one, understand the experience of leaving one world and approaching another – the experience called death? To begin with, they hint that death does not begin at the time of what *we* call death. The righteous, at least, incline toward death, prepared by God and preparing others at the same time.[1] Rabbi Judah the Patriarch, the editor of the Mishnah, is reputed to have given final directions before his death, directions relating to his widow, his funeral and his burial (Kil. 9:3, 32a = Ket. 12:3, 34d). Though we are unable to capture the emotion of his voice, it is clear that Judah was in control, dispensing directives that would determine his own immediate fate and the fate of those close to him. As for all important transitions, preparation is evidently recommended in advance of death. This is not a time for fear on the part of the dying person, not yet a time of lament. Death is to be faced with sobriety, even a degree of confidence.

The source of this apparent confidence may be in Rabbi Judah's presumed knowledge that he, like other righteous individuals, awaits reward after death. This is not merely a general belief. Rather, God is said to show the righteous their future reward *before* death, allowing them to die "soul-satisfied." Doing this, God is doing no less than a human king, who would naturally show his invited guests what they can expect in advance. According to the midrash, proof of all this may be found in the experience of R. Abbahu who, upon death (presumably shortly before death) was shown thirteen rivers of balsam oil, all his in the future world (B.R. 62:2, y. A.Z. 3:1, 42c). The righteous, at least, approach death with satisfied confidence.

What modern individuals call death is for these rabbis the exit of the soul. When the soul exits the body, it emits a great noise – a noise which, though generally not audible to the human ear, is so great that it can fell cedars (B.R. 6:7). (Crucially, in the midrash's story, the noise may be detected by the brother of the dying person, suggesting a special connection between the dying individual and his or her close relatives; more on this connection later.) This noise may be a cry of agony for, in a very obscure midrashic text, the exit of the soul is said to be like "a twisted rope [which is drawn with difficulty] through a hole [in a ship]" or, possibly, a wet thorn, stuck in a throat, which is now forcibly extracted (L.R. 4, 2).[2] Whatever the precise meaning of the images recorded in the midrash, it seems clear that the exit of the soul is believed to be difficult, even tumultuous, and perhaps painful. The composure of pre-death is displaced before the agonizing experience of death itself.

Between Death and Burial

When the soul has exited, the close relative who is in the presence of the deceased is, as we learned in the Mishnah, exempt from the obligation to read the Shema, wear tefillin (prayer straps) and (presumably, though the Mishnah does not make this explicit) recite prayer. Above all other concerns, this relative (called an *onen*, one who is grieved or oppressed) must now take responsibility for funeral preparations. The Yerushalmi, for the first time, records the full range of rituals which pertain to an individual at such a time:

He should eat with a friend or, if he has no friend with whom to eat, he should at least eat in another house [away from the deceased] or, if there is no other house, he should make a partition between himself and the deceased or, if he has nothing with which to make a partition, he should at least turn away from the deceased. He should not recline comfortably when eating, nor should he eat or drink all that he might desire. He should not eat meat nor drink wine. He does not join in the communal blessing after meals. If he blesses, others do not answer "amen," and if others bless he does not answer "amen."

The Yerushalmi adds that none of this applies on the sabbath, when burial may not take place in any case. Furthermore, as the same text puts it, "When he [the deceased] has been transmitted to the public" or "to the shoulders" of those carrying the bier for burial, "he [the *onen*] may [once again] eat meat and drink wine" (Berakhot 3:1, 6a; M.Q. 3:5, 82b).

How are we to understand these various ritual restrictions? Let us approach the list in reverse order. Exclusion from communal blessings after meals, including the restriction on responding "amen," most obviously signals a separation of the *onen* from the community – even the small community constituted around a meal. Such a separation echoes the ritual placement of the mourner seen in earlier rabbinic tradition, so its repetition here occasions no surprise. What is more interesting is the association of this symbol with eating ritual, for this list is primarily about what may or may not be eaten during this period, and in what way. Why is eating central to the symbolic construction of this time?

Avoidance of meat and wine is commonly thought to have "mourning" connotations in rabbinic practice, for these were to be avoided in observance of the destruction of the Jerusalem Temple (see m. Ta'anit 4:7). But meat and wine had particular associations in the Temple ritual (meat = sacrifice; wine was poured on the altar), so we should hesitate before extending this symbolism to mourning in general. In fact, a ritual recorded in the same Talmudic context as the above list makes a "mourning" interpretation of abstention from meat and wine thoroughly implausible. I refer to the practice of "drinking ten cups [of wine] in the house of the mourner." Whatever the purpose of these ten cups (see below in this chapter), it is clear that wine is not to be avoided by the mourner – quite the contrary! So there is no symbolic conflict between wine and mourning. There is also no teaching prohibiting meat to the mourner. Thus, whatever the meaning of this avoidance, it cannot be "mourning" as such.[3]

It is tempting to interpret the avoidance of meat and wine as a symbolic avoidance of joy (which is not, however, the same as mourning). The Bavli records a teaching, which it claims originates in the period of the Mishnah, that associates meat and wine with joy; in its words: "R. Judah ben Beteira said – When the Temple stands, there is no joy except with meat . . . And now, when the Temple is not standing, there is no joy except with wine" (Pes. 109a). This teaching finds no earlier record, so we cannot be sure whether it was available to the teachers of the above ritual list. However, for other reasons it seems to me that the avoidance, or at least diminution, of joy is precisely the issue in this ritual symbolism. Joy, of a distinctly fleshy and physical sort, is the realm of the living. Such joy stands at odds with the position of the *onen* as he relates to the deceased before him.

Particularly notable in the same ritual list is the fact that, whatever one eats, *one should not eat it in the presence of the deceased*. This is spelled out in unusual detail, accounting for all imagined possibilities which might make observance of the ritual difficult. What is the meaning of this insistence? Self-evidently, eating is an act of giving life – of sustenance of the living. Engaging in such an activity in the presence of the deceased is, therefore, an unparalleled contradiction in terms. Life and death will not mix in this proximity. Separation is urgent.

This urgency may be a product of another consideration as well. To be sure, symbolisms may be extremely powerful, and symbolism alone might indeed provoke the concern expressed here. But the Jews whose opinions are recorded in the Yerushalmi and contemporary midrashim – like the Jews in the several centuries before them – "knew" that the dead are sentient. This is stated most explicitly at B.R. 96 (in manuscript, and found also at y. A.Z. 3:1, 42c), where we are told that, according to some, at least, the only difference between the living and the dead is speech. The dead hear the praise of the living as though in a dream. If the deceased knows what is going on in her or his presence, then those around the deceased must exercise extreme caution. So, for example, if the survivor were to engage in the activities of life (i.e. eating) in the presence of the deceased, her experience would be rendered more bitter. She would feel the limitations of her new condition – that she is no longer able to sustain herself, to take food. She would see her surviving relative enjoying the small pleasures of life and her pain would be that much greater. Of course, this pain would be heightened even further if the substance being enjoyed were meat or wine, those rare and special sources (along with sex, also prohibited at this stage and through the seven days of mourning) of the joy of human flesh. More than mere symbolism, these prohibitions may well be intended to assure that the dead not be "mocked" by the living (to borrow an expression from the Bavli's later interpretation). The deceased has barely left life. We should be careful that his dignity be maintained, that her pain not be increased.

Having gone this far in interpreting the rituals of the *onen*, we should not neglect the Yerushalmi's own attempt to identify the root of the *onen's* exemptions. In reference to the Mishnah (Ber. 3:1) granting exemption from the Shema and tefillin, this Talmud records a teaching which declares, "if he wants to be more stringent with himself [and recite the Shema even despite his exemption], we do not listen to him [= he is not permitted to do so]." "Why not?" the Talmud wants to know, "Is it because of the honor of the deceased or because there would be no one else to assume his burden [and attend to preparation for burial]?" The Yerushalmi does not succeed in answering its own question, being unable to find an authoritative source which would require one interpretation or the other. Both, therefore, presumably remain live possibilities. Both are relevant to the situation at hand: the deceased *does need his burial to be prepared* and the deceased *does need his honor to be protected*. The meaning of the former statement is evident. But what is the meaning of "the honor of the deceased?"

We have just learned that the honor of the deceased is protected by refraining from reciting the Shema and wearing tefillin. In the course of its deliberation, the Yerushalmi adds that the same purpose is served when we refrain from shaking the palm-branch on Sukkot and from blowing the shofar on the New Year festival (again, we are speaking of the *onen* who must avoid all of these activities). Why would refraining from the performance of mitzvot (divinely ordained obligations) protect the honor of the deceased? If we return to the interpretation suggested above, we will readily understand: if the deceased knows what is done while he as yet lies unburied – particularly what is done by his surviving close relative – then performance of mitzvot such as these will again be the source of despair and indignity. "Look at the noble, pious acts I may no longer perform!" the deceased will say to himself. "Look at what my loved one does while I lie here, reminding me of my diminished state! He should be directing himself to my needs. At the same time, he should not force me to confront the blessings of life which I have lost."

The state of being an *onen*, which began at the time of death, continues either until burial (in the opinion of R. Judah the Patriarch) or for the entire day (according to other sages; see y. Pes. 8:8, 36a–b). But this definitional dispute assumes we are speaking of a "normal" ancient case, when the deceased was buried on the day of death. All agree that the ritual status does not apply at night, nor does the prohibition of eating "holy things" (such as the paschal lamb) extend beyond the first day.

As the Mishnah already directed, burial should take place as quickly as possible. In the language of the Yerushalmi: "For all deceased, he [the surviving relative] pushes the bier [to quick burial] and doesn't overly involve himself in [elaborate] preparation, but for his father and mother he involves himself in much preparation and doesn't push the bier [to quick burial]" (y. M.Q. 3:8, 83d). Under ordinary circumstances, in other words, the honor of the deceased is served by quick burial. But parents are different. Children should not hurry a parent into the grave. This would be hurtful, a sign that the child wants to part with the parent quickly. The child should experience great sorrow at the death of the parent, and the ritual is constructed so as to assure this will be so – at least symbolically. The distinction between the ritual for a parent and for others begins before burial. As this Talmud's subsequent deliberation makes clear, the distinction should define the entirety of the mourning period as well.

Burial

How was burial itself conducted? The earlier rabbinic record provided considerable detail concerning the place of burial, the structure of the burial cave, appropriate dressing of the deceased, and so forth. Unfortunately, we can say little concerning how much of the earlier practice was maintained at this stage, for the record of the fifth century is scattered and incomplete. But we do find some new and suggestive details, details which hint even of lost practices and forgotten beliefs.

The most striking such detail is the mention, in Leviticus Rabbah (5:5), of the synagogue as a place of burial. This record has generated much perplexity: it finds no parallel elsewhere in rabbinic literature and it seemingly stands in contradiction to much-accepted notions that the synagogue should be a place of purity while the corpse is a powerful source of impurity. In fact, that the synagogue might be a proper place for burial was so unthinkable to later Jews that subsequent versions of the midrash (including the printed text) change "synagogue" (*beit haknesset*) to cemetery (*beit haqevarot*).

The manner in which the midrash speaks of this possibility ("A person should have a nail or stake affixed in the synagogue in order that he merit being buried in that place") suggests that the concern is for acquiring a regular, "fixed" presence in the synagogue. In other words, if a person makes his life – his home – in the synagogue, he will have the merit of locating his eternal home there as well. Whatever the apparent problems of such a burial might be, there is an indubitable sense to this connection as well. Moreover, Ariès documents a parallel phenomenon in medieval Christendom. Originally, Christians, like other ancients (including, of course, Jews), buried their dead at a distance from their settlements. In Ariès' words, "the dead were impure; if they were too near, there was danger of their contaminating the living. In order to avoid all contact, the abode of the dead had to be separated from the domain of the living" (Ariès 1981: 29). But thereafter there occurred what Ariès terms a "rapprochement" between the living and the dead, including the relocation of burial grounds to the sides and, in the case of particularly respected individuals, insides of churches (Ariès 1981: 36ff.). The church was holy ground; the dead, despite their impurity, were also holy. Thus, what had once been unthinkable came to be accepted, and with good reason.

Jewish vocabulary, from this and later periods, gives evidence of the notion that the dead were indeed thought to be holy. Martyrs were termed *kedoshim* ("holy ones"), the society that serves the dead was the *hevra kadisha* ("holy society"). We cannot insist, therefore, that death and holiness stand in opposition. We can also not dismiss the possibility that the midrash preserves remnants of a long-lost practice – burial at the synagogue. The midrash's modern critical commentator, M. Margulies, takes this tradition at face value. His is a reasonable conclusion.[4]

The story of the death of R. Judah the Patriarch (y. Kil. 9:3, 32a; y. Ket. 12:3, 34d; B.R. 96 and B.R. 100) preserves important opinions concerning proper burial, as well as information explaining the motivations behind these opinions. You will recall that Rabbi issued several directives in anticipation of his death. In addition to the three spoken of earlier, R. Hezekiah declares that Rabbi issued two others: that he not be buried with many shrouds (the text records that he may have been buried in a single simple sheet) and that his coffin have holes through the bottom to permit contact with the earth. Concerning the former directive, the Yerushalmi explains that Rabbi was of the opinion that "a person will not come [again into the world, at the time of resurrection] as he left." Thus, he need not worry that his burial garments be appropriate for resurrection. At burial, a simple sheet is sufficient and, if he merits a place in the World to Come, he will be wardrobed appropriately at the proper time ("the One who brings the generation will clothe it").

Others, in contrast, believe that one's state at resurrection will be the same as at the time of burial. So R. Yohanan is reported to have requested that he be buried in garments that were neither black nor white – so that, whether he find himself standing among the righteous or the wicked in the future world, he would not be ashamed. Speaking in disagreement, R. Yoshaya commanded that he be buried in proper white garments; why, after all, should he be ashamed to recall, in the color of his resurrection garments, his righteous deeds? Finally, R. Jeremiah is reported to have directed that he be buried with proper garments, sandals and a walking-staff, then laid to rest near a road, so that, when the Messiah arrives, he will be prepared to arise immediately.

As these traditions, several times repeated, make clear, death and burial are preparatory to future events: judgment, Messianic awakening, the World to Come. One's condition at the time of burial may therefore be crucial. True, according to one opinion, one need not worry at the time of death about one's future wardrobe; it will be provided miraculously in any case. But others believe that steps must be taken now, even to the extent of providing practical support. Thus, the objects of life, commonly found in burial caves, may not be intended to comfort the deceased, or not that alone. These may be supplies for a future journey, death being merely a resting-place along the road.

After burial: mourning

The mourning period, the broad contours of which have long been established according to the rabbinic record, commands significant attention in this community of texts. It is detailed, elaborated and explained, providing a full picture of and commentary on the life of the survivor following the death of a loved one.

For the first time, the source of the seven-day mourning period is sought out (y. M.Q. 3:5, 82c; B.R. 100, 7). A variety of possible derivations is suggested, each intimating an interpretation of the practice as well. The shiva

(= seven) may find its origin (= parallel) (1) in the seven-day mourning for Jacob following his interment in Canaan (Gen. 50:10), or (2) in the period of priestly preparation for service at the altar (Lev. 8:35) which is seen as parallel to God's anticipatory mourning for humankind seven days in advance of the flood (Gen. 7:4 and 10), or (3) in the isolation of the surviving sons of Aaron for seven days following the death of their brothers (Lev. 10:7), or (4) in the seven-day exclusion of Miriam from the camp when she became leprous (Num. 12:15), or (5, by fanciful reading) in the mourning for Moses (Deut. 34), or (6) in the seven days of the pilgrimage festival, or (according to B.R. 97) in the seven days of the wedding feast. What is the meaning of these purported sources, alone or in combination?

First, we must note that the most direct source, the mourning for Jacob by his family following his interment in the Land of Canaan, is rejected; in the Yerushalmi's view, it is improper to derive such a halakha from a practice which preceded the revelation of the law at Sinai. The mourning for Moses would provide an equally compelling source if the Torah actually spoke of a seven-day mourning period; it doesn't. Still, the sage behind this proposal clearly wants to see the mourning for Moses as a model, so he reads the "seven" into the text just the same. The association with Miriam is also relatively simple. Aaron explicitly speaks of the leprous Miriam "as though dead" (v. 12), and thus, if the people of Israel wait (mourn) for the "dead" Miriam for seven days, it is reasonable for later Jews to mourn for their dead for the same period.

The other proposed derivations are more challenging. The prophet Amos associates festivals and mourning (Amos 8:10 – thus the proposal attributed to R. Shimeon b. Laqish in the name of R. Yudan the Patriarch: just as the pilgrimage, Sukkot, lasts for seven days, so should mourning). Amos threatens that, as punishment for their sin, Israel's festivals will be turned into mourning. If death, leading to mourning, is punishment for the people Israel, so too may it be for the individual; surely, we have seen this notion before. But there is, at the same time, an ironic nexus between mourning and festival celebration. One is the reverse of the other; one yields to the other. Does the exegete want to build on this connection, saying that, if celebration yields to mourning, the opposite must be true as well? Does he mean to claim that just as Amos' mourning-as-punishment will give way to redemption, so too will the mourning that follows common death yield ultimately to redemption?

The association between mourning and the wedding-feast, posited already in an earlier chapter (see p. 45), supports such a conclusion. In fact, the association is strong and the parallels multiple. In what appears a contradictory tradition to the one referred to above, the Yerushalmi (Ket. 1:1, 25a) reports that the seven days of the wedding feast and the seven days of mourning were both *enacted* by Moses (this would grant these practices a kind of "rabbinic" status because, according to this present opinion, they cannot actually be derived from the letter of the Torah). Laws concerning the blessings of each occasion are also associated in the same context. Thus, scriptural support or not, the sages of this community perceive an undeniable association. On what is this association based? In addition to the explanations proposed in Chapter 4 (the wedding and death are both significant life-transitions; marriage and death are both seen as births into a new life), we must add the recognition that both marriage and death carry with them profound redemptive connotations. The redemptive promise of marriage is well expressed in the marriage blessings, which speak of the ingathering of the exiles to Zion in joy (see b. Ket. 8a).[5] With proper expiation-by-death and subsequent judgment, death will similarly lead to salvation, now finally and perfectly. Thus, marriage and death perform similar functions at different stages of one's life. Their similarity is marked, in the opinions of the sages whose teachings we read here, by similar ritual observances.

The closely related "priestly" derivations (2 and 3) of the mourning period depend upon the narrative contexts of the cited verses. The first, appearing near the end of Leviticus 8, brings to a close the detailed description of the service for the inauguration of the priesthood. The full conclusion (beginning with verse 33) is this:

> And do not go out from the opening of the Tent of Meeting for seven days, until the days of your inauguration are fulfilled, for seven days will he consecrate you. As he did on this day has the Lord commanded be done, to atone for you. And you shall sit by the opening of the Tent of Meeting, day and night for seven days, and observe the watch of the Lord, and you shall not die, for thus have I been commanded.

In the original context, the intent of this service is to atone for the priests who are now entering upon the holy service. If they observe the commanded preparation, in all of its details, they will not die.

But, crucially, this same law appears shortly before the story of the death of the sons of Aaron, Nadav and Avihu, who offer a "strange fire which He [God] had not commanded them." As a consequence of their improper offering, they are immediately consumed by fire (Lev. 10:1–2). In the midrashic imagination, the seven days during which the priests are commanded to sit in the Tent of Meeting is transformed from an inauguration ritual into an *anticipatory* mourning period for the soon-to-be-dead Nadav and Avihu.

Such anticipatory mourning is then justified by claiming a parallel practice on God's part. In the story of Noah and the flood (Gen. 7), God announces that God will destroy all living things from the face of the earth save for selected samples of each species. God gives Noah seven days to collect the survivors, including his own family, onto the ark. At the end of the seven-day period, the flood comes and wipes out the creatures who have not found haven on the ark.

In context, the seven days obviously serve to provide an opportunity for the creatures to gather onto the ark. The Yerushalmi claims here, however, that the seven days is, in effect, God's shiva for the world; anticipating the death of these many creatures, God mourns for them seven days in advance of their death. So both God and the family of Aaron (following God's command!) mourn for seven days before the death of their loved ones. This, it is claimed for a brief moment, is the source of the shiva practice.

But the Yerushalmi immediately admits a problem: mourning normally follows death, whereas the seven-day period described in these cases occurs *before* death. How could this, then, serve as a proper source for the practice of shiva? The Talmud answers that "[a human, made of] flesh and blood, who does not know what will happen in the future, doesn't mourn until the person dies, but the Holy One, Blessed be He, who knows what happens in the future, mourned for His world first [= before the fact]."

This brief passage makes a remarkable claim. In its view, it would be better to mourn for the deceased *in advance* of death: God, the ultimate model for human behavior, did so. Knowing what would become of Nadav and Avihu, God commanded the first priestly family to do so. And if we could know when a person would die, we too would mourn in advance of his or her death.

What could this claim mean? We noted earlier that death should properly be anticipated. The model of Rabbi Judah the Patriarch suggested that, when one inclines toward death, certain preparatory steps should be taken. By the same token, we now learn, the (not-yet-) surviving relative would also take such steps if he could be sure that his loved one is going to die. He would mourn in advance, expressing the pain of impending separation, indicating in the presence of the still living relative that the separation of death is a hated event.

But, because (unlike God) humans cannot know in advance when death will come, the Yerushalmi pushes ahead to find a more appropriate source for human shiva. In the same narrative just considered, the Torah describes how, following the removal of the remains of Nadav and Avihu, Aaron and his surviving sons are commanded, in effect, not to mourn (v. 6). Moses then adds: "Do not go out from the opening of the Tent of Meeting [presumably, but not explicitly, for seven days] *lest you die.* . . . " This Mosaic command, insisting that the surviving family remain in the Tent, might appear to have a natural connection with shiva. But several problems confound the association. First, what is described here is partial mourning, at best. In the same breath, other mourning practices are prohibited to Aaron and his surviving sons, forcing us (those who are looking for a biblical source for mourning practices) to turn a blind eye. In addition, a seven-day period is not mentioned explicitly here. Thus, the connection is anything but simple. Obviously, something else about this priestly narrative must attract the eye of the rabbinic readers.

It seems to me that what is compelling about these stories (whether the story of the death of Nadav and Avihu or of the "anticipatory mourning" alleged to be described in Leviticus 8) is the claim that one who observes such an isolation is protected from death. For the mourner, such protection is crucial. Having come so close to death and narrowly escaping, the survivor remains in danger. As the Yerushalmi and Midrash both express it, "for all of the seven days, the sword is drawn . . . " (y. M.Q. 3:7, 83c and B.R. 100). In some indiscernible way, the survivor is also deserving punishment. It is therefore essential that she take steps to protect herself. As the Torah says here clearly, staying inside and refusing to cross the threshold of one's "tent" will protect one – in this case the mourner – from death. Crucially, the term employed in the midrash to describe what God purportedly did during the seven days before the great deluvial destruction, which I have imprecisely translated as "mourn," is better translated as "guard" or "stand watch." If God's shiva is a "standing guard," should the human shiva be understood as one also? In the opinion of the present midrash, the answer seems clearly to be yes.

Whatever the source of the practice, mourning begins with a "shiva," a seven-day isolation (more on which below). Significantly, the seven days are not a uniform period. In the Yerushalmi's law, the first days are distinguished in several ways from those that follow. First, the mourner is not to wear tefillin (prayer straps) on the first or (according to another opinion) first and second day of mourning; the law is decided in favor of a single day. This discussion assumes a reality in which men wore tefillin all day, not just at the time of prayer (as in later Jewish practice). Therefore, the absence of tefillin – itself a biblical obligation – would be a powerful distinguishing symbol: for a reason or reasons as yet undefined, the first day is different from the rest. Second, even under circumstances of extreme hardship, work is prohibited for two or three days (again, there is a dispute). To be specific, if the mourner's neighbors have failed to provide her with food, during these first days she may not work to provide for herself. Thereafter, she may work only in private. This all relates to the recognition that the first three days are distinct from what follows, a recognition we saw already in the pre-rabbinic record (see Chapter 2). To designate this difference, the Yerushalmi describes these first days as the "strength" of mourning, that is, the period during which grief is strongest. Distinct in emotional power, these days are also, therefore, distinguished through special ritual markings.

The Yerushalmi (again, this is all found at M.Q. 3:5, 82b and following) adds that the first three days are also singular for the deceased. As the Talmud relates:

R. Abba the son of R. Pappi, R. Joshua of Sikhnin in the name of R. Levi: For all of the three days the soul hovers above the body, thinking that she will be able to return to it. When she sees that the face [of the body] has changed [presumably with the first strong evidence of decomposition] she gives up and leaves. After three days, the belly splits [spewing its contents] upon his face and says to him, "here is what you stole and took by force and put in me!" . . . At that moment, "but his flesh will feel pain upon him and his soul will mourn for him" (Job 14:22, translated for context).

As we can see, during the first three days, death is apparently not yet definitive, at least as far as the soul of the dying (we would prematurely say "dead") person is concerned. As long as the body remains intact, without more extreme signs of deterioration, the soul hopes to return to the body and resume normal life (much as it presumably does when the person wakes from sleep). But when the face changes, and then the belly splits, the soul finally understands its fate. With no hope, now, of returning to the body, it resolves to undertake its journey to the next world.

This Talmudic exposition is, in fact, largely a midrash on the last verses of Job 14. There we read (beginning with verse 20): "You overpower him forever and he perishes; You alter his visage and dispatch him. His sons attain honor and he does not know it; They are humbled and he is not aware of it. He feels only the pain of his flesh, And his spirit mourns in him" (Jewish Publication Society translation). Death (perishing) comes first, then his face changes. When this has occurred, he no longer knows what happens in the world of the living. Still, he can feel the pain of the deteriorating flesh, and the soul ("his spirit") then mourns for him as well.

The distinction of the first three days is grounded not only in the emotional state of the mourner but also in the physical state of the deceased, as this text makes perfectly clear. This would also have been clear to the authors of these traditions, for, as we saw in Chapter 5, it was an ancient and accepted custom for Jews in Palestine to visit their deceased who had been laid in burial caves. They thus would have known that physical changes become apparent at approximately this stage.

As we saw in passing in Chapter 2, the stories of the death of Jesus also attest to the custom of visiting the (apparently) deceased on the third day. The version in Matthew (27:57—28:1) attests to the practice most dramatically. According to that version, Jesus was laid to rest "wrapped in a clean linen cloth" on the Day of Preparation (for the sabbath), that is, Friday. The chief priests and Pharisees, concerned that Jesus' disciples would steal his body and then claim that his prophecy had come true ("After three days I will rise again"), approached Pilate and asked that the tomb be guarded until the third day. On that third day, Sunday, the two Marys "went to see the tomb" and discovered that Jesus was gone.

The question is, why did Mary and Mary come to visit the tomb on the third day? According to this version, their visit seems to be a response to the resurrection drama. But in the versions preserved in Mark (15:33—16:2) and Luke (23:44—24:1), this drama is absent completely: no petition by the priests and Pharisees to Pilate, no fear of a resurrection on the third day, no guards. Instead both versions agree that the purpose of the third-day visit is to anoint the body of Jesus with spices and ointments. This is reminiscent of the practice, described in the Mishnah, of anointing the body of the deceased before burial. Here the same practice seems to be repeated at least until the third day. At this time, of course, as the visitors would see, the physical effects of death would be increasing, the deceased would therefore experience greater pain, and the soothing qualities of the oils would be that much more necessary.

We might also go so far as to propose that, as in the story of the miracle of Lazarus, the drama in Matthew depends upon the belief that when three days have passed (or, in the Gospel's record, from the third day) death is irreversible; until that point, it is always possible that the soul will find its way back into the body. Thus, to assure that Jesus not reawaken to life – whether in fact or by ruse – guards would have to be posted until the third day. After that time, "everyone knows" that such a reawakening is impossible (until, that is, the general resurrection of the dead).[6]

Returning to the Yerushalmi's deliberation, we should also take note of the parallel between the experience of mourners and that of the deceased. As the first days are painful and confusing for mourning relatives, so are they also for the deceased. Just as survivors mourn the death of a loved one, so also does the soul of that (now deceased) loved one mourn for the same death. The parallel suggested in Chapters 3 and 4, captured in the ritual enactment of the mourner who plays as though dead, is here claimed as literal. We shall have more to say concerning this parallel below.

This literature permits us to recover the most comprehensive picture of mourning practices available in the classical rabbinic record (the major sources for what follows are again y. M.Q. 3:5 and B.R. 100). According to a tradition which claims origins in the Mishnaic period, during the shiva, mourners are prohibited from washing, anointing, wearing shoes, having sexual relations, cutting hair, laundering clothes, reading the Torah, repeating (= studying) midrash, laws and rabbinic stories, asking the welfare of another, and doing work. Other teachings add that the mourner is obligated to rend his garments (which he must then wear during all of shiva), to cry out, to shun the wearing of tefillin (as we saw already above), and to cover his mouth. He must also uncover his head and overturn his beds and couches. Many of these rituals attract comment and elaboration.

The Yerushalmi suggests the source of several of the mourning practices. The teaching, attributed to R. Abbahu, calls our attention to the prophet

Ezekiel (ch. 24), whom God directs *not* to mourn for "the delight of his [Ezekiel's] eyes," the wicked Israel. Each thing that Ezekiel is directed *not* to do is taken as evidence of what normal mourners *should* do. So, God directs Ezekiel to "sigh in silence" (v. 17), therefore a mourner must cry out. God directs Ezekiel to "bind his turban"; a mourner, therefore, must avoid wearing tefillin (metaphorically, a turban) or, according to another interpretation, properly laundered clothes. God directs Ezekiel to put on his shoes; a mourner, therefore, must avoid wearing shoes. God directs Ezekiel not to cover his lips; the mourner, therefore, must cover her mouth. Finally, God directs Ezekiel "not to eat the bread of men"; the mourner, therefore, must eat food provided by others.

The proposed derivations are quite straightforward. In fact, regardless of whether they were practiced in the intervening centuries, it is hard to escape the conclusion that these were indeed ancient mourning customs. But, of course, for the author of this midrash, the actual history of these practices hardly matters. What is important is that they are defined by God. Recognizing this source, we (that is, readers of the Yerushalmi) will say that they are virtually the law of the Torah.

The practice of overturning beds and couches, which we saw already in earlier rabbinic texts, is here both grounded in scripture and explained. The purported source is found in Job 2:13, where Job's colleagues, joining him to offer comfort for his losses, sit with him "*to* the earth seven days and seven nights" – not *on* the earth but close *to* it, that is, (according to this interpretation) on overturned beds. What is the purpose of this practice? Several explanations are suggested. Bar Kappara attributes the following reasoning to God: "I had one good icon [i.e. the human, created in 'the image of God'] in your house and you [the mourner] caused me to overturn it. So too must you overturn your bed." Others propose that the bed is, in effect, the "middle-man," that is, the place where the parents had sexual relations and thus a partner in the creation of the person. Overturning this "partner" represents the overturning of the created person. In a more practical vein, R. Shimeon b. Laqish suggests that forcing the mourner to sleep on an overturned bed will keep him awake at night, thereby reminding him that he is a mourner (see y. M.Q. 3:5, 83a and y. Ber. 3:1, 5d–6a).

The latter two of these interpretations invite little comment. According to the last cited opinion, the mourner should not be able to escape consciousness of his mourning status, even through sleep. In this view, mourning is an obligatory state of consciousness, and the various rituals which define the period are intended to serve as constant reminders of this condition. In the interpretation which associates the bed with procreative sexual relations, the bed symbolizes the product of those relations. By this view, the symbol reminds the mourner of the deceased, but nothing more.

But the first interpretation makes a bold statement. Bar Kappara speaks of the mourner as the *cause* of the death – spoken of as the overturning of the image of God. This can only be because the death of a loved one causes pain and suffering to the survivor and must therefore be punishment for his sin. People suffer, this teacher and others with him believe, because they sin. Assuming this perspective, the symbol of the overturned bed takes on an accusatory aspect: *You* have done something of which you must be reminded. *You* have overturned a life. Your comfort, your rest, must also therefore be overturned.

However the mourner understands the symbol, the question arises how literally the obligation to overturn beds is meant. Are substitutions or approximations possible? The Yerushalmi preserves the following modification: "If he said, 'I will not overturn the bed; behold, I will sleep on a bench,' we do not listen to him, because he said [explicitly] 'I will not overturn the bed.' But if he said 'I will overturn the bed' [and yet still sleep on a bench] we do listen to him." But this teaching is challenged, and the challenge is not clearly resolved. Thus, whether or not a bench may substitute for an overturned bed is not known. Only one exemption is unambiguously enunciated: if the mourner is the resident of an inn, he is not obligated to overturn his bed, for he might be suspected of being a sorcerer.

The prohibition of washing is also modified (y. M.Q. 3:5, 82d and y. Ber. 2:6(7), 5b). First, some are of the opinion that washing is like eating and drinking and therefore permissible. What this means, apparently, is that washing, like eating and drinking, is a basic human need. Whatever the symbolic intent of the ritual prohibition, then, the denial of washing for an entire week may not be tolerable. Further, even those who prohibit washing are said to agree that the prohibition applies only to washing for pleasure. Bathing for one's health, however – even when there is no risk of grave consequences should bathing be avoided – is permitted.

According to the Yerushalmi's clarification, the prohibition on wearing shoes should not be allowed to place the mourner in danger. So if for some reason the mourner is forced to travel from one town to another, he is permitted to wear shoes on the journey. In the words of the tannaitic teaching which expresses this clarification, "A mourner and banned person who were walking on the road [between towns] are permitted to wear shoes, and when they come to the town they should remove them. And the same is true on the Ninth of Av and during a public fast." Of course, this is, in other words, none other than the teaching of the Tosefta we saw in Chapter 4 (t. Taan. 1:6). And, like that other teaching, this again upholds the ritual equation between the mourner, the banned person, and Jews observing a fast. The meaning of this equation we discussed earlier (see pp. 41–3). Regrettably but characteristically, the Yerushalmi does not elaborate on the equation.

Finally, the Yerushalmi adds, if someone is "on fire" to study Torah, he may disregard the prohibition against such study.

The most important "exception" to the mourning ritual – actually a regular but notable interruption of its practice – pertains to the sabbath. In fact, the power of the sabbath to transform the status of the survivor begins when the deceased is as yet unburied; the variety of restrictions which pertain to the *onen*, discussed earlier in this chapter, are not in force on the sabbath (see y. Ber. 3:1, 6a). This same power extends to the period of mourning itself. A brief list of regulations attributed to Samuel directs that, on or in preparation for the sabbath, the mourner is obligated to uncover his head (which had been covered for mourning), to turn the tear in his garment to the rear (where it will not be seen), and to raise the beds which were overturned for mourning. Moreover, if he so desires, he may wear shoes, have sexual relations and bathe. Rav declares that uncovering one's head for the sabbath is not obligatory. Furthermore, a story quoted in context makes it clear that Samuel's approval of sexual relations for the mourner on the sabbath is merely theoretical. One of his students is said to have made the mistake of carrying theory into practice and found himself the object of Samuel's anger (an anger so powerful that it caused the death of the student).

Explicitly described as subject to local custom is the question of whether one should greet a mourner on the sabbath – some communities deem it proper and others do not. R. Hoshaya the Great is said to have greeted mourners in a location with whose custom he was not familiar by saying, "I do not know the custom of your place, but peace be with you according to the custom of my place." Still, despite the lip-service paid to respecting local custom in this matter, the accompanying narrative makes it clear that greeting – representing a public denial of mourning on the sabbath – is indeed preferred.

What is the reason for this profound sabbath transformation? According to this same Yerushalmi text, "there is no mourning on the sabbath, as it is written, 'the blessing of the Lord will make wealth' – this is the blessing of the sabbath, 'and no sorrow will be increased with it' (Prov. 10:22) – this is mourning." The same midrash is repeated at Genesis Rabbah (11, 1), in exposition of the verse, "God blessed the seventh day and hallowed it" (Gen. 2:3). According to this midrash, the sabbath is a day of special blessing, a day whose essence and spirit contradict the spirit of mourning. As a day commemorating creation, a day of rest sanctified by God, the recollection of death cannot be tolerated. Death is contrary to creation; there was yet no death in creation; observing the rituals of death would disrupt blessing and rest. Thus, the day takes precedence. The needs and obligations of the mourner, whatever they may be, must yield before the grand power of the seventh day.

The claim that there is no mourning on the sabbath is attributed, in the Yerushalmi, to R. Meir. To demonstrate the truth of his teaching, R. Meir intentionally extends greetings to mourners on this day (the mourners object to the greetings, and the above midrash is then cited to support his actions). In the narrative version of these events preserved in Genesis Rabbah (100, 7), the mourners to whom the greetings are directed are found "standing in line" on the sabbath, that is, they are engaged in the ritual of receiving comfort (see above, pp. 40–1). The point of the narrative, repeated twice (once with R. Meir and once with R. Hoshaya the Great, as quoted above), is that such a ritual cannot be tolerated. Mourners may desire the ritual – they may need the comfort – but the centrality of the sabbath demands that the needs of individual mourners be suppressed.

Still, the triumph of God's day, and its communal celebration, is a symbolic one, and of necessity incomplete. It is only the more public symbols of mourning that are reversed. Those rituals that are not clear signs of mourning, such as maintaining bare feet (others who are not mourners also may go barefoot), need not be reversed. Emblematic of the persistence of "private" mourning is Samuel's insistence that the most private of all mourning rituals, abstaining from sexual relations, be maintained, even "on pain of death." There is only a conflict, therefore, on the level of public symbolisms. As a member of the public community, the mourner must rejoin that community when the sabbath so demands. But the heart, in its privacy, cannot be commanded to abandon mourning. Private symbolisms are therefore appropriate even on the sabbath.

The sabbath-modifications in the mourning practice, and their apparent meaning, provide important insight into the broader symbolism of the cluster of mourning prohibitions and obligations. As we have seen, there is a crucial distinction on the sabbath between public and private practices; private practices might be upheld, public practices must be reversed. So, for example, while sex is not tolerated, greetings must be publicly extended. What pertains to the realm of society – what might be viewed by neighbors or visitors and understood as a mourning practice – must be erased, what would be seen or understood only by the mourner herself still has a place.

In earlier chapters, based upon a far more limited record of the mourning ritual, I already suggested that one of the primary symbolisms of mourning is the distancing of the mourner from common society. This interpretation may be repeated and expanded here. So, once again, we may note that an individual who refrains from washing, anointing (to disguise bodily smells), and laundering clothes will, within a few days, be offensive to others. Allowing his hair to grow, wearing torn garments, he will transgress public norms and therefore distance himself from social intercourse. Covering his mouth and refusing to ask the welfare of another, he will both symbolically and literally isolate himself from his neighbors. Not allowing himself to wear shoes, access to the public domain will be restricted in any case.

But this interpretation does not account for other mourning rituals. For example, how do we explain the prohibition placed upon sexual relations and the study of Torah (in the broad sense)? We may perhaps understand these as intended to diminish joy (presumably, both sex and Torah study were seen as sources of joy in the culture reflected here). But, as I have already argued, the prohibition on work will be difficult to explain from the same perspective.

Though I think it would be a mistake to dismiss these readings – all symbols may carry multiple meanings at the same time – it seems to me that the interpretation which most comprehensively explains the mourning rituals is one which understands them as marking the experience of the dead, *which the mourner in part shares*, in contradistinction to that of the living. Living persons *participate in* and *build* society. One who does not work, greet, beautify or procreate, *like the dead* does neither. The living (that is, living Jewish rabbinic males) wear tefillin and study Torah. Again, *the dead and the mourner* do neither. His bed overturned, the mourner, *like the deceased*, places himself on the ground. As Robert Hertz observed, "Mourning, at its origin, is the necessary participation of the living in the mortuary state of their relative . . . " (Hertz 1960: 86). The mourner is living, but he shares the experience of the dead; he has been touched by death, and the practices he must observe demand that he stare it in the face.

But even while the mourner participates in the experience of the deceased, the living community of Israel intercedes to begin to invite him back into their world. The customs or rituals enacted by those gathered in the house of mourning make this purpose clear. First, we have seen in earlier rabbinic compilations that neighbors are required to provide sustenance for mourners. This first meal following burial is called "the meal of giving health." In light of the interpretation of the mourner's practices proposed earlier, this meal may be understood as the community's first invitation to the mourner: "You have been touched by death, but you are alive. We invite you, when you are ready, to rejoin us – the society of the living."

To what was known from the earlier rabbinic record, the present works add (in a teaching claiming tannaitic status) that "they drink ten cups [of wine] in the house of the mourner, two before the meal, five during the meal, and three after the meal" (y. Ber. 3:1, 6a). The cups before and during the meal are not explained. But concerning the three following the meal we are told that "one is for the blessing after meals, one for 'deeds of loving-kindness' and one for 'the comforting of mourners.'" I have placed the latter phrases in quotation marks because there are evidently technical terms, referring to special blessings recited in the homes of mourners. If this understanding is correct, then in this respect, too, is the death-mourning transition analogous to the marriage transition; special blessings accompany the blessing after meals for seven days on both occasions.

At Yerushalmi Pesaḥim 8:8, 36b,[7] the phrase translated as "the comforting of mourners" is coupled with "the blessing of mourners," and explanations are provided: "What is the blessing of mourners? That which they say in the synagogue.[8] What is the comforting of mourners? That which they say in the line." Both contexts support the conclusion that we are speaking here of a specific formulation, though, again, we have no record of what the formula might be. Thus, we may assume that, in the opinion of the Yerushalmi, special blessings should be added to the after-meal recitation in the house of the mourner, one directed at those who have come to offer comfort and one at the mourners themselves.

From the Yerushalmi's definition of "the blessing of mourners," we also learn that specific recitations are thought appropriate for the synagogue. These may have been associated with the mourner's return to the synagogue (see below in this chapter), but to accept this scenario, we would be forced to assume that what was called "the blessing of mourners," earlier identified with the meal in the mourner's home (or perhaps with the post-funeral line), was now reappropriated for other ritual purposes. Perhaps, therefore, the Yerushalmi's association of the blessing of mourners with the synagogue reflects a new practice of conducting parts of funerals in synagogues. Admittedly, this is speculative. But we know that the synagogue underwent tremendous growth in Palestine in the fourth century (the century before the composition of the Yerushalmi), and rabbinic involvement in the synagogue grew at precisely the same time.[9] If the strength of the institution grew, it may have become the arena for Jewish rituals which earlier found a home elsewhere. Certainly, many parallels of such a development could be found in modern times (such as the custom to hold weddings, and even funerals, in modern synagogues). In any case, the living quality of the ritual of "blessing mourners" is clear.

Returning to the cups before and during the meal, we may only speculate on their purpose and/or meaning. (I consciously avoid reference to the parallel version preserved in the Bavli, where explanations are provided even for these cups.) Are these cups of wine intended to bring levity into the house of the mourner? Given what else we know about the rabbinic mourning ritual and its probable affective consequences, this is unthinkable. Are they meant, instead, to comfort the mourners, to lessen the severity of their shock and help them go on? In view of the association of this custom with the restorative meal, such an interpretation is far more reasonable. The emotional turmoil of the mourner is not to be ignored or ritually effaced (even on the sabbath!). The custom of drinking wine, even far more than normal, is evidently a concession to the mourner's perceived personal needs.[10]

While speaking of meals of restoration and alcoholic concessions to personal grief – both apparently "healthy" affirmations that "life goes on" – we should not ignore crucial evidence that fasting, too, may be considered a proper ritual response to death, at least on the part of some individuals. The relevant discussion in the Yerushalmi commences with a remarkable equation: "One who sees a disciple of sages who has died, it is as though he sees a Torah scroll which has been burnt!" (M.Q. 3:7, 83b). In response to this statement, R. Abbahu declares, "May [a curse] come upon me if I tasted anything that entire day [i.e. the day I saw a disciple of sages who had died]!" The Yerushalmi adds: "R. Yona was in Tyre. When he heard that the son of R. Abbahu died, even though he had eaten cheese and drunk water, he completed the day fasting." Crucially, neither of these stories speaks of the relative of the deceased – the mourner proper. But we see clearly that, for others, fasting may indeed be an appropriate expression of grief. Why not for the mourner? We may speculate that, in the case of the mourner her- or himself, fasting would be too dangerous or, perhaps, too literal an imitation of the condition of the dead. There must be limits, markers that, despite everything else, distinguish between the living and the dead. Eating may be that limit. The mourner, unlike others, should not go this far.

Back to the community of the living

Emergence of the mourner from the most intense period of mourning comes slowly and in stages. We saw above that the first three days of mourning are understood to be particularly intense, and we recall from earlier generations that the seven-day mourning period is followed by a less severe period (called *shloshim*), up to the thirtieth day following death. This emergence and return of the mourner to society is symbolized by the "place" of the mourner in the synagogue on the sabbath. Again the Yerushalmi quotes a source of purported tannaitic origin, and again it records a dispute. According to the quoted teaching:

> On the first sabbath, the mourner doesn't go to the synagogue. On the second, he goes to the synagogue but does not sit in his [customary] place. On the third, he sits in his place but does not speak, and on the fourth he is equal to all persons. R. Judah says: ... [what is actually] the second is [here called] the first [thus postponing the mourner's return to "his place" by a week], the third is the second, the fourth is the third. R. Shimeon says: On the first sabbath, the mourner goes to the synagogue but does not sit in his [customary] place. On the second, he sits in his place but does not speak, and on the third he is equal to all persons. R. Shimeon b. Levi said: the law follows the one who adds days [that is, evidently, R. Judah; this is not, however, the necessary meaning of R. Shimeon b. Levi's words].
>
> M.Q. 3:5, 82b

The debate is clear, the decision is not. But the resolution matters little for present purposes. What is plain is that the mourner is displaced from his public place and may return thereto only slowly, week by week. At first, he is divorced from public society completely. Then he begins his return, but he does not arrive immediately. Even when he does arrive, finding himself in his accustomed "place," he does not return to normal; he still eschews the exchange of words. Only after many weeks – three or four or five – does he return to normal. Needless to say, the present ritual literally enacts the separation and reconnection of mourner and community earlier suggested in interpretation of the mourning rituals. It also punctuates the stages of return, at the end of shiva and beyond.

The rituals of the thirty-day period (shloshim), marking the same "in-between" status of the mourner, are finally detailed in the Yerushalmi. During the shloshim, the torn clothing of the mourner may not be rewoven (though it may be roughly re-sewn), clothes may not be properly finished (ironed, starched), hair may not be cut (y. M.Q. 3:5, 82a). Returning slowly to society, some of the dishevelment characteristic of separation from society is maintained. The mourner again participates in the building of society (though only in a restricted way: local trade is permitted, long-distance trade is not); at the same time, the evidence of her separation is not forgotten.

The end of the shloshim marks a significant transition, as we may see in a number of pertinent ritual transitions. At this point, most mourners may re-sew their torn garments and may again wear freshly laundered garments (y. M.Q. 3:8, 83d). They may again cut their hair and may finally venture out on long-distance trading. Literally and symbolically, the mourner is again a full participant in society.

The exception, a crucial and common one, is the mourner who has lost a parent. Such a mourner may never re-sew garments torn upon hearing of the death. He may not wear properly laundered garments until the passing of a full year. He may not travel abroad on business "until his colleagues rebuke him" (y. M.Q. 3:8, 83d). Is this all because the death of a parent touches one more closely, more brutally? Is it because the ritual wishes to insist that such a loss is more severe, with more extended consequences? Both are reasonable surmises; indeed, they are not contradictory.

The two-tiered mourning structure, which comes to conclusion at the end of a month and the end of a year, is reflected in a discussion which asks the question: After how long a period following the death will mourning obligations no longer commence? In a brief report of what are described as earlier sources, the Yerushalmi (M.Q. 3:5, 82c) discusses the status of a relative who hears of the death of a loved one at some point after inhumation. Two possible scenarios are imagined: what are called *shemua kerova* and *shemua rehoka* (literally, "a proximate hearing" and "a distant hearing"). According to the quoted tradition, one who hears "in proximity" to the death is obligated to observe shiva and shloshim, but one who hears "at a distance" is not obligated to observe these periods. The definition of proximate and distant is the subject of debate. According to one opinion, the point of division lies at the end of thirty days, according to another, at the end of a year; the law is decided in favor of the shorter period.

The law is rendered to reflect what is the more common term of extended mourning: thirty days. Only mourning for parents will extend for a greater duration. But, notably, the dispute echoes both options, showing that, for different categories of relatives, it is reasonable to mourn – *even to begin mourning* – for a month or even for a year. Ritual mourning ends when mourning is over (yes, this is redundant). Thereafter, mourning is evidently not a reasonable response.

Does the end of the mourning periods reflect this rabbinic community's judgment concerning the end of a certain emotional state? Perhaps. But then these rabbis would be not merely presumptuous but also wrong. Does it reflect their judgment concerning when that state *ought* to end? Again, though not impossible, this would be tragically misguided; such emotional engineering is bound to fail. Rather, a theological teaching, quoted in both the Yerushalmi (M.Q. 3:7, 83c) and Genesis Rabbah (100), supplies a more likely explanation. A family (and a colleague circle!), we are told, is like a dome built of rocks: if you remove one rock, the entire structure is threatened. The "removal" of a relative, in other words, endangers the entire family. The lesson continues:

> For the entire year, judgment is "spread out" against the family. For all
> of shiva, the sword is drawn; for shloshim, it [the sword of judgment]
> shakes, and it does not return to its sheath until twelve months [have
> passed].

Earthly rituals have heavenly counterparts. Shiva, the time when the mourner is almost like the dead, when he has been touched though not taken by death, is the period of greatest danger: the sword of judgment is drawn and strong; it might take him at any time. Shloshim, during which time the mourner rejoins the society of the living while not leaving the presence of death completely behind, is marked by weaker symbols of mourning. The sword of divine judgment is also, during this period, somewhat weakened. And, in the case of the parent at least, mourning is not gone until a year has passed. Neither is the fear that judgment might, at the last minute, bring death.

Though not mentioned in this text, it is also at the end of a year that the bones of the deceased are collected, after the flesh has completely decayed. The Yerushalmi instructs that reburial is not an occasion for formal mourning or wailing, though the survivor of the deceased should say words of praise to God (see Pes. 8:8, 36b and San. 6:9, 23d). Why is praise appropriate? A closely related teaching supplies the key: At Talmud Yerushalmi Sanhedrin 6:10, 23d, we learn that the executed criminal was originally (according to this traditional "memory") buried in mounds for the flesh to decay. When only the bones were left, they would be reburied in wood, and on that day, the surviving family would mourn (because they could not do so originally, since their relative was a felon convicted of a capital crime). The next day, however, they would rejoice. The flesh having decayed, the suffering of death having been experienced, the deceased had been atoned for. He was no longer, properly speaking, a criminal. He could, therefore, be properly mourned.

Thereafter, relatives could rejoice that he had escaped the fate of gehinnom. Obviously, all people – not only executed felons – would enjoy the same atonement by virtue of the pains of the grave. In recognition of the cessation of pain, the end of the process of death leading to a peaceful life after death,[11] it was considered appropriate, at this time, to express praise to God.

7

LAW AS COMMENTARY
The Bavli on death and burial

To the east, there was another Jewry. Descended from the Judean exiles of old, these Jews found themselves scattered along the great rivers, enjoying the relative tolerance of a different empire – the Persian. We know little about the memories or traditions of this community, for we have not preserved whatever literature it may have composed. But of its commitment to the ancestral faith there can be little doubt. These Jews of Babylon were already, in the centuries of the rabbis, the world's most ancient exiles.

Rabbis did not find their way to Babylon until the generation following Bar Kokhba, in the middle of the second century, and they did not begin to forge their own tradition in Babylon until the beginning of the next century. At first a movement of messengers and refugees from Palestine, the rabbis' seeds soon began to bear native fruit, and in relatively few years the rabbinic community of the east began to compete with the rabbinic community of the west for pre-eminence. But the communities remained small, even more so in Babylon than in Palestine, and the rabbis did not have an easy time persuading the ancient Babylonian Jewish community of the superiority of their Jewish ways. The road to rabbinic religious dominance of Jewry in Babylon would be a long one. Not until the fifth or sixth century, at the earliest, did the rabbis speak as recognized leaders of this eastern diaspora.[1]

In the matter of death and burial, as in other matters, the eastern rabbis looked for guidance to the first great record of rabbinic teachings, the Mishnah. So they knew that, according to the Judaism they deemed right, the dead had to be buried immediately, not only in contact with but actually in the ground. After approximately a year, the bones of the deceased should be gathered and reburied, again under the surface of the earth. Unburial was a sin and more: if the protection of the grave did not eliminate the pains of death, how much worse would the pains of unburial have been!

But in these respects, the religious laws of their neighbors stood in stark contradiction to their own. In the opinion of the dominant Persian religion, Zoroastrianism, the earth and its purity had to be protected from the stain of impurity at virtually any cost. And (ironically, just as in Judaism) corpses, human or animal, were believed to be a powerful source of impurity.

Whenever a person died, therefore, it was essential to keep the corpse and corpse-matter (as the body decomposed) above the earth. Burial was anathema. The dead were exposed in the open, either on *dakhmas* ("towers of silence") or mountain tops, to be consumed by corpse-eating birds or dogs. One who buried the dead was a sinner and, if he failed to exhume the corpse, he would be punished with increasingly severe punishments. These concerns were apparently so urgent that the largest bulk of preserved ancient Zoroastrian law addresses questions relating to corpse impurity (Zend-Avesta, Vendidad, fargards III–VII). At least partially overlapping in spirit, rabbinic and Zoroastrian practice regarding the dead could not have been more at odds.

We know little of how Persian beliefs in this matter may have affected the practices of the ancient Babylonian Jewish community. We can certainly imagine that the rabbis found themselves in an immensely awkward position; the relevant Avestan ruling makes it clear that the concern for preserving the purity of the earth doesn't end with Zoroastrians (Vendidad, fargard III, iv). Still, we can only imagine, because there is almost no record of conflict or difficulty in the teachings preserved by the Babylonian rabbis in their Talmud. A story recorded at Baba Bathra 58a speaks of a "magus" – probably a Zoroastrian priest – who was digging up the buried dead of Israel. But this is an isolated incident, speaking (at most) of a single zealous soul. And a statement attributed to Ravina at Bezah 6a, declaring that "now that there are 'fellows' we are concerned," is very ambiguous. This statement says something about burial on the second day of a festival, but it is not clear what. It may mean that Jews had to bury their dead as soon as possible out of fear that "fellows" of the Zoroastrian faith would interfere, but other interpretations are equally reasonable. In any case, these testimonies are few and unclear. What is clear is that the Babylonian rabbis directed their gaze not at meddling neighbors but at the teachings of their rabbinic forebears. If more than one or two zealous Zoroastrian priests refused to tolerate an alternative Jewish practice, we preserve no evidence to this effect.

The Talmudic record comes to its preserved form some time after the Christian year 500.[2] It is a massive work, a formulation composed of deliberation and detail. In its discussions of death and burial, as in so many things, the Talmud seems to miss little; the entire prior rabbinic tradition stood before the authors of these texts, or so it seems. But the unique contribution of the rabbis behind this corpus lies not in the preserved details. Their genuine and lasting contribution is found in what we might call their "law as commentary," their reflections upon the details of life which add up to commentaries on the meaning of life. Accordingly, no purpose will be served by telling the rabbinic story of death again (though, to be sure, we will notice important divergences from the earlier Palestinian record). Instead, we must read the major deliberative essays that comment on death, those sugyot (literary weavings) which tell us most about what this community believed.

Here, we will have the opportunity to interpret the interpretations of law and practice, to plumb the imaginations of the greatest rabbinic minds.

FOR THE LIVING OR FOR THE DEAD?

We begin with the Talmud's deliberation on the basics of a funeral – the eulogy and burial. In the first section of the central text (Sanhedrin 46b–47a), which I will not discuss here, the Talmud unsuccessfully (!) seeks a biblical source for the obligation to bury the dead.[3] Notably, in one of its efforts, the Talmud describes the Sassanian king, Shapur, as inquiring concerning the source of this obligation in the Torah. R. Hama is unable to provide him with an answer because Persian kings are not persuaded by rabbinic midrash. Could this be an ironic reference to the contrary Persian practice forbidding burial? We shall never know. Crucially though, the Persian inquirer is a king known in the Talmud for his sympathy toward his Jewish subjects. If in the real world there is lack of understanding or tolerance for the practices of the Jews (at least those who follow rabbinic law), there is no hint of this in the present text.

In any case, having failed to identify an unambiguous biblical source for the obligation to bury the dead, the Talmud asks the reason for burial (if there is no authoritative source, there must at least be a good reason; otherwise, why be so concerned about burial – particularly since it contradicts local custom?). The Talmud's discussion, in its basics, is this:

A: They inquired: Burial – is it because of [the] disgrace [which exposure of the dead might cause the survivors] or is it because of [the] atonement [that the burial will effect for the deceased]?

B: What difference does it make?

C: [It would make a difference] if he [= the dying person] said: I do not desire that that person [meaning himself] be buried.

D: If you say it is to avoid disgrace, he hasn't the power to do this, but if you say it is because of atonement, lo, he [effectively] said that he wants no atonement . . .

A variety of authoritative sources are quoted which might tip the scales in one direction or the other. In this immediate context, no conclusion is arrived at. The Talmud then continues with a related question: Is the eulogy for the honor of the living (the survivors) or the honor of the deceased? Again, evidence is cited and again it appears that there will be no definitive conclusion. But, as the sugya approaches its end, its typical "Talmudic" attempt to avoid such a conclusion becomes disingenuous, absurdly forced. For example, the Talmud quotes part of the Mishnah upon which its discussion is based: "If they left the deceased [unburied] overnight for his honor, [such as] to bring him a coffin and shroud, there is no transgression." This text seems to state clearly that the primary concern is the honor of the deceased. And even when the Talmud claims that "his" may refer to the living, not the deceased, we are hardly convinced. The same is true in the following step, where the quoted source speaks explicitly of the "honor of the dead;" the Talmud's claim that this does not really refer to the honor of the dead rings hollow. We are already inclined, therefore, to conclude that these practices are intended to uphold the honor of the deceased. Thus, we are prepared for the gemara's ultimate and conclusive step:

> Come and hear: R. Nathan says – "It is a good sign for the deceased
> if payment is exacted from him after death. A dead person who is not
> eulogized or not buried or who is dragged by an animal, or if rain falls
> on his [exposed] bier – this is a good sign for the dead." Learn from
> this that it is because of the honor of the deceased; learn from it.

What is the meaning of this conclusion? Why is this evidence conclusive when other evidence was not? We can make sense of this final step in the gemara's deliberation only if we understand that, in the opinion of the authors of these texts, the dead have direct and conscious experience of what happens to them. If they are left unburied or if no one cries over them in lament, they will experience disgrace and suffer on its account. And, as we know, according to the common rabbinic view, suffering effects atonement. Therefore, if the deceased experiences uncommon disgrace following death, it may be viewed as "a good sign." Because it will effect the ultimate atonement of the deceased, his current disgrace and suffering should be understood as beneficial. If he has not been properly honored, then he has at least been quickly atoned.

Of course, if the absence of burial and lament is experienced by the deceased as indignity, then proper burial and lament must be experienced as honor. For this reason, the Talmud here concludes that these things (both eulogy and burial) are for the honor of the dead or, in the case of burial, for the atonement of the dead. We avoid causing indignity (though, ironically, such indignity may ultimately redound to the good of the deceased), we strive to bring honor. And the deceased will know what we do or do not do. These concerns must therefore direct all of our actions with respect to the dead.

In other Talmudic texts, discussing eulogy and burial in other ways and from other perspectives, we find the same conclusion supplemented and reinforced. As we shall see immediately, there are important consequences which flow from the belief that the deceased are conscious and sentient.

SPEAKING OF THE DECEASED

The earlier rabbinic record frequently refers to the so-called "eulogy," the expression of lament and sorrow which constitutes the rabbinic funeral (= accompaniment to the grave). But nowhere does it hint at the sorts of words that might have been spoken on this occasion. We can imagine the clapping and wailing, the sound of the flutes. But we have nothing to direct us when we seek to imagine how one is to speak of (or to?) the deceased.

In two brief texts, barely *sugyot*, the Bavli finally breaks the rabbis' silence. In two difficult and sometimes impenetrable discussions, the Bavli finally tells us how to speak of and to the dead. In doing so, it at the same time reveals much of how, in its opinion, death is to be understood.

The first recorded eulogies are found at Mo'ed Qatan 25b, beginning with a story about the deaths and burials of Rabbah b. R. Huna and R. Hamnuna. According to the Talmud's story, both sages were being "brought up to there" (presumably to the Land of Israel) at the same time. They came to a narrow bridge simultaneously and proceeded to argue with one another (remember: they are dead!) over who should cross the bridge first. After the matter was resolved – Rabbah b. R. Huna crossed first – a child who was standing nearby "opened [his mouth]" in praise of the deceased. His words, as the Talmud relates them, were these:

> The shoot of ancient ones came from Babylonia and with him was a book of wars.
> The pelican and bittern saw in double measure the ravage and destruction that comes from Shinar.
> The Rock was angry with His world and robbed souls,
> But He took pleasure in them [the souls] like a new bride riding on clouds.
> He took pleasure and rejoiced over the coming to Him of a righteous soul.

(I have provided an overly literal translation, following slight emendations based upon manuscript variants. For an excellent translation that captures the spirit of this and the following eulogies, see *The Soncino Talmud*.)

Without engaging in too detailed an analysis, and allowing for difficulties of interpretation, certain traits and qualities of this speech may readily be observed. First, the language of this "child" draws heavily upon biblical usages. The word translated as "shoot" is the same word used in the phrase "shoot of Jesse" in Isaiah 11:1; the reference is unmistakably messianic. Reference to the pelican and bittern echoes Isaiah 34:11, where these birds are described as ready to inherit the ruins of Israel's enemies against whom the Lord has exacted vengeance (a similar usage is found at Zephaniah 2:14).

Again, the language has unmistakable redemptive connotations, and so too, therefore, does its presumed reference – the deceased righteous person concerning whom these words are now uttered.

Second, we see that the deceased is spoken *of* (in the third person), not *to*. Though he lies before the speaker, he is not actually addressed with these words. Instead, he is praised in extraordinary terms, now a character in a redemption narrative. Third, though the exit of this soul from the world is described in violent language ("robbed"), the soul is unhesitatingly characterized as righteous, and God is represented as being immensely joyous at the arrival of this soul in the world beyond. Indeed, God is said to be like a bride greeting her loved one – a remarkable reversal of common prophetic imagery, in which God is the groom and Israel the bride. Finally, the speech is brief and carefully formulated, filled with allusions and poetic flourish; it may properly be described as poetry.

The next recorded eulogy, speaking of the deceased Ravina, exhibits many of the same traits. Its substance is this:

> Ye palms, sway a head for the one who is righteous like a palm.
> Let us make nights like days [with our lament] for the one who made nights like days [with his Torah study].

Again, the deceased is spoken of, not addressed directly. Instead, the actual addressees of the speech are elements of nature who are directed to respond to the death of a righteous person. The deceased is described in biblical terms: he is the righteous one who "flourishes like the palm," spoken of in Psalm 92:13. And, once again, the statement of the "eulogizer" (precisely this term is used by the Talmud) is brief and poetic. An unmistakable model begins to emerge.

Several more such praises are recorded as the text unfolds:

> [for R. Ashi:]
> If a flame fell among the cedars, what will the moss on the wall do?
> If Leviathan was raised with a hook, what will the fishes of the swamp do?
> If the rushing stream became dry,[4] what will the marshy waters do?

> [another eulogizer, for R. Ashi:]
> Cry for those who lose,[5] and not for loss, for it [loss, death] is for
>   rest, but we for grief.

In the first of these eulogies, the same qualities we saw above repeat themselves. R. Ashi, referred to in the third person, is spoken of in hyperbolic poetic imagery: he is a cedar, Leviathan, a rushing stream. Common persons, in contrast, are moss on the wall, small fish, shallow waters. Explicit biblical

100

references are fewer, but the biblical usages of cedars (of Lebanon) and Leviathan resound clearly. And the reference to the dried stream is particularly poignant; in chapter 14 of the book bearing his name, Job speaks of mortals who "languish and die; Man expires; where is he?" He continues: "The waters of the sea fail, and the river dries up and is parched. So man lies down never to rise; He will awake only when the heavens are no more, only then be aroused from his sleep" (vv. 10–12). The dried stream symbolizes the human whose strength flows no more. The empty stream-bed that remains reminds us of what is lost and cannot be recovered.

The alternative eulogy, motivated by its speaker's sense that it is improper to use such violent images as "flame" and "hook" with reference to the righteous, says virtually nothing about the deceased.[6] There is, in his words, none of the exaggerated praise which previously characterized these statements, none of the biblical images or references. Instead, in an extremely terse poem, the speaker comments on the relative fate of the deceased and of those who survive. In his view, the deceased is in a superior position because death will bring him to eternal rest. In contrast, survivors experience not rest but grief – whether this is intended to speak of the immediate grief of loss or of the greater, more pervasive grief of life is not certain. But, whatever the formal differences, this speech and the one preceding it agree on a fundamental reality: common folk, in this life, have little to hold on to. If even the "cedars" among us will be felled, how appropriate it must be for us to grieve and groan.

Below in the same text, we read of a certain R. Ḥanin, son-in-law of the Patriarch's house, who had no children. He prayed to God for a child, and his prayer was answered. But on the day of the birth of his son, he himself passed away. Thereupon, the eulogizer proclaimed:

> Joy has turned to sorrow,
>   happiness and pain are joined.
> At the time of his joy he sighed [his last sigh],
>   At the moment of his receiving caresses
>   died he who was to caress him.[7]

This eulogy is, as were earlier examples, a brief piece of poetry, carefully crafted. But it is again devoid of explicit biblical references, and it makes no attempt to praise the deceased concerning whom it speaks. Instead, the eulogizer speaks directly to the occasion of the death. His point, without question, is to highlight the bitter sorrow of the moment, to call up the pain and sorrow of those who might hear his words, encouraging them to cry out in anguish. In fact, whatever their precise approach, whatever the qualities of the person being eulogized, it is clear that such speeches have one central task: to open the wellsprings of tears in the hearts of those who now accompany the deceased.

All of the eulogies just examined have spoken of particular, usually august individuals and the circumstances of their deaths. Below, at page 28b, the gemara offers other model eulogies, now general expressions that might befit any funeral.

First, the most general statement, the irreducible minimum of a funeral cry: What do the wailing women say? the Talmud wants to know. "Woe for the departed! Woe for the wound!" But, of course, much more can also be said. The alternatives recorded in the Talmud are these:

I. Draw the bone from the jaw [alternative: from the pot],
   Let water be put into the pot.

The meaning of this statement, whatever the formulation may originally have been, is impossible to recover. Fortunately, the next is clearer:

II. Muffle and cover [yourselves], you mountains,
   for he is the son of high and great ones.
III. Borrow a robe of fine wool [alternative: Sheol is a robe of fine wool]
   for the free-man whose outfit is complete [alt.: has come to an end].
IV. He runs and falls at the ferry,
   and he takes a loan.
V. Our brothers are merchants who
   [a.] are searched at the customs house.[8]
   [or, b.] are tested by the goods they sell.
   [or, c.] are judged by the brood they left.[9]
VI. One death is like another,
   and our bruises are the interest [paid].

These several statements are obscure in a variety of their details. Still, certain observations may be made with confidence. As before, eulogizing is a form of poetry-writing; the poetry is laconic, the use of images free and wide-ranging. As we have come to expect, the individuals who have passed-on are praised (II). But these examples add important details. In one, the deceased is described as a free-man (III), a description which more likely pertains to his state after death than to his status during life. In the same statement, death (Sheol) is possibly seen as a fine garment; in any case, the praise not only of the deceased but also of death is clear. In other statements (IV and V), death is characterized as a passage or a journey. It is a time when goods are examined, when payments must be paid. The reference to the ferry is particularly noteworthy: as in Greco-Roman mythology, death is a river-crossing, for which the vessel is essential. This image confirms our interpretation of the many ship-drawings found on the walls of the Beth Shearim burial caves (see Chapter 5). These drawings are obviously not meant to represent journeys of this life. Rather, they express, in pictures instead of words, the notion that death is like an over-water passage. Only when payment is made and the passage accomplished will the deceased find her final rest.

If any quality ties these many funeral-speeches together, it is their expression of sorrow, and their attempt to raise up that sorrow in us, the listeners. We who listen are meant to cry and even to cry out. Whether from Ecclesiastical resignation (see VI above) or recognition of the magnitude of the loss, our tears are meant to flow. The question we must ask is why? Why is it so important that we cry as we accompany the deceased to the grave?

The answer to this question has already been provided in the Sanhedrin text, examined earlier. As we saw, the Talmud definitively concludes that the "eulogy" – that is, speeches or other rituals that provoke wailing over the life now ended – is meant to honor the dead. What this means is that the deceased will know what we do and what we say. If she sees that we are in great sorrow over her passing, she will be honored on this account. She will feel loved, wanted, missed. In contrast, if we fail to cry bitterly over the loss, she will sense that she made little difference in our lives. This failure would bring her pain and disgrace.

On this basis, we may understand why the deceased is spoken *of* in the ways modelled above, and why, despite the fact that she will indeed hear our words, we do not address her directly. Honor derives from the recognition that the loss has been immense. The community expresses the gravity of its loss by wailing, beating breasts, playing flutes. The greater the sense of loss, the greater the wailing and the greater the honor done the deceased. If, instead, the deceased were to be addressed directly, the tears of the community would not be directly provoked and might therefore be less abundant. Former friends and neighbors would now be mere witnesses to a final communication but not participants. Furthermore, if the deceased were addressed, emphasis would fall on what continued, not on what was lost. She still hears and feels and knows, witnesses would say to themselves, and their sorrow might therefore be diminished. Honor would thereby be reduced, and this we should want to avoid at all reasonable costs.

DEATH, BURIAL, AND ATONEMENT
(Sanhedrin 47a–b)

The Talmud likewise supplements our understanding of the relationship between death, burial and atonement of the dead. The relevant sugya builds upon a Mishnah which describes the execution of a criminal, his initial interment in a grave set aside for convicted criminals, and his subsequent reburial in "the graves of his fathers" (see m. San. 6:5–6). This brief sugya seems at first to have little to do with normal cases of burial. Nor does it evidently shed light on our understanding of the condition of death. But as we read, we will find that its contributions are invaluable. It shows once again that, in the opinion of the Talmudic rabbis, death is, at its base, an *experience* much like any other in life.

The gemara begins by explaining that the executed criminal was to be buried in a separate grave "because a wicked person is not buried next to a righteous person." But, the gemara suggests, there is a problem: If death effects atonement, then, following execution, the former criminal is no longer a wicked person. Why then should he not be afforded proper burial? Rava is more precise, adding that the fact that the executed criminal dies in an abnormal fashion should itself be the source of his atonement (in contrast, a wicked person who dies naturally may not be atoned through his death).

Abbaye objects to Rava, suggesting that a violent death, not following normal procedures, would indeed be the source of atonement, but that a proper procedural death, such as at the hand of the court, would not effect atonement. His proof? The very Mishnah on which the Talmud here is commenting! As we already noted, if death atoned then there would be no justifying a separate burial. So the very fact that the Mishnah requires separate burial of a criminal shows that death, by itself, does not atone. Maybe then, the gemara suggests, both death *and burial* are necessary to effect atonement.

But, R. Ada b. Ahava[10] objects, the Mishnah also says that the criminal, when buried, should not be mourned for. If death and burial atoned, then what reason could there be for not mourning? So, the gemara responds, "disintegration of the flesh is also necessary!" Indeed, the Mishnah supports precisely this conclusion, for it directs that, when the flesh has decomposed, the bones of the executed should be collected and reburied in a proper grave.

To here, this appears to be a technical discussion, using the evidence of the Mishnah and other authoritative traditions to determine the point when the atonement of the dead is effected. What has not, for the most part, been asked is "why?" To be sure, we do see hints of an answer. It is clear that the less normal a death, the more likely it is to atone. But why should this be so? And what is it about burial or disintegration in any death that should effect atonement?

The answer comes in a dissenting view attributed to R. Ashi. "When is atonement effected?" he asks. "When he [the deceased] sees [= experiences] a bit of the pain of the grave." The crucial detail is *pain*.[11] Again, the deceased is understood to continue to *feel*, in much the same way as the living. Obviously, then, burial will be uncomfortable and the decay of the flesh painful (we all know how painful decaying flesh is!). But what does pain have to do with atonement? The answer, which we have suggested before, is by this point obvious: Suffering of any kind atones. Indeed, the more suffering, the more complete the atonement. So the question here is, essentially, how much of the suffering of death, burial and decomposition is necessary before atonement is effected? Two opinions are recorded here: one saying that only the beginning of the process of decay is necessary and the other that complete decay, until only the bones are left, is required. Of course, both agree that the dead do feel and suffer. Otherwise there would be no meaning to this debate at all.

Though it may be clear by implication, we should not fail to reiterate the meaning of the notion that death effects atonement. Atonement is the repair of relationship with God. If one is atoned it means that he has been forgiven by God. If God has forgiven the sinner, God will declare the deserved decree of punishment null and void. Thus, if one transgressed a sin for which the appropriate punishment would be death, atonement would mean that death has been averted. God would allow him to continue living.

But what could atonement during and following death mean? Clearly, if atonement during life assures an extension of this life, atonement during death must assure future life, that is – as the Mishnah in Sanhedrin states explicitly in connection with the felon who confesses his sins – life in the World to Come. Ultimately, it is all about the same thing: suffering brings atonement, atonement brings life. Suffering in this world brings life in this world. Suffering in death brings life in the World to Come.

DEATH AND BURIAL II (Berakhot 17b–19b)

The several texts we have already examined suggest unambiguously that the deceased are believed to know and to feel. Theirs is, in other words, a sentient life, though we do not (yet) know the details of their condition. Fortunately, the Talmud does not leave us to rely on our imaginations in this matter. As we shall see, a lengthy sugya discussing the not-yet-buried dead, the survivor and the funeral, in the end comments on – more than anything else – the *life* of the deceased.

Mishnah Berakhot 3:1, we will recall, announces a general exemption from religious obligations for the person whose dead relative lies yet unburied before him. How far does this exemption extend, the Talmud wants to know? Does it apply only to the one whose dead lies unburied "before him," as the Mishnah explicitly states, or is the exemption more comprehensive? Whom does the unburied dead affect, and what is the nature of his or her power?

The Talmud's answer (beginning at Ber. 17b) begins by quoting the lengthy teaching, found earlier in the Yerushalmi (see above, pp. 74–5), which details the ritual status of the *onen*: he must eat in another house, or in another room, or on the other side of screen, and so forth. Such an individual is, we are told, exempt from religious obligations, even when eating his meal in another house. Thus, we see clearly, the language of the Mishnah is *not* to be understood literally. But how is that imprecise language to be understood? The Talmud explains: "Since it is his obligation to bury him, it is *as though* he [the deceased] is laid out in front of him," even if he is actually out of sight (Ber. 18a). What matters is not presence, but condition.

What if a person is guarding a corpse who is not his relative? Is only the one whose own deceased lies unburied exempt from other religious obligations? The answer is definitively given: anyone who guards the deceased is exempt. But there is another question, one which follows far less naturally – What if one is merely walking in a cemetery? the Talmud asks. The response is embodied in this teaching, identified as a tannaitic tradition:

> A person should not walk in the cemetery with tefillin on his head and a Torah scroll on his arm, and read therefrom. And if he does so, he transgresses [the scripture which says], "He who mocks the poor affronts his Maker" (Prov. 17:5).

The commentary concludes that within a distance of four cubits from the dead – any dead, at any stage of death – these things are not permitted.

Already, the Talmudic deliberation seems to have led us far beyond the issue immediately at hand. The Mishnah speaks of the unburied and of the exemption of his relative from certain religious obligations. Such a surviving relative is exempt whether in the presence of the dead or not, presumably because the obligation for burial is primarily his. Others are exempt only if they serve as guards for the dead, and again the obvious explanation is obligation to the deceased. As the Talmud says elsewhere, one who is involved in the performance of one obligation is (at that moment) exempt from others (Suk. 26a). But in such a context, the third question makes little sense. Who, after all, said anything which might lead us to consider the case of one walking in a cemetery? The answer is, in truth, no one. In the latter case, there is no unburied corpse, no obligation to the dead. So we must be suspicious of this line of questioning. Are we being led on and, if so, where does the Talmud want to lead us?

The answer surprises just as much. Various acts normally considered religious obligations are prohibited in the cemetery not because of an alternative obligation (as in the cases above) and not because of ritual impurity (as we might expect), but because one who wears tefillin in the presence of the buried dead as though "mocks the poor and affronts his Maker." "The poor" is obviously understood to refer to the deceased. Performing religious obligations in his immediate presence is by extension called "mocking." How are we to make sense of this fanciful interpretation – of the application of this verse to the deceased? There is only one reasonable answer: The deceased must know what is done in his presence and so, if he sees you doing what he can no longer do, you are unwittingly mocking him. Because this is true, we must be sensitive to how the deceased may feel. Our actions in the presence of the deceased should be directed by this sensitivity.

If the deceased when buried and gone is aware of what happens in his presence, how much more must the recently deceased, as yet unburied, be aware! This is indeed relevant to the earlier discussion, but in an unexpected way. We discover that, in the opinion of the Talmud here, what motivates the exemptions hinted at in the Mishnah and detailed in the baraita is not the principle that "one who is involved in one mitzvah is exempt from another," as we thought. No, the motivation is concern for the deceased. If we eat in his presence, bless in his presence, enjoy the pleasures of the life of the living in his presence, we are being insensitive and foul, mocking him and affronting his maker. The deceased knows; survivor, take care.

Two teachings now follow in the Talmud, one closely related to the foregoing deliberation and one less so. The latter speaks of a person who transports the bones of a deceased person (after the flesh has decomposed) from one place to another; we are warned not to treat the bones disrespectfully. They are said to be equivalent to a Torah scroll with regard to the honor due them. Then comes a teaching which pertains to the funeral: "Anyone who sees the dead and does not accompany him [to burial] transgresses [the scripture which says], 'He who mocks the poor affronts his Maker.'" The connection with what precedes is clear. The same verse from Proverbs is again quoted to make a similar point: The deceased knows what you do and you must therefore treat him with utmost respect. He will know if you fail to honor him by accompanying him to burial. Because of the feelings of the deceased, participation in the funeral procession becomes a mitzvah of the highest order.

The importance of this obligation is highlighted in the comment with which the Talmud continues. "And if he accompanied him [to burial], what is his reward?" the Talmud asks. "Concerning him scripture says, 'He who is generous to the poor makes a loan to the Lord' (Prov. 19:17) 'and he who honors him [God] is gracious to the poor' (ibid. 14:31)." The deceased, again, is "poor," and the one who does him honor at the same time honors God. At the simple level, paying honor to the deceased is said to be equivalent to paying honor to God. But this equivalence is claimed to be more literal than may, at first, appear. The first biblical text quoted as "proof" of the greatness of one who accompanies the deceased contains a meaningful linguistic ambiguity. The biblical phrase is strangely (that is, poetically) out of order. More literally translated, it would say "makes a loan to the Lord he who is generous to the poor." But even this does not do justice to the meaning of this verse as quoted here, out of its primary context. The Hebrew letters rendered in translation as "loan" are the same letters which form the Hebrew word "accompany," that is, *funeral*. In fact these very same letters appear (without pronominal suffix) just a few words earlier in this teaching, speaking of "he who does not *accompany* him [the deceased]." So when the reader arrives at this biblical proof, prejudiced by the prior context and not knowing which biblical verse will be quoted nor what meaning it will be given in its new context, she is tempted to translate: "he who accompanies God is gracious to the poor." One who accompanies God? But one who attends a funeral accompanies the deceased! Rather, a connection is here suggested between the "poor" who is accompanied and God – one who accompanies the deceased as if it were accompanies God. A remarkable claim indeed!

We have long since understood that this deliberation is, at least in part, about what the deceased knows. This concern now becomes central and explicit. The Talmud commences with a story:

> R. Ḥiyya and R. Yonatan were out walking in a cemetery. The blue fringe [= the ritual fringes, called *ẓiẓit*] of R. Yonatan was dragging. R. Ḥiyya said to him: Lift it, so that they don't say "Tomorrow they are coming to be with us and now they mock us!" He said to him: "And do they know this much? But is it not written, 'And the dead know nothing' (Ecclesiastes 9:5)?" He said to him: "If you have read, you have not repeated; if you repeated, you did not read a third time; if you read a third time, they did not explain it to you. 'For the living know that they will die' – this refers to the righteous who are called living even in their death . . . 'And the dead know nothing' – this refers to the wicked who, even in their lives, are called dead . . . "

A simple story, offering the first challenge ("Do the dead know so much?") and response. If the dead know, then our conduct in the cemetery must account for their knowledge. We must not "drag our fringes over their heads," reminding them of the religious obligations that we can fulfill but they cannot. Naturally, the party who would deny the dead their knowledge turns for proof to Ecclesiastes – "the dead know nothing." But according to the response of R. Ḥiyya, it is R. Yonatan who knows nothing, at least about the present subject. The righteous, in their deaths, are alive. Surely they know what we do in their presence.

Another story and then another:

> The sons of R. Ḥiyya went out into the city. Their learning became too "heavy" for them and they took pains to recall it. One said to his fellow: "Does our father know of this pain?" The other said to him, "From where would he know? And isn't it written, 'His sons will become heavy and he does not know' [Job 14:21, translated for context]? The other responded to him: "And does he not know? And isn't it written, 'when his flesh is upon him [even after death] it will hurt and his soul will mourn for him' (ibid., v. 22)! And R. Isaac said, "The worm is as difficult [= painful] for the dead as a needle in the flesh of the living." [Thus, the proof is clear. The dead certainly do know!] They say [in response, trying to defend the view of R. Yonatan], "they do know of their own pain; of the pain of others they do not know."

A temporary resolution. The dead do know, but only in a limited way. Of their own immediate experience they have awareness; of the experience of others, they have none.

But this conclusion is, at least for the moment, not satisfactory. Do they not know? the Talmud asks. "But has it not been taught:

> It once happened that a certain pious person gave a *dinar* to a poor person on the eve of the New Year, during years of scarcity, and his wife became angry with him. He went and slept in the cemetery, and he heard two spirits [of the dead] speaking to one another. One said to the other: My friend, come, let us roam the world, and we will hear from behind the curtain [of heaven] what sort of punishment is coming to the world. Her friend said to her: I cannot, for I am buried in a mat of reeds. But you go and tell me what you hear.
>
> She went and roamed and returned, and her friend said to her: My friend, what did you hear from behind the curtain? She said to her: I heard that anyone who sows seed during the time of the first rain, hail will destroy it. So he [the pious man who had overheard all of this] went and sowed during the time of the second rain. Everyone else's crop was destroyed, but his was not.

The following year, this same pious man returned to the same cemetery and again took away good advice. His wife, amazed at his good fortune, asked him how this happened, whereupon he told her the whole story. Shortly thereafter, the wife got into an argument with the mother of the young woman who was buried in the reed mat, insulting her for permitting her daughter to be buried in such a fashion. News of this incident got back to her dead daughter so, the next year, when the pious man returned for information concerning the upcoming crop season, the spirits refused to talk. Aware that they were being overheard, they decided to keep quiet. It follows from this story, the Talmud declares, that the dead do know! The response, defending the alternative possibility, is that someone else may have died in the meantime and then come to report what was happening. In other words, the living can surely hear what is being said by the dead, though the dead may not be able to hear the living!

The deliberation is not over, so we cannot yet say definitively whether the dead do or do not know what happens in this world. Still, based upon the evidence of this story – evidence with which the Talmud takes no issue – there are important things we may say about the condition of the dead. First, it is evident that the souls (or spirits) of the dead continue to live after death, and they live in the vicinity of the body or bones with which they were once joined.[12] These souls have a physical quality, for they can get stuck in a mat of reeds.[13] But they also have what we might call "spiritual gifts," including the ability to travel abroad in the world and to hear what is happening in the other, divine world. They converse with their neighbors (is this why it is important to know whom you are going to be buried next to?). They care about those who survive them, even if they do not necessarily have direct access to the lives of the living.

Two more stories follow, both testing the same questions. In the first, Zeira entrusts some coins to his landlady, who dies while he is out. Wanting to recover his money, he follows her "to the courtyard of the dead," where she tells him where to find his coins and adds a request: "Tell my mother to send me my comb and eye paint with so-and-so, who is coming tomorrow."[14] This dead woman, in any case, communicates with the living, and takes care to maintain her appearance.

In the second story, Samuel seeks out the soul of his dead father, who died while holding property belonging to orphans; Samuel wants to find the property so that he can return it to its owners. Approaching certain unknown souls in the cemetery, Samuel is told that his father is in "the yeshiva of heaven." When the soul of his father finally arrives, Samuel sees that he is both laughing and crying. Asking him why, Samuel discovers that his own honor in this world is a source of joy to his dead father, but his impending death, which his father of course knows about, is a source of sorrow.

These stories, like those which came before, paint a clear picture. The dead do know. They communicate with the living and with one another. They live lives which, though not full in the way of the living (they cannot eat or perform mitzvot), are full in the way of the dead. And, though following each story the Talmud weakly tries to show that the dead may not know what is happening in this world – at least in normal cases – the testimony of the accumulated stories speaks far more loudly than these paltry defenses of the alternative opinion. In fact, the Talmud now reports that the author of the opinion it is trying to defend (that the dead do not know), R. Yonatan, changed his mind.

Still, the debate concerning the awareness of the dead is not over. R. Yitzhak declares, "anyone who speaks concerning the dead speaks as though concerning a stone." What does this mean? the Talmud wants to know. "There are those who say [it means] that they do not know [at all] and there are those who say that they know and do not care." Here, in the end, the parameters of the debate are clear. What is at issue is whether the dead know what is said by the living. Concerning this debate, some believe the dead do know and some believe that the dead do not. But no one – not even R. Yonatan – denies that the dead know what is happening in their world. There they speak together with full consciousness, as several of the stories we have seen illustrate. In addition, no one denies that the deceased have physical sensation, at least so long as their flesh continues to exist. These kinds of awareness may be taken for granted. Only that awareness which bridges the realms of the dead and the living is doubted by some, and it is clear that such denial is a minority opinion. The bulk of the evidence cited by the gemara makes it clear that the dead are believed to be aware even of what occurs in the world of the living.

Finally, we see, this text seeks to define the state of death – what it *feels* like to those who have passed on. Its claims are simple: death is a conscious, sentient state, much as is life. Life and death are not, therefore, radical oppositions. They are instead points on a continuum or, perhaps more accurately, steps along a single path. On the one end is the awake state of life, a condition distinguished by the highest degree of consciousness and feeling. Closer to death is sleep, when we experience comfort or pain – though not consciously so – and know little of what goes on in the world around us. When we cross the line to death, we still feel pain and we still know what goes on in our world – in this case, the world of the dead. And we may even know something of what transpires in the other, living world. Death is not oblivion. Death is not the end. Death is something like life, however altered.

DEATH AND BURIAL III (Shabbat 151a–153a)

If, as we have seen, the deceased is believed to be in some sense "alive" – that is, sentient and aware – this must affect our understanding of the rituals pertaining to the dead. Indeed, we have already interpreted the Talmud's discussions of the obligation to eulogize the dead in light of this belief. Other rituals of death and burial may surely be scrutinized under the same lens.

The Talmud itself fails to elaborate upon the many rituals of preparation of the deceased and burial in a direct and detailed way. Instead, it offers scattered comments on these rituals, preferring to devote more extended attention to the various experiences of the deceased: of death itself, of burial, and of the acts of survivors who accompany her on her path to the grave and beyond.

The Talmud's most extended deliberation relating to these concerns begins with reference to m. Shabbat 23:4–5, which, as we saw in Chapter 3, outlines the preparation of the deceased for burial. The Mishnah, which speaks of the "needs" of the deceased, specifies those needs as including anointing, washing, placing the body on the ground and tying the jaw. Building on this foundation, the Talmud adds (151b) that cooling vessels should be placed on the belly of the deceased in order that it not swell, and the person's orifices should be stopped up so that air not enter the body. All of this is intended to minimize the signs of death which, after three days, will be gross and extreme in any case. At that point, as the earlier Palestinian tradition also knows, "his gut splits and spills out upon his face, saying to him: take [back] what you have put in me."

The Talmud continues its expansion of the Mishnah, segment by small segment. The Mishnah declares that one must not shut the eyes of the dying person until death is clear. In the gemara, R. Shimeon b. Gamliel offers advice for indirectly closing the person's eyes on the sabbath, when to do so directly is prohibited. He then remarks that, though the sabbath may be profaned to save the life of a day-old infant, it may not be profaned for even a great Israelite king who is dead. Why not? Because "when a person dies he is exempt from [performing] the mitzvot."

This latter comment, found also in the Yerushalmi, takes on new significance by virtue of its present contextual placement. We have already seen that the deceased have feelings and needs. But, with some few exceptions, those needs do not take precedence over the sanctity of the sabbath. Why is this so? Now we discover that the most crucial difference between the living and the dead, at least in the view of the rabbis behind the Bavli here, is that the former may perform God's commands in the flesh while the latter may not. Like the living, the dead know and feel. In some ways, as we have seen, their knowledge may be superior to that of the living. But they are deficient in their inability to wear tefillin, to recite the Shema, to light the candles of the sabbath. The soul, as it lives on independent of the flesh – indeed, long after the flesh has deteriorated – is unable to fulfill the physical commands of God's Torah. For this reason is life, when soul and flesh are united and may together perform God's will, superior to death.

This assertion of the ultimate indispensability of the flesh, of the excellence of mitzvot that are performed in the flesh, characterizes rabbinic Judaism more fundamentally than perhaps any other belief. As noted by Boyarin and others (Boyarin 1994), the rabbis, unlike early Christians or more thoroughly Hellenized Jews, refused to read the mitzvot (and other "in the flesh" elements of the Hebrew Bible) allegorically. For those other readers of Hebrew scripture, the "spirit" of the divine commands became their essence and, in some cases, their more literal meanings were suspended entirely. This valorization of the spiritual meaning, and diminution of the value of the flesh, corresponded to – indeed, was generated by – the same valorization of the spirit over the flesh in Neo-Platonism. It was the world of Platonic ideas that mattered. The world of matter, in contrast, was ideally to be transcended.

Of course, according to this alternative vision, the release of the soul from the body following death led to a vastly superior state. The corrupted and corrupting body now gone, the soul was free to live in all of its purity. But the rabbis, who resisted allegory because they insisted on the value of the flesh, posited that life was superior – the life of the flesh that performs mitzvot. This is not to say that there aren't also ways that death is superior. It is simply to say that, as the present text affirms, this Torah-of-the-flesh, this life in-the-flesh, will never lose its value.

Immediately following, the Talmud goes on to other things. But before too long (at 152a, bottom), it quotes R. Yitzhak, who declares that "the worm is as painful to the deceased as a needle in the flesh of the living." We have returned to the experience of the dead, now to be elaborated still further. In the next moment, the Talmud records this remark: "A person's soul mourns for him for all of shiva [= the seven days], as it says 'and his soul mourns for him' (Job 14:22)." It continues:

> Rav Judah said: A dead person who has no comforters, ten people [should] go and sit in his place. A certain person died in the neighborhood of Rav Judah, and he had no comforters. Each day, Rav Judah would take ten people and sit in his place. He [the deceased] appeared to him[15] in his dream and said to him, "may your mind rest [= may you be comforted] for you have put my mind at rest."

I have translated the Hebrew word *menaḥamin* literally and correctly as "comforters," despite the discomfort this translation might cause us.[16] Both the statement that precedes it ("A person's soul mourns for him for all of shiva") and, more directly, the story that follows, make it clear that the dead is capable of – nay, *in need of!* – being comforted for his or her own death. This brief fabric of traditions, unprecedented in earlier rabbinic literature, thus expands considerably our appreciation of the current understanding of death and our relation to the deceased. A forgotten ritual and a story shed light on the meaning of death as few other teachings have.

Death is understood as a catastrophic rupture, a source of sorrow for both the deceased and her or his survivors.[17] Since both are presumably grief-stricken by the demise of the body, both must mourn. So both participate in the same ritual, mourning for seven days. And, just as the living mourner must be comforted by others, so too must the dead mourner be comforted by others; in both cases, the needs of one individual generate obligations for others. If someone is in need of comfort, others must respond to that need.

We also discover here that one of the purposes of the mourning of the mourner is *to comfort the deceased*. This is clear because, in the absence of mourners, the community must undertake to perform this same task. But, under normal circumstances, the mourners themselves will accomplish these ends. Presumably, the deceased will be comforted by seeing that survivors lament his passing. Seeing that he is valued, perceiving the grief that his demise has caused, he will find immense solace.

Crucially, as we already surmised in our interpretations of earlier rabbinic texts, there is a "mirroring" here: the experience of the mourner mirrors the experience of the deceased and vice versa. Both parties share a similar if not identical condition. So the Bavli's interpretation of the rituals of mourning cannot be doubted. Its language makes the parallel explicit. Mourner and deceased are touched by death, mourn, are comforted, find themselves limited, removed from society, unable to build. The only difference is that, for the moment at least, their journey will lead them in different directions: one back to the society of the living and one to the society of the dead.

As has been evident, this Talmudic exposition is largely about what the deceased knows and feels. The text continues by addressing this matter explicitly. According to one opinion, the deceased knows everything that is said in her presence until the sealing stone is placed over her resting-place; according to another, she knows everything that is said until the flesh has completely deteriorated. Whichever is correct (no determination is made), the soul ultimately "returns to God," that of the righteous in peace and that of the wicked in trouble. In fact, the souls of the righteous will find a place beneath God's "Throne of Glory," while their bodies will "return to the dust."

"Not so fast!" the Talmud in effect now says. There is evidence to the contrary, evidence suggesting that the bodies of the righteous do not turn to dust:

> Certain diggers were digging on the property of R. Naḥman. R. Aḥai the son of Yoshaya [who was buried there] became angry at them. They came and said to R. Naḥman: A person became angry at us. He [R. Naḥman] came and said to him: Who are you, sir? He said to him: I am R. Aḥai the son of Yoshaya. He said to him: But didn't R. Meri say, "the righteous will in the future turn to dust"? He said to him: he who taught you Ecclesiastes did not teach you Proverbs, for it is written, "envy is the rottenness of the bones" (Prov. 14:30) [meaning] anyone who has envy in his heart, his bones will rot, but anyone who does not have envy in his heart, his bones will not rot. He [R. Naḥman] touched him [R. Aḥai the son of Yoshaya] and saw that he had substance. He said: get up sir, and come with me to the house. He said to him: . . . it is written, "you shall know that I am the Lord when I open your graves" (Ezekiel 37:13). He said to him, but is it not written "you are dust and you shall return to dust" (Gen. 3:19)? He said to him: that [is speaking of] the single hour before the resurrection of the dead.

First, it is necessary to emphasize, this story is not offered as miraculous, as a rupture of the natural order. It assumes that the dead may speak, may get angry, may interpret Torah. All of this is true because, as we have seen amply illustrated before, the dead are alive, though in a different sense of the term. What is new here is only the suggestion that the bones of those who do not harbor envy in their hearts will not turn to dust. While their flesh will presumably deteriorate, their bones will not. This claim is not a phantom or an illusion, the story insists. You may touch such dead people with your own hands! But they are still dead, and, therefore, must await God's miraculous awakening before "returning home." In the meantime, they will remain in their graves, hopefully undisturbed by those digging in the vicinity.

The next small step, apparently an effort to test the claim that "the souls of the righteous are stored under the Throne of Glory," contributes a crucial insight. If the claim is true, then how could the Witch of Endor have raised Samuel? The answer: the events described in 1 Samuel 28 occurred within the first twelve months following Samuel's death, and "it has been taught: for the full twelve months, the body exists and the soul rises and descends. After twelve months, the body is no more and the soul rises, never again to descend."

Again, the profound connection between body and soul is asserted. The latter may not leave the former until it (the body) has decomposed completely. At that point only has the soul been freed for its final journey. At that point only is death complete. Of course, it is difficult not to read this teaching in association with the obligation to mourn for parents for a year. It is impossible to ignore the parallel between what is described here and the practice of reburying the bones of the deceased when the flesh has decomposed. At approximately the end of a year, word and ritual teach us, death has come to an end. If life resides in the flesh, life is not fully over, death not fully realized, until the flesh is gone and the soul may finally ascend.

Before leaving its deliberation on the awareness of the deceased, the Talmud (at 153a) tells one more brief story. In this story, Rav directs a colleague to "heat up" his eulogy when he dies – that is, to express his grief with fervor, igniting the sorrow of others – for "I will be standing there." In a way that by now occasions no surprise, the Talmud insists that the deceased do know what is said about them, at least before their hearing is cut off by the sealing-stone of the grave. The eulogy is for the deceased, beckoning the living to be grieved in his honor. Ritual and casual conduct must together be sensitive to the experience of the dead, we again see. This, as we have said, is what is meant by the honor of the dead.

****

What we have seen in these Talmudic expositions represents a natural extension of the rituals and teachings of earlier rabbinic Judaism. In earlier chapters, we often had occasion to "read" the rituals associated with death and burial as statements of our sensitivity to the felt needs of the living deceased. Whether or not we were correct in those contexts – and I see no reason to doubt that we were – we see that the Bavli, in any case, fully concurs. Death is the other side of life, a late – but not the last – stage in the full life of the individual.

Crucially, if our interpretations have been largely correct, then ancient rabbinic Judaism remained relatively constant in its beliefs concerning death over the course of its history, from the second to the sixth centuries. This is notable because, in other important matters – including responses to human suffering (Kraemer 1995), revelation and the nature of Torah (Kraemer 1991:

613–30; Kraemer 1996: 20–48) – this same Judaism underwent significant changes. But death, as understood by these rabbis, remains the same phenomenon. Perhaps this is because death is a universal human phenomenon, one which probably most peoples in the ancient (and not-so-ancient!) world understood in ways similar to the rabbis. Humans from antiquity to the Enlightenment believed that after death the person lives on in a different but real and conscious state. Why should the rabbis have been different?

8

THE BAVLI INTERPRETS THE MOURNER

The mourner, the leper and the banned person

The Mishnah in the third chapter of tractate Mo'ed Qatan lists those individuals who, contrary to the general rule, may shave or have their hair cut during the intermediate days of a festival (Passover or Sukkot). The feature which ties all of the exceptional cases together is the fact that they were unable to attend to such grooming before the festival began. Thus, someone who returns from abroad or is released from prison immediately before the festival is permitted to shave during the festival's intermediate period. So too is someone who was released from a rabbinic ban or emerged from his period of "leprous" impurity (for want of better terms, I will use "leper" and "leprosy" throughout this chapter despite the fact that this is probably a misidentification of the condition (Milgrom 1991: 816–18)). Though a mourner whose mourning came to an end with the advent of the festival would seem to fall into the same category, the mourner is not mentioned in the Mishnah's list.

Nevertheless, the mourner soon becomes the focus of the Talmud's extended discussion (14b–16a). Attention to the mourner proper begins with the Talmud's declaration that "a mourner does not observe his mourning during the festival, as it says, 'and you shall be joyous on your festival' (Deut. 16:14)." Then, ignoring the simple power of the unadorned biblical proof, the Talmud adds a logical analysis/justification: "If it is [a state of] prior mourning [having begun days earlier], the collective obligation [of rejoicing on the festival] comes and pushes aside the individual obligation [of mourning]; if it is [a state of] mourning which begins now [during the festival], an individual obligation does not come and push aside a collective obligation." The issue, in other words, is the relationship between the individual and the collective, and, by extension, between public and private observance. In a society where the needs of the collective generally take precedence, the obligation to rejoice with the collective will take precedence over the obligation (notice: it is not viewed as a *need*) of the individual. Permission may be granted to observe the most private restrictions of mourning, such as abstention from sexual relations (see my discussion of Yerushalmi M.Q. 3:5 in Chapter 6, and also below at M.Q. 24a). But, in matters obvious and public, the individual must yield to the community. For related reasons, the Talmud records in the name of R. Pappa that "there is no festival in the face of [the death of] a sage" (M.Q. 27b). Because, in the opinion of the sages, the death of a sage is a communal tragedy, the community may mourn for a sage even during the intermediate days of a festival. In such a case, there would be no conflict between a communal and an individual obligation, only a conflict between one communal obligation and another.

Having expressed the opinion that mourning is not practiced during the festival, the Talmud proceeds to ask whether the restrictions placed on a person banned by the court (henceforth: *menude*) and on a leper are in force during the festival. The details of the subsequent deliberations, each asking whether a particular restriction is operative on the festival, are unimportant for present purposes. Suffice it to say that the answer to each question is yes — restrictions pertaining to the *menude* and the leper *are* in force during the festival. Scriptural proofs are cited in context to support each answer, but we may speculate that the Talmud's reasoning goes further: both banning and leprosy are public events (the *menude* is banned for refusing to heed the directives of the rabbinic court, the leper may render large sectors of the community impure) and therefore are practiced even during the festival. Be that as it may, what requires attention is the fact that these questions are asked at all.

Why does the Talmud follow its designation of the status of the mourner with questions concerning the status of the *menude* and the leper? It is not sufficient to reply that both are mentioned in the Mishnah at the beginning of this sugya. The Mishnah mentions other sorts of individuals as well, yet their status is not questioned here. More crucially, the mourner is not even listed in the Mishnah, as we observed earlier. So this series of questions is at the very least curious, and perhaps more than that. Were this the only time these categories of people were related in the course of the Talmud's discussion, we should perhaps not detain ourselves by seeking to interpret this combination. But, in fact, precisely this combination is the defining characteristic of the entire deliberation. We cannot leave it alone.

Beginning with the questions just seen and continuing literally for pages, this sugya follows the same recurrent pattern. First, the Talmud quotes a teaching pertaining to the rituals and restrictions of the mourner. (Recombined, this series of teachings is nearly identical with what we saw earlier in the Yerushalmi.) Following each quoted ruling, the Talmud proceeds by asking, in one way or another, "What about the *menude*?" then "What about the leper?"

The actual sequence of questions and discussions is this: Following the first series, just described, the Talmud records a ruling which declares, "a mourner is prohibited from cutting his hair." What about those who are banned and lepers? the Talmud then asks. The answer, deriving from a tradition of tannaitic provenance, is unambiguous: both are subject to the same prohibition. Not mourner nor *menude* nor leper may trim his or her hair.

Next, we learn that the mourner must "cover his head." Precisely how this is to be done is not clear, but the proof text, quoted from Ezekiel 24:17 (where God directs Ezekiel not to mourn for the sinful Israel that is to be destroyed), suggests that what is intended is covering the lips or mouth. Thus, the present directive seems to refer to a muffling, a broad covering of the head and face. Symbolically, this would signal the hesitancy of the mourner to communicate in normal fashion. He would in this gesture be enacting his estrangement from social intercourse.

Does the same ritual obligation apply to the *menude*? In response, the Talmud quotes a baraita from Ta'anit which describes the ritual responses to a severe drought. According to this tradition, those who observe a fast in the event of such a drought must "cover themselves and sit like those banned and like mourners, until they [?] have mercy upon them from heaven." The answer would seem to be clear (as would the crucial equation of banned persons and mourners!). But the gemara, in the voice of Abbaye, equivocates – Perhaps one who is banned by heaven, as evidenced by the drought, is different; perhaps a heavenly ban is more severe.

In contrast, the answer regarding the leper is quick and direct. The Torah itself demands that the leper should cover his lip (Lev. 13:45). Thus, in this detail, the ritual of the mourner and the leper is identical. The mourner, the leper and the one banned by heaven, at least, must muffle themselves, covering their heads and mouths.

"A mourner is prohibited from putting on tefillin [so-called prayer straps]" the Talmud goes on to relate. Whether the *menude* may wear tefillin it does not know, but an interpretation offered by R. Pappa shows that a leper probably may.

"A mourner may not inquire of the welfare of another," we next learn. Does this restriction apply to the *menude*? Mishnah Ta'anit 1:7 – declaring that those fasting for a severe drought may not inquire of another's peace, just "like those with whom God is angry" – suggests that banned persons should be like mourners in this matter. But, again, the Talmud reminds us, those rebuked by heaven may be different. And what is the law for the leper? An authoritative source is cited: "His lips should be bound together, he should be like a *menude* and like a mourner, and may not inquire of the welfare of another." It is difficult to imagine a clearer statement of law. But a clever interpretation makes the obvious conclusion unnecessary. In all likelihood, if I understand the inclination of the gemara, the leper probably should not extend such greetings while the *menude* probably may. Whatever the law may be, the strong suggestion of an equation of mourner, *menude* and leper is repeated again. Again the combination cries out for notice and interpretation.

The next law restricts the mourner from studying Torah. In contrast, brief discussions reveal that both the banned person and the leper may do so. We are led to wonder whether, in certain respects, the condition of the mourner is more severe than that of the *menude* or the leper. The Talmud follows with the ruling that mourners may not do laundry. In this case, the law of the *menude* and the leper is the same.

The list and the comparisons continue. A mourner, we know, is obligated to rend his garments. The same is true of the leper, but the Talmud does not know about the *menude*. A mourner must overturn her beds and couches. The Talmud is unable to determine whether lepers and banned persons must do likewise.

A mourner may not perform common labor. A teaching quoted in context seems to equate the mourner and the *menude* in this respect, but a brief interpretation shows that this is not necessarily so. In the next moment, the Talmud shows that a *menude* may, in fact, work. Whether the leper is permitted to labor or not, the Talmud fails to determine.

A mourner is not permitted to wash. A banned person probably may wash, but no conclusion is suggested for lepers. A mourner may not wear shoes. A *menude* probably may; whether or not a leper may, the Talmud does not know. A mourner may not have sex. A leper, similarly, may not, but the law concerning the *menude* is not clear. A mourner may not send sacrificial offerings to the Temple. Neither may a leper, and the law concerning a banned person is unclear. With this detail, the Talmud's list of mourning practices and its consideration of the related laws of the *menude* and the leper come to an end.

Before turning to the comparison on which this sugya is built, it is necessary to comment on one detail of the law of the mourner. As I commented earlier, the Bavli's law is virtually identical with what we saw earlier in the Yerushalmi. The only addition to the prior list, and the most irrelevant because least practicable, is the restriction upon sending offerings. The reasoning behind this restriction does, however, shed important light on our understanding of the status of the mourner, at least as interpreted in the Bavli. According to the tradition quoted in the gemara, the sacrificial offering is called *shelamim*, reasonably interpreted as "whole" or "complete" offerings (from the Hebrew root *sh–l–m*). According to the interpretation offered in the cited teaching, this term means to restrict such offerings to a person "while he is whole, and not when he is an *onen*," who is assumed to be incomplete. The *onen* and the mourner are incomplete, having lost the relative who was somehow part of them. Or, perhaps we would be more correct to say that they are incomplete because death has touched them, taking a part of them with it. Both explanations are plausible, both are suggestive. We shall return to these possibilities after we consider this sugya's defining feature, its comparison of the mourner with the *menude* and leper.

A *menude* is, as I explained, someone who is banned for having refused to heed the directive of the court (an extended discussion of such banning interrupts this sugya at 16a–b). The term describing such an individual employs the same root as the term used for a woman during her menstrual impurity, a *niddah*. Just as she must be avoided due to her ritual impurity, so too must a *menude* be avoided – publicly shunned – because of what we might call the impurity of his actions. He is estranged, isolated, ostracized – condemned for what he has done if not for what he is.

A leper, too, must be sent outside, expelled from the camp (Lev. 13:46 and Num. 5:2–4). He must tear his clothes, let his hair grow, cover his upper lip and avoid all social contact by crying out "Unclean! Unclean!" (Lev. 13:45). Clearly, his ritual is closely related to that of the biblical mourner (see Ezekiel 24:17–18); which "comes first" makes no difference. But more than being impure, more than being ostracized, the leper is seen in the Torah "as one dead . . . half of whose flesh is consumed" (Num. 12:12). It is reasonable to suppose, in fact, that his impurity is a consequence of what is viewed as his partial death (Milgrom 1991: 819–20).

This latter point requires elaboration. Whether or not the disease of Leviticus 13 is leprosy, it is clearly a condition which causes the scaling or decaying of the flesh. We have often seen that Jews of Palestine, in the biblical as in the rabbinic period, visited deceased relatives in their burial caves and thus had occasion to witness the decay of the flesh of the dead directly. Of all of the developments of death, it must surely have been this more than any other which represented death in the popular mind. So if someone experienced decay of the flesh, her or his immediate association would have been with death. Someone afflicted by the condition described in Leviticus 13 would have been seen as dying before death. For this reason would she be impure. For this same reason would she be required to mourn – for herself – so long as her death-decay persisted.

On this basis, we may now make sense of the Talmud's extended comparison. Earlier interpretations will provide a first explanation. As we noted in Chapter 4, the most obvious similarity between the mourner, on the one hand, and the *menude* and the leper, on the other, is that all are placed outside of common society.[1] But this is too obvious, and therefore not particularly helpful. The more important question is, of course, *why* are they all placed outside of society? Does the comparison and partial equation go deeper?

Let us begin with the banned person. As we review the answers to the questions posed in the sugya, we find that, in the end, the *menude* has little definitively in common with the mourner. Only cutting the hair and laundering clothes are clearly prohibited to him. In contrast to the mourner, he may study Torah, do labor and wash. And all of the other restrictions and obligations may or may not apply to him; his status in all of these matters is unclear. So we are tempted to say that the comparison of the mourner and the *menude* has not been terribly fruitful, for they appear to be more dissimilar than similar.

But we should not succumb to this temptation, because such a conclusion would be misguided. First, we should note that the mourner is in a more restricted and therefore more severe state than a *menude*. However serious being banned by the rabbinic court may be, mourning is more serious. And why is this so? In passing, the gemara (in the name of Abbaye) has suggested an answer. We will recall that the gemara distinguished on a couple of occasions between the person banned by a court and the person banned by heaven. The only reason the *menude* may not be bound by certain restrictions or obligations is because he is subject to an earthly, not a heavenly ban. But were his ban heavenly, then he would surely be bound by these obligations – to cover his upper lip, to refrain from greeting another – as well. Of course, these are obligations which do bind the mourner, and so we may say, using the gemara's own language, that *the mourner is in some sense banned by heaven.* His or her state of mourning, precipitated by the death of a loved one, is an expression of God's displeasure. The mourner is a *menude* of the most severe degree, his restrictions a symbol of his banned status.

The mourner and the leper are ritually more alike in the gemara's estimation. Neither may cut hair, launder his clothes, have sex or send sacrificial offerings. Both must cover their upper lips and rend their garments. The leper, like the mourner, is probably not permitted to greet another. Other rituals are in doubt, and the only time the leper and mourner are clearly distinguished is with respect to studying Torah and wearing tefillin. Though not identical, these states have much in common.

Because the leper carries the symbolism of death literally on her or his body, this is the characteristic of the leper that is most prominent – she is touched by death. The Talmud elsewhere expresses its appreciation of this connection explicitly: "Four are considered as though dead . . . lepers . . . " (Ned. 64b). The same association also pertains, we earlier suggested, to the mourner. In fact, the teaching which most directly leads us to make this association, found first in the Yerushalmi, is repeated later in this Bavli chapter; in the Bavli's version: "a mourner, for the first three days he should see himself as though a sword is placed between his two thighs [or, in another version, his two shoulders]. From the [end of the] third until the seventh [day], it is as though it is placed opposite him in the corner [of his room]. From here onward it is as though passing before him in the marketplace" (M.Q. 27b). The mourner, in this vision, has come face-to-edge with the sword of death, escaping only narrowly. The Bavli's extended comparison of the mourner and the leper, with the ritual similarities noted in process, reinforces and extends the same vision. The mourner is in the presence of death, diminished by it and still threatened.

Another quality of the leper also brings us back to the *menude*. The story told of the leprosy of Miriam (Num. 12) leaves no doubt that this condition is seen as punishment for wrongdoing, as an expression of God's displeasure. The same is illustrated by the cases of Gehazi (2 Kings 5:27) and Uzziah (2 Chron. 26:18–21). In the opinion of the rabbis also, leprosy is punishment from God. The extended exposition on the law of the leper found in Leviticus Rabbah (ch. 16) repeats this point over and over again. In the opinion expressed there, the leper (*mezora'*) is seen as one who sins through libel (*mozi'* [*shem*] *ra'*); leprosy is punishment for the sin. The same opinion is repeated by the Babylonian sages at Arakhin 16a–b. Thus, the leper is not merely one touched by death. He is touched by death *because* he is a sinner, having committed what is, in the view of the sages, a severe sin. Partial death comes as punishment. It is God's way of *banning* the sinner from the society upon which his sin has impacted so destructively.[2]

To synthesize what we have seen: This Talmudic deliberation interprets the mourner in terms of the *menude* and the "leper." Both of the latter have sinned, in each case sins against the fabric of society. Both are therefore expelled from society, one by the human court and the other by God. The expulsion of the leper is precipitated by his death-like condition, itself a punishment and signal from God, an expression of God's wish that the sinner be expelled.

The mourner is also "banned by heaven." He or she is touched by death and therefore excluded from common society. Why does this happen? Evidently, the death of the loved one is seen not only as punishment for *his* sins, but as punishment for the sins of the mourner as well. This extreme, grievous personal suffering is, like most suffering, punishment. But this should not be viewed in isolation from the punishment – that is, death – of the deceased. Both are in some measure punished. Both, therefore, die – at least in part. As I have suggested in earlier chapters, this also explains many of the rituals of the mourner: his abstention from sex, work, grooming, social intercourse, etc. The equation is incomplete, of course; the mourner is not yet dead. But his death-like qualities, highlighted by his more severe observance of the rituals of the leper, who has also partly died, leave no doubt that a partial equation is indeed intended.

The Three Days

We have seen in the Bavli as in earlier rabbinic texts that the first three days following death are understood to have a special quality. This is the period during which the soul is believed to hover nearby the body, hoping to re-enter its former home. Only with the coming of the third day, when the physical signs of death first become undeniably apparent, does the soul give up hope and begin its journey of transition to the world of the dead. The first three days or, according to other records, up to the third day, are also distinguished for the mourner. This is said to be the period of most severe mourning, of bitter crying. It is the period during which the mourner is inconsolable.

In the opinion of the Bavli, it is also much more. The Bavli finds the opportunity to elaborate the qualities of the first three days in connection with Mishnah M.Q. 3:5, which declares that if a person buries his dead three days before the beginning of a festival, the shiva is cancelled when the festival arrives. Echoing this ruling, the Talmud's expansions are multiple and noteworthy.

After testing the precise effect of the festival on the counting of shiva and shloshim, the gemara begins to accumulate laws relating to the first three days of mourning. Specifying a detail that would already be implied in the Mishnah, the Talmud (at 20a) quotes a dispute (found earlier in the Tosefta) which begins with the opinion that "if someone performed the obligation of overturning beds for three days before the festival, he need not overturn it after the festival – [these are] the words of R. Eliezer." An alternative opinion suggests that even one hour of observance of this obligation before the festival would exempt the mourner from any further obligation. This dispute is said to repeat the same dispute of the Schools of Hillel and Shammai (with the School of Shammai taking the more stringent position), and later sages are reported to persist in this disagreement, with Rava saying that "the law follows our [tannaitic] teacher, who said three [days]."

After continuing with related matters, the Talmud returns to its discussion of the three days at 21a, where it records the dispute, seen (in slightly different form) earlier in the Yerushalmi, concerning the mourner and tefillin. Again, according to the first recorded opinion, the mourner should not wear tefillin "for the first three days . . . [but] from the third day forward, inclusive of the third day, he is permitted to wear tefillin." The second opinion, given in the same source, reduces the prohibition by a day. Clearly, we see here once again a dispute between those who desire to protect the first three days by means of ritual markers and those who feel less need to do so. (In fact, the apparently contradictory statements of the baraita, "for the first three days . . . but from the third day," may be a manifestation of this same dispute; the phrase "inclusive of the third day" has all of the characteristics of a later clarificatory addition, perhaps by someone who wanted to reduce the period during which wearing tefillin is prohibited. Without this phrase, it would be perfectly reasonable to read the phrase "from the third day" as saying "after the third day has passed.") But I think we should not read too much into this dispute. There may be no agreement concerning the relationship between the emotional state of the mourner – or the condition of the deceased – and the need for a corresponding ritual symbolism. But, as we shall see, the unique status of the first three days is beyond question.

The Talmud continues, quoting further tannaitic teachings which pertain to the first three-day period. We next learn that during these days a mourner may do no work, even under the most dire circumstances. Thereafter, if he is desperate, he may labor in private, though properly speaking (as we have seen) he should refrain from work for the entirety of shiva. Compromises may be made during shiva, but not during the first three days.

During the three days, a mourner may not go out even to the house of another mourner. Thereafter, she may go to another mourner's house, but she should sit with the mourners, not with those who offer comfort. During the three days, a mourner may neither ask of the welfare of another nor respond to an inquiry concerning his welfare. Thereafter, he may respond to such a question (however inappropriate such a question may be! – see below), but for all of shiva he still may not ask others. After shiva but during shloshim (or the entire year in the case of the death of a parent), he may even ask others of their welfare, but it is clear that others should still not ask him because it should be obvious that the mourner "is not dwelling in peace."

This series of regulations, the immediate symbolism of which is clear (does the mourner experience "peace" or doesn't she?) helps us understand the emotional progress of the entire mourning period. During the first three days the mourner is so afflicted by grief that he is silent. He may not even respond to the gauche and insensitive inquiry by another, "What is your peace?" After the three days, he may begrudgingly respond, but he has not yet rejoined society and so must not engage in social discourse; there should be no joining in relationship by asking the other, "What is your peace?" After shiva he has left his isolation, so he may begin to rebuild the social bridges that such a greeting will support. At the same time, it should still be clear to others that his peace is not well. Not until after thirty days – or a year when a parent has died – is it safe to assume that he is at peace. Only then, when there is no longer danger of causing the mourner greater grief, may others greet the (former) mourner as they would greet others.

The Talmud concludes its series of laws pertaining to the three days with the following directive: "During the first three days, if the mourner came from a nearby place, he counts with them [= the other mourners]. If he came from a distant place, he counts by himself [a full shiva]. From this point onward, even if he came from a nearby place, he counts by himself." Two factors are necessary for one to be "close" to mourning, that is, close enough to others in mourning to join their mourning and not commence one's own cycle. First, one must literally be close – sufficiently close to the other mourners that one may be viewed as part of their company; close enough that one might easily have been notified of the death within a reasonably brief period of time. Second, one must be close chronologically. One must come into the company of the other mourners when they are still in their most intense period of grief, when the death is, as it were, still "fresh." During the first three days, the death has as though just occurred. We might even speculate that not until the end of the three days can we be sure it has occurred (remember: the soul isn't yet sure during this period!). In any case, three days is the period of closeness, of immediacy. During this period, therefore, one may begin mourning with others who are similarly still at the beginning of their mourning.

The evident ambivalence of this sugya is worthy of comment. We saw above two specific cases where the ritual integrity of the three days was subject to question. With respect to the question concerning the overturning of beds, the final recorded opinion declares that the obligation has been fulfilled if the mourner overturned his beds "even one hour" before the holiday. Following the general principle that the law follows the lenient position in laws of mourning (b. Mo'ed Qatan 18a and parallels), this turns out to be the accepted position in post-Talmudic Judaism. But whatever the accepted law, the prominence of those positions that seek to mark and protect the three days ritually is unmistakable. Indeed, what is remarkable is the persistence of these laws despite the fact that Babylonian practice seems to prefer lenient rulings in the matter of the three days. Why give such prominent record to laws protecting the three days? Why record laws which fail to find a place in any earlier rabbinic collection?

The Bavli identifies laws regarding the three days as originating in rabbinic Palestine and, whatever the actual history of specific rulings, there is no reason to doubt the general claim; as we saw, the three days already have a place in the Palestinian Mishnah. The special nature of these three days is grounded in two realities: one, the emotional state of the mourner and, two, the death-status of the deceased. As we have noted, Palestinian Jews visited their deceased in burial caves and looked for positive signs of death (that is, obvious decay). Before these signs were evident, they believed that the soul of the deceased, at least, had not yet given up hope. Emotion and perceived reality united in setting the first three days apart, and ritual practice followed in stride.

But Jews in Babylonia could not have visited their dead in the same way (the topography of the land did not permit cave burial). Thus, one of the two foundations of the three-day rituals disappeared in their experience. This may explain, at least in part, why the preference of later Babylonian sages was to reduce or eliminate the three-day restrictions. Nevertheless, the Bavli does not wish us to forget the special qualities of this period entirely. Some practices are evidently maintained and, more importantly, others are recalled. Reviewing the details, we, the students, cannot help but be struck by the degree to which this period is distinct from what follows. We know that it is a period of intense grief, a period of silence, a period of proximity to death. We may recall that it is a period during which the sword is drawn and ready, during which our judgment is near as well. The three days is the first distinct period of mourning. Only when we get past the three – the *shlosha* – can we begin to speak of shiva, shloshim and beyond.

A Ritual of Comfort

In all of rabbinic literature, we have seen relatively little concerning the comforting of mourners beyond the broad obligation to do so. We have read of the "lines" of comforters who greeted mourners with words of condolence as they left the burial, but, with a few exceptions, we do not know what was supposed to be said.[3] We have seen mention of the "blessing of mourners" and "comforting of mourners," but until the Bavli we find no suggestion of what the substance of these recitations might be.

Finally, at Ketubot 8a–b we find an important deliberation relating to the ritual status of the mourner which sheds considerable light on ancient rituals of comforting. The sugya, which begins by comparing and contrasting the bridegroom and the mourner, includes a lengthy report of one meal in the house of a mourner and of the ritual recitations which punctuated that meal. The report, whether representative or not, is an unparalleled testimony to a custom now long since lost.

The exposition that concerns us begins by setting up a contradiction: R. Yohanan[4] teaches that bridegrooms are counted in a ritual quorum (a minyan) and mourners are not, whereas a baraita teaches that bridegrooms and mourners are both counted in a ritual quorum. The first proffered resolution of this apparent contradiction suggests that R. Yohanan, who states that mourners should not be counted, is speaking about the post-burial "line." But, the gemara suggests, this resolution is unsatisfactory, for R. Yohanan also expressed his opinion in a slightly different way, saying that "the blessing of mourners requires ten, and mourners are not included in that number;" there is no "blessing of mourners" in the funeral line, the gemara points out. So, the text now suggests, R. Yohanan must be speaking of the ritual "in the open square." But, the gemara objects, R. Yohanan also said that the exclusion of the mourner lasts for all of shiva; is "the blessing of the open square" recited all of shiva? Yes, the gemara answers, when "new faces" have come, guests who have not previously visited the mourner to offer their comfort.

Before continuing, we should note the crucial connection being made here. The question before the gemara is whether the bridegroom and mourner, respectively, are included in quorums for rituals that pertain to their status. We have encountered this pairing of bridegroom and mourner before. This gemara makes it clear that the parallels between the two are, at least in Talmudic practice, more numerous than is commonly recognized.

The parallels begin with the special blessings recited for both the bridegroom and the mourner. These blessings are recited for a week for both, but only if "new faces" (new visitors) are present. Moreover, in both cases, the blessings are recited at a meal, some as part of the *birkhat hamazon*, the blessing after meals.

On the prior page (8a), the gemara indicates that a special formula is added to the *birkhat hamazon* in the home of newlyweds for the entire first month of the marriage and, under certain defined conditions, even up to a full year. In other words, not only is there a shiva (seven-day ritual) for both the newlywed and the new mourner, but there is a shloshim (thirty-day ritual) and year-long ritual as well. And just as death is prepared for through certain rituals, so too should a special blessing be added to the *birkhat hamazon* during the period in which immediate preparations for the wedding are being made.

This detailed exposition of the ritual parallel of bridegroom and mourner invites us – even requires us – to re-examine our earlier interpretations of the same phenomenon. It should be evident that what we have learned in the Bavli, particularly in the prior chapter, indeed affirms those interpretations. As we have noted, the newly married person is said to be as though newly born. The deceased is also considered to be born into a new life, for he is, like the bride and bridegroom, atoned of all sin (see b. Yev. 63b). It is undoubtedly appropriate, therefore, to mark both experiences with similar if not identical rituals.

But there is a problem: the deceased, unlike the bride and groom, cannot celebrate the ritual. As he or she is removed from other mitzvot, so too is he or she removed from this one. So it is the mourner, who in some ways shares the experience of the deceased, who participates in the appropriate ritual. She hears the expressions of comfort which the deceased would also take comfort in, she hears the blessing which he would also enjoy.

But what, precisely, is the ritual? The Talmud goes on to illustrate:

R. Ḥiyya b. Abba was the Bible teacher of the son of Resh Laqish . . . His child died. The first day, he [Resh Laqish] did not go to him [to comfort him]. The next day, he led Judah b. Naḥmani, his spokesperson [to pay respects].

[1] He said to him: Rise and say something with respect to the child. He opened [his mouth] and said: "The Lord saw and spurned, out of anger for His sons and daughters" (Deut. 32:19) – a generation in which the parents spurn the Holy One, blessed be He, He becomes angry with their sons and daughters and they die when they are small. . . . (He came to comfort and he caused him pain [with such a statement]! This is what he said to him: You are considered [righteous enough] to be caught [= to suffer] for the generation.)

[2] He [Resh Laqish] said to him [his spokesperson]: Rise and say something with regard to the praise of the Holy One, blessed be He. He opened [his mouth] and said: The God who is great in the abundance of his greatness, mighty and strong in the multitude of awesome acts. *Who brings the dead to life with His word*, Who does things so great that they cannot be scrutinized, wonders that cannot be counted. Blessed are You, O Lord, *who brings the dead to life*.

[3] He said to him: Rise and say something with regard to the mourners. He opened and said: Our brethren who are worn out, who

are crushed by this mourning, let your hearts examine this – This stands forever, it is a path from the six days of creation. Many have drunk [its waters], many will drink. As the drinking of the earlier ones is the drinking of the later ones. Our brethren, the Master of comfort will comfort you. Blessed is the One who comforts mourners. . . .

[4] He said to him: Rise and say something with regard to those who comfort mourners. He opened and said: Our brethren, bestowers of kindness children of bestowers of kindness, who uphold the covenant of Abraham our father . . . Our brethren, the Master of reward will pay you your reward. Blessed are You, who pays the reward.

[5] He said to him: Rise and say something with regard to all of Israel. He opened and said: Master of the Worlds! Redeem and save, deliver [and] save your people Israel from the pestilence and from the sword and from plundering and from the blast and from mildew and from all manner of troubles that break forth and come into the world. Before we call you will answer. Blessed are You, who stops the plague.

(emphasis added)

The story, with the blessings it reports, is meant to illustrate the gemara's earlier claim that "the blessing of the open space," equated by the Bavli (Meg. 23b) with "the blessing of mourners" mentioned in the Mishnah and elsewhere, is recited once again when new comforters are present. Resh Laqish, who came the second but not the first day of the shiva of R. Ḥiyya b. Abba, shows in his actions that this is indeed the case. While at the mourner's house, Resh Laqish directs his spokesperson to recite certain blessings. It is the substance of those blessings that is of greatest interest here.

Following Resh Laqish's direction, Judah b. Naḥmani begins by praising the deceased son, however indirectly, and thereby offering comfort to the father. To do this, Judah justifies the death of the child, saying that it was on account of his unblemished quality that he died. Following a suggestion first found in an early midrash, the Mekhilta, that the righteous of a wicked generation will die first (Kraemer 1995: 86–7), Judah offers the child's death as proof of his goodness. Presumably, by recognizing this goodness, the father will be sure that the child has a place in the World to Come.

Next, Resh Laqish directs Judah to "say something with respect to" (1) the Holy One, (2) the mourners, (3) the comforters, and (4) all of Israel. Resh Laqish's direction seems to invite a spontaneous response, but each of the statements that follow is a blessing, ending with a formal concluding phrase. It seems clear, therefore, that this is testimony of a fixed ritual, with accepted formulations, and even if the precise wording of the blessings is fluid, the concluding phrases and therefore the themes are not. Moreover, this is, as I said, the only Talmudic record of such an expression, so, whether or not there is room for creative expansion of the defined themes, we are surely meant to see – and to interpret – *this* formulation (that is, to the extent that a particular "original" formulation is preserved; of course, manuscripts preserve multiple variants of the precise wording). Interpretation is now our task.

The first blessing praises God. The praises are, for the most part, quite general and of a type: the same phrases are used, in different combinations, in other rabbinic blessings. What stands out in this formulation is the emphasis on God as the One who restores the dead to life. It hardly needs be said that, in the context of a meal at the home of a mourner, this emphasis is particularly appropriate. Of all of the qualities of God, at this moment the most crucial – and most comforting – is God's mastery of life and death, and God's power to bring the dead back to life.

The second blessing is directed to the mourner himself. It begins by reminding him that what he is now experiencing, however horrible, is far from unusual. It is, rather, part of the fate of all humans, from the moment of their creation.[5] He is thus in the company of all humans; he may be comforted by remembering that he does not stand alone. Furthermore, he should know that, ultimately, it is the Lord who comforts mourners. This is one of God's special attributes, one perhaps often forgotten but mentioned appropriately in the presence of the mourner. "Know," the blessing says to him, "that your comfort is in God's hands."

The next blessing, directed at the (human) comforters themselves, praises those who engage in this mitzvah by reference to the covenant of Abraham. Those who show kindness by comforting mourners emulate Abraham who is renowned for his acts of kindness. They thus show themselves to be of the stock of Abraham, uniquely committed to his covenant with God. On account of this commitment, comforters will be rewarded by the Lord who gives reward. The message to the comforter is straightforward: For performance of such an act, a *mitzvah* of the highest degree, reward is surely appropriate. Ultimate reward is what you may expect.

Finally, a blessing is recited for all of Israel. The blessing amounts to a prayer for God's protection and salvation. Its conclusion, as much a request for mercy as an assertion of faith, describes God as the One who "stops the plague." Clearly, the expression emerges from the fear that the death now mourned may be the first of many deaths. If death is in the hands of God, if it is punishment from God for sin, then who (aside from God) knows whether the punishment is appropriately applied only to the individual or to the community as a whole? So what "all of Israel" needs in the face of death is protection from death which may spread – salvation from the fate of common sinners.

The substance of these blessings is fitting and the themes expected. The nature of the ritual seems clear enough as well: blessings – corresponding to the *dramatis personae*, broadly conceived – are recited at the meal in the house of a mourner by individuals who have come to offer comfort. Unfortunately, we can say little more than this, because the ritual which finds its fullest description here was lost already in the centuries immediately following the composition of the Talmud. As one Babylonian master of the subsequent period comments: "and now it has vanished" (Levin 1938: 32). In fact, the Talmud's blessings seem to be only part of a larger liturgical repertoire that fell into desuetude in the subsequent centuries. One testimony to this reality is found in the following rabbinic responsa:

> And [concerning] what is written, that "in our place, when they return with the mourner from the grave, they bless over a cup [of wine, saying] Blessed are You, Lord our God, Judge of Mercy . . . and the mourners [then] drink, and this is their entry into mourning. Is this custom in effect or not, and this blessing, must it be said with ten [people present] or not?" [Response:] And is the establishment of [the state of] mourning dependent upon the drinking of a cup [of wine]? And this blessing [concerning which] you have written, we have never heard of it, and it has no mention in the Talmud, and we have never heard that someone says it in the two Yeshivas [in Baghdad], and we have not heard of it from our teachers.
>
> (Levin 1938: 32–3)

To me, it is clear that the ritual described by the questioner is (at least) one community's interpretation of the obligation to conduct a ritual of "blessing the mourners" at a meal – preferably the first meal – following burial. Because of the failure of the earlier rabbinic sources to define the substance of this blessing, at least in the record transmitted to subsequent generations, those who wished to perform their obligation had to depend on interpretation and local custom. We may imagine that this led to a rich range of possibilities. But, whether or not this was so, little of this custom – Talmudic or post-Talmudic – has been preserved. How, ritually speaking, the comforter is to do his or her job is very much left to the imagination.

Appropriately, the present Talmudic deliberation ends with reference to another comforting ritual that was no longer practiced in subsequent centuries. I am speaking of the obligation, mentioned first in the Yerushalmi, to consume ten cups of wine in the house of the mourner, "three before eating, to open his intestines, three during eating, to dissolve the food in his stomach, and four after eating, one for the 'provide' [blessing of birkhat hamazon, the blessing after meals], one for the blessing of the land, one for [the blessing] 'builder of Jerusalem,' and one for [the blessing] 'the One who is good and does good.'" The wine, the Talmud reports explicitly (in what is now a supplemented version of this tradition, one which includes explanations), is to calm the mourner, to enable him to eat, and to mark the occasion with ritual cups during birkhat hamazon. Though, as we have seen, wine is elsewhere associated with joy, and might therefore seem inappropriate for the meal in the house of a mourner, concern for comfort and ritual here takes precedence, allowing this source of joy to at least provide consolation.

In addition to prescribing a ritual cup of wine for each of the blessings of *birkhat hamazon*, the Talmud (Ber. 46b) also relates a custom of supplementing the "the One who is good and does good" blessing with special appropriate additions. The earliest recorded version of this supplement (which is, however, post-Talmudic; see Lewin 1931: 45) preserves the following formula: "The living King, who is good and does good, true judge, who judges in righteousness and truth, who is sovereign over all His acts, we are His servants and His people, and for everything we are obligated to thank Him and to bless Him." Another addition, hinted at in the same early record and preserved in the printed Talmud, speaks of God who, on the occasion of this mourning, should "seal this breach for us." These formulae are clearly intended to be recited for the entirety of the shiva, whether or not new guests are present. They are additional to the "blessing of mourners" itself. And, in the opinion of the geonic authority whose version I have quoted here, the law in his days (the Islamic age) continues to require the recitation of these words. This ritual, surviving the end of the Talmudic period, would not disappear until a later time.

Perhaps (this is pure speculation) the loss of these rituals is a consequence of the joyous connotations of wine in rabbinic culture. Such a motivation is suggested in the writings of later authorities, who, though making reference to the practice of drinking ten cups of wine, distort it almost beyond recognition. Maimonides (12th cent.), for example, writes that no more than ten cups of wine may be drunk in the home of a mourner lest those who do so become inebriated (*Mishneh Torah*, Laws of Mourning, 13:8). For Maimonides, this is a limitation, not an obligation as it is in the Talmud. There is no sense, in his record, that the point of at least several of these cups is comfort, nor is there recognition that the latter cups have a ritual function. In actuality, though his source is clear, his appreciation for the ritual is absent entirely.

Whatever the subsequent history of the practices described or alluded to at Ketubot 8b and elsewhere, there can be no doubt that the Talmud knows a rich ritual of comforting to be enacted at the home of the mourner. In some degree prescribed, in some degree spontaneous, the ritual was thought essential. For this reason it is described as a unique expression of the covenant of Abraham. For this reason, the rare person who in the time of the composition of Midrash Song of Songs knew how to recite the "blessing of mourners" was called "a lily among the thorns" (Song of Songs 2:2). The Talmud, in the details examined above, recalls the garden.

9

POST-TALMUDIC
DEVELOPMENTS IN JEWISH
DEATH-PRACTICE

Readers familiar with contemporary traditional[1] Jewish practices relating to death, the funeral and burial, will have been surprised by some of what they saw in prior chapters. "How did the practices and beliefs described here develop into those with which I am familiar?" they will have found themselves asking, perhaps many times. The surprises emerge on both sides of the ledger. On the one hand, practices taken for granted by the classical rabbinic works, such as anointing the deceased, the standing and sitting ritual, overturning the beds, covering the upper lip, and reburial – to enumerate only a few examples – seem to find little or no memory in later Jewish practice. On the other hand, practices later generations view as central to death and mourning ritual, such as recitation of the *kaddish*, are totally unknown in this connection in the early rabbinic sources. Indeed, it is difficult to avoid the question: How did *that* come to be *this*?

In this chapter, I intend merely to begin answering this question. This is not meant to be a comprehensive history of post-Talmudic developments in Jewish death and mourning rituals, and I make no claim of having researched these developments as such a history would require. Furthermore, I will not remark upon all of the details of these rituals, nor will I offer extended interpretations of them. Rather, I hope simply to trace the major changes in Jewish death-practice, addressing primarily the most outstanding Talmudic[2] rituals, now lost, or those later rituals which do not find an obvious source in the earlier record. This will, I hope, answer the questions readers have been most likely to ask. A proper history of Jewish death-practices in the medieval period will await the attentions of another scholar.[3]

The earliest evidence we have of the practice of Jews in the post-Talmudic age is the writings of the so-called *geonim* ("illustrious ones"), the heads of the Babylonian rabbinic academies from the eighth to the tenth centuries. These writings preserve ample testimony regarding developments in Jewish death and mourning rituals, testimony which allows us to see that, already in the centuries immediately following the redaction of the Talmud, accepted custom in these matters had begun to change significantly.

Regrettably, we do not preserve geonic comments relating to the preparation of the deceased, what was described in the Mishnah as attending to his or her "needs." Maimonides, writing in the twelfth century, does include a full description of this preparation (*Mishneh Torah*, Laws of Mourning 4:1–2), a description that is virtually identical to what we saw in the classical rabbinic documents. But because of the identity of Maimonides' laws with the Talmudic sources – an identity that pervades his entire exposition on burial and mourning, even when, according to the prior geonic record, some of these practices have been abandoned – we cannot rely on Maimonides' testimony for drawing historical conclusions. It is likely, in fact, that Maimonides anachronizes, imagining perfect practice in light of the deliberations of the Talmudic masters. For this reason, we shall not often return to Maimonides' testimony in this chapter.

Approximately two centuries later, R. Jacob b. Asher, in his *Arba'ah Turim* ("The Four Pillars"), quotes Maimonides on the law of preparing the deceased, apparently indicating his approval of what Maimonides writes (Yoreh Deah 352). He does not indicate if there have been any changes in the customs of preparation. But shortly thereafter, in his exposition of burial itself, R. Asher has much to add. He emphasizes that each Jewish community should follow its own custom, indicating that some bury their dead in *kokhim* (as in Mishnaic and subsequent rabbinic practice), some in ditches. Some use coffins, some bury their dead directly in the earth. Where the climate permits, the deceased need not be covered with dirt (thus the earlier custom in Palestine), but elsewhere, as in Babylonia, the dead should be covered completely to avoid putrefaction (Yoreh Deah 362). Clearly, this authority assumes that practices have changed from the Talmudic model, and even in some important matters the custom of the community is allowed to decide.

The Mishnah assumes, as we saw, that a public "standing and sitting" ritual will occur as the deceased is transported to burial (see my discussion of m. Meg. 4:3 in Ch. 3). But the Babylonian tradition, as represented in the Bavli, B.B. 100b, already understands this ritual as a ritual of comfort, directed to the new mourners as they exit the burial place. In the Bavli's record, the mourners are addressed with the declarations: "Stand, O dear ones, stand; sit, O dear ones, sit." The number of prescribed standings and sittings, seven, are said to correspond to the expressions of "futility" found in Ecclesiastes. Not surprisingly, the geonic authorities, following their canonical text, the Bavli, similarly know of the "standing and sitting" as a post-burial comfort ritual.

Rav Hai and Rav Sherira (both 10th cent.) describe the ritual in this language:

> The custom of the "blessing of the open place," this is it: After they bury the dead, they gather and stand in the open place, that is the field in which they take leave of the deceased, and conduct the

"standing and sitting". . . . And they say, "Sit, O dear ones, sit," and
they sit and wait. And they stand, and announce and say, "Dear ones,
stand!" And they stand up [and move] to another place, and they
[again] announce "Sit, O dear ones, sit," and they sit. And during that
standing and sitting they comfort the mourners . . .

(Lewin 1931: 44)

A close reading of this description shows that it mixes various rituals which
in the earlier rabbinic record seem to be distinct: the standing and sitting, the
standing in line to comfort, and the blessing of the open place. Perhaps out
of recognition of this confusion, Rav Natronai (9th cent.) claims that the
"standing and sitting" practiced during his age is not the Talmudic ritual. In
his words:

We neither recall, nor have we learned, in the generations before us,
in either of the two [great Babylonian] academies, that they practice
according to the gemara, neither individually nor communally, neither
in the city nor in the cemetery. Rather, the rabbis of our academies
are accustomed, when they return from burial, to sit and stand seven
times for mere [symbolic] interruption, *but not to fulfill "standing and
sitting"* . . .

(Lewin 1931: 42–3).

In other words, the writer is aware of the Talmudic practice, but says that it
has not been formally practiced in his memory. It survives, to his awareness,
as a *mere* custom, not as a fulfillment of the canonical directive.

The Mishnah's ritual for leaving the burial place, known also in subsequent
rabbinic documents, is referred to by the term "standing in line" (see m. Ber.
3:2; m. M.Q. 3:7; and my comments in Ch. 3). In the Mishnah, this ritual
is clearly intended to serve as the first occasion for offering comfort to the
mourner (in the language of M.Q. 3:7, "we stand in the line and comfort").
Rav Hai Gaon explains the details of the ritual, but then proceeds to
comment, "In Babylonia we do not stand in the line except for a great sage, in
which case the sages pass before them [the people] in a line and the entire
people stands" (Lewin 1931: 41). A vestige of the practice remains, but only
in the community of sages. If a great teacher dies, his students, the other
sages, are all mourners, and the community must offer comfort. But otherwise
this Talmudic ritual, at least as ancient as the Mishnah, is no longer in
practice.

In the midst of the discussion of funeral rituals, two rituals central still to
modern Jewish funeral practice, but unknown, in this connection, in the
Talmudic record, are first mentioned – *zidduk ha-din* ("justification of the

divine judgment") and kaddish. I quote the most complete description of these rituals in full:

> And the rabbis' custom is to say [biblical] verses of "justification of the judgment" and eulogies at the grave, and when they turn their faces [from the grave] they recite [kaddish]: "May His great name be magnified and sanctified, in the world that He will in the future renew, and restore the dead to life, and bring them into eternal life, and rebuild the city of Jerusalem, and restore the Temple in its midst, and uproot foreign worship from our land, and restore the worship of His name to its place. And the Holy One, Blessed be He, will give dominion to His kingdom, and His glory, in your lives and in your days, and in the life of all of the House of Israel, quickly and in a time that is near, and say, Amen. May He be blessed . . . May there be great peace. . . . " And after this they take dirt and wipe their hands and say, "And now, Lord, You are our Father. We are the substance and You are the One who forms us. We are all the work of Your hands," – in order that the Holy One, blessed be He, be filled with compassion and stop our death [from coming]. And before they go into the house of the mourner, they wash their hands two times in order that [divine] anger be cancelled from us as water that is poured out.
>
> (Lewin 1931: 41)

This exposition is rich with new funeral rituals, including the two specified above, and each requires comment.

The "justification of judgment" ritual derives from the Mishnah's demand that "upon [hearing] bad news, one should say 'Blessed be the judge of truth'" (Ber. 9:2). Hearing of the death of a loved one would certainly be included in the category of "bad news." In fact, the Talmud (b. Ber. 59b) teaches explicitly that one should recite the "blessed be the judge of truth" formula upon hearing of the death of one's father. However, the Talmud does not explicitly connect this formula with the funeral ritual. Moreover, though the geonic record does not specify the substance of the "justification of [divine] judgment," it does make clear that it involves the recitation of biblical verses; the formula specified in Berakhot is not a biblical verse. Later practice will designate Job 1:21 – "The Lord gave and the Lord took away; may the name of the Lord be blessed" – a verse used in the Talmud to "prove" that one is obligated to bless God even upon hearing bad news (Ber. 60b). Indeed, it is not unreasonable to assume that this was at least one of the verses already recited in geonic practice. But, be that as it may, the ritual as here described has no clear precedent in the Talmudic record.

According to the present opinion, the "justification" is to be recited "at the grave," along with eulogies, which in the Talmudic record were recited both during the funeral procession and at the grave. But, as we saw, the "standing and sitting" ritual is no longer part of the funeral procession in Babylonia, so it would appear that there is little choice but to recite the eulogies – the calling forth of tears – at the grave alone.

Crucially, the ritual of ẓidduk ha-din just described is regarded by Rav Hai Gaon as "the custom of one place" which was first mentioned in the time of "the early geonim." But, in his opinion, it is not a proper Babylonian custom and he clearly prefers that it not be recited (Lewin 1931: 55). Despite his preference, the custom persisted, and it remains a part of Jewish funeral ritual to this day.

Next, upon turning from the grave, comes the kaddish. The formula recorded by the gaon is notably more expansive than that known in later practice. Its emphasis is unmistakable: the prayer (stated as an affirmation of faith) is for messianic restoration. Evidently, upon turning from the just-inhumed deceased, the mourner turns his or her attention to resurrection, which itself is but one part of the awakening of the World to Come. There are, of course, various versions of the kaddish, this one for the graveside, others for recitation during prayer. But, whatever the formula, its association with burial is unprecedented,[4] and therefore requires explanation.

The geonic explanation which survives is this:

> You should know that kaddish, that is "*yitgadal* . . . ," we have not found it at all [that it should be recited] by [the side of] the deceased, but only after the eulogy or the ẓidduk ha-din, for any place where there are words of Torah, we respond after them [by saying] "Amen, May His great name. . . . "
>
> (Lewin 1931: 49)

Kaddish, the gaon admits, is not for the dead. In fact, according to another geonic testimony, kaddish is not to be recited until the mourner distances him- or herself[5] from the grave at least four cubits, ritually enacting the separation of the recitation from death (See She'arei ẓeddeq, pt. 3, she'ar 4, pt. 9). Instead, the present authority suggests, this is a ritual to be enacted after speaking words of Torah. Indeed, in its abbreviated, better-known version, the kaddish seems in no way associated with death, as has often been noted. The explanation proffered here, therefore, is intuitively sensible. But whatever the origins of the connection of kaddish to the funeral, and thereafter to commemorations of death in general, there can be no question that, by the time the version quoted above had developed, the connection was a powerful one. Only on the foundation of this association can the redemptive thrust of the grave-side formula be understood.

Returning to the fuller exposition of the ritual, we see record of a practice, long since forgotten, which is intended to protect the mourner from the danger of death. The ritual involves a symbolic act and a recitation, both clearly expressions of the belief, originating in Genesis 2, that humans are formed by God out of the soil of the earth. The mourner wipes his hands in dirt while speaking of himself as the substance (the clay) and God as the craftsman; the mourner's hope is that, as the One who forms or shapes humans, God will protect him, His handiwork, from destruction. A similarly explicit symbolic ritual is described as taking place at the portal of the house of the mourner: water is poured over the hands of the mourner to suggest the pouring away of God's wrath, the wrath which has been expressed against the deceased but which, the mourner hopes, will not be expressed against him.

These hand-wiping or washing rituals are not, however, supported by all authorities. One gaon, commenting on the custom of wiping one's hands in dirt, says that "it is not done here." And Rav Hai, though he begrudgingly permits the practice, shows no enthusiasm for it. In a similar fashion, both Rav Natronai and Rav Paltoi (9th cent.) say there is no need to wash one's hands upon returning from the grave, though both say there is no objection if a person undertakes this custom (Lewin 1931: 41–2). In view of the frequency with which such washing or wiping rituals are found world-wide (Parker 1983: 36; Toynbee 1971: 50), it seems likely that the geonic authorities are here noticing and commenting upon a more popular custom, one they do not support but which they have no power to suppress. For that reason, perhaps, it continues in many Jewish communities to this day.

Also part of the "exit" from grave to mourning are various other rituals, including blessings and expressions of comfort directed to the mourner. Though the Mishnaic references to these blessings are undecipherable, and the Talmudic discussions still far from clear, it would nevertheless appear that the blessings are intended to mark the advancing stages of the mourning process: its beginning following burial, its transposition to the mourner's home, the passing days of the shiva. The geonim offer interpretations of the Talmudic references. But, for the most part (as we saw in Chapter 8), the practices to which they refer are no longer enacted in their day.

The geonic record preserves various opinions and versions concerning these transition rituals. According to Rav Hai and Rav Sherira:

> Before the first sitting [for comforting] after the burial, they immediately recite the "blessing of the open place" before the wrapping of the head of the mourner, then they immediately wrap his head in order to say that the mourning has begun.
>
> (Lewin 1931: 44)

This is a strikingly dramatic ritual, involving the choice of one mourning ritual – the wrapping of the head and, with it, the covering of the upper lip –

138

as representing the acceptance of the condition of mourning. This precise function is not ascribed to this ritual in the Talmud and it is impossible to recover its source. Be that as it may, this ritual of transition was quickly abandoned in any case.

Later rabbinic authorities are, of course, familiar with these various practices, which find their source in the earliest rabbinic record, and most faithfully spell out the Talmudically authorized steps. But after the geonic period is seems clear that their descriptions are mere history. Writing in the fourteenth century, R. Jacob b. Asher states the situation simply:

> All of these matters are dependent upon [local] custom . . . and in our generations, these customs are forgotten. . . . rather, this is how we practice now: we place the deceased in the grave, and cover the grave, and remove shoes and sandals and distance ourselves a little from the cemetery, and recite kaddish (*Arba'ah Turim*, Yoreh Deah 376).

Talmudic ritual is long forgotten in practice. The modern traditional Jew will be familiar with customs more-or-less as described by R. Jacob.

According to the geonic record, the transition to the home of the mourner follows these steps:

> They enter into the house of the mourner and prepare for him a cup of wine and bless the "cup of comfort," that is the "blessing of the open place," in this way: "Blessed be the Judge of mercy, judge of truths, who has judged us with a judgment of His truth, as it is written, 'The Rock, His work is perfect, for all of His ways are justice, a trustworthy God without iniquity, righteous and straight is He.' (Deut. 32:4) Blessed are You, O Lord, comforter of mourners." And they don't drink, rather they give it to the mourner and he blesses " . . . creator of the fruit of the vine," and he drinks.
>
> (Lewin 1931: 43)

In another source, a questioner knows this ritual but is not sure whether or not it is practiced. The response of the gaon is clear; as we saw in an Chapter 8, this entire cluster of rituals finds no support among these authorities (though the persistence of the discussion and questions suggests that it remained a part of popular practice in at least some circles).

But, following the Talmud, the geonim do support the addition of special formulae to the blessing after meals in the house of a mourner. To be specific, the "One who is good and does good" blessing is supplemented with the words "true judge [who] judges with justice, and all is His and we are His

139

people and His servants, and He will stop this breach for us." Or, at least this is offered as a preliminary opinion. Further on, the same authority recommends following the practice of Mar Zutra in the Talmudic story (Ber. 46b) who, following a loss, added the following formula to the same blessing after meals:

> The living King, who is good and does good, true judge [who] judges with justice and truth, and rules over all of His creations, for we are His servants and His people, and in all matters we are obligated to thank Him and to bless Him.
>
> (Lewin 1931: 45)

Despite all of this discussion and a clear decision in favor of this addition to the blessing after meals, even it was forgotten in later generations.

The geonim suggest no significant changes to the rituals of the mourner during the shiva, so it would appear (though this is not a necessary conclusion) that the Talmudic customs remain in force. But not all of the requirements pertaining to the mourner – the overturning of beds and couches is the most obvious example – are known in later generations. With respect to this particular practice, R. Jacob quotes his father, R. Asher, as ruling that it is unnecessary for mourners to overturn beds because Jews, in their day, live among non-Jews who visit their homes regularly. They will view this custom with suspicion, as an act of sorcery, and thus Jews may refrain from performing it (*Arba'ah Turim*, Yoreh Deah 387). The authority of these sages was accepted in Germany (Ashkenaz) and France, at least, so it is clear that the ritual was no longer practiced by Ashkenazic Jewry at least by the fourteenth century.

The geonim describe a noteworthy ritual for the transition from shiva to the next, less restrictive stage of mourning. This ritual involves the following steps: On the morning of the seventh day, immediately after the morning prayer, they bring oil and anoint the head of the mourner, reciting at the same time "for the sake of the mourners of Zion." They then wash the corners of his head with a little bit of water and feed him a small morsel. Crucially, "they recite before him the blessing of mourners before they anoint him, in order to make clear that he already practiced mourning that day. And this [ritual] is the sign of his exit from mourning." Having completed exit, he uncovers his face (remember: the covering of his face was the symbol of his entering the state of mourning) and changes his clothes. Other authorities add that when his head is first washed, those attending to him comb his hair, presumably preparing him to re-enter society (Lewin 1931: 27). All of these rituals, dramatically marking the end of the mourning period proper, were evidently forgotten after these centuries.

Finally, perhaps one of the most important death customs spoken of in the earlier literature, assumed as a matter of course from the Mishnah to the Bavli, was the reburial of bones approximately a year after death itself. As we saw in Chapter 5, the archaeological evidence suggests that this custom fell into desuetude in the mid-fourth century in Palestine – though the subsequent rabbinic sources continue to discuss ossilegium as though it were still practiced. What do we know of this practice among post-Talmudic Jews?

The geonic responsa preserve a question concerning members of a family who bring the bones of their deceased relative (apparently to their family burial place) after a year. The questioner wants to know whether such reburial requires the recitation of "the justification of the judgment" (*zidduq ha-din*) and kaddish. Rav Hai responds: "It is not our custom to remove the deceased from his burial place, but there are those who bury the deceased in Baghdad and after some time remove him a distance of several parsangs to the other side of western Persia, to the desert that is close to 'yeshimon'" (Lewin 1931: 49). Hai's opinion could not be clearer; reburial is not, as far as he is concerned, an accepted practice in Babylonia, but not because there is anything wrong with it. Furthermore, some Jews do practice reburial according to a particular custom, providing their loved ones a resting-place close to the mythical wilderness ("yeshimon;" see Deut. 32:10 and Psalm 107:4), evidently associated in the popular mind with the land of the dead. In view of the currency of this custom in popular practice and (following a different custom) in the authoritative sources, contemporary rabbinic masters have no reason to condemn it.

R. Jacob b. Asher (in the *Arba'ah Turim*) describes reburial as a custom that was done "at first." But he goes on to quote another responsa of R. Hai which makes it clear, again, that while R. Hai might object to certain reburials – those motivated by the need to free up graves for others, for example – he approves of other reburials, motivated by other, more praiseworthy considerations. Thus, reburial in the Land of Israel is approved, as is reburial in a person's family plot.[6] And if it is the custom to allow the flesh to decompose and then rebury the bones that remain, that too is permitted, R. Jacob writes. It is unclear, though, whether he knows of the latter from actual practice or only from the Talmudic record, so it is impossible to assess whether the earlier rabbinic practice itself actually survives these many centuries later (Yoreh Deah 362–3).

Of course, the history of Jewish death and burial practices in the Middle Ages is far more complex and nuanced than suggested in the brief review given in this chapter. Practices were different for Jewish communities in different areas of the world. Customs continued to develop from one century to the next. But the select snapshots we have chosen already make it clear how and when Talmudic practice yielded to what would later, and even in our own day, be known as traditional Jewish practice. As I said in my introduction to this chapter, more than this will have to await a more sustained scholarly effort.

10

A PERSONAL THEOLOGICAL POSTSCRIPT

No scholarship is thoroughly objective. If for no other reason than that a scholar chooses to research and write about this subject and not that, the scholar's subjective interests and inclinations inevitably enter into the scholarly process. Thus, in obvious and not so obvious ways, the scholar's subjective self powerfully affects the nature of what he or she writes.

Also obvious but less often noted is the power of the scholarship to affect the scholar. Simply put, we are affected by what we discover; the conclusions of our researches have an impact on the ways we think about our subjects and even on the ways we think about ourselves. As an active scholar who has asked questions that have interested me – questions I have thought important – I have been aware of this impact before. But nothing I have studied has affected me as profoundly as my researches for this book. What I have discovered has changed forever the way I will understand Judaism, ancient and modern, and therefore myself.

My first significant realization deriving from this research is the degree to which Jews, rabbinic and non-rabbinic, were, in their beliefs and rituals surrounding death, common "savages." I was long ago persuaded by Howard Eilberg-Schwartz's argument, in his *The Savage in Judaism*, that ancient Jews were not as distinct from "primitive" peoples as is commonly imagined (or apologetically argued). But Eilberg-Schwartz doesn't address death-practices, and I had not initially thought to examine death rituals to establish the commonality of Jewish and "savage" practices and beliefs. Thus, I did not anticipate that ancient Jewish death-practices would provide a significant example of the phenomenon he describes, and powerful support for his overall thesis. I was both shocked and moved by the degree to which Jewish death-ways and beliefs, as reflected in Talmudic literature and contemporary archaeology, were shared with peoples in societies near to and distant from the population I studied. I was challenged to consider again the meaning of the collapse of the boundary between "advanced" or "sophisticated" rabbinic Jews and other, more "primitive" peoples. The common fate of humans – our mortality – leads us to common beliefs and practices, even without influence and mostly without recognizing what we hold in common. We seek to make distinctions, but we are foiled in this attempt by God's failure to distinguish our most fundamental qualities. Fundamentally, then, rabbinic Jews are just another tribal culture, as much "primitive" in their construction of categories as they are philosophical, as much "savage" in their reflections upon the meaning of death as they are theological.

Affecting me more profoundly, though, was my recognition of just how much the loss of the belief in a life-of-death in modernity transforms our theology more generally. I have come to the conclusion that the inability of many modern people to believe with confidence that death is merely the next stage of life – believing, instead, that death means the extinction of the individual – distances us from the beliefs and experiences of our ancestors perhaps more than anything else. I will explain by reference to specific examples.

Consider the reception of the story of Abraham's binding of Isaac (Genesis 22) in Jewish communities of various ages. I have rarely heard or read a contemporary comment pertaining to this story that does not begin by remarking on its grave difficulty (no pun intended) or troubling nature. How, after all, can God ask Abraham to take the life of his child?! But reference to pre-modern comments on (or liturgical usages of) this story quickly reveals that our ancestors had few such difficulties. So, seeking an answer for the question why, on Rosh Hashana (the Jewish New Year), Jews are required to blow a shofar made from the horn of a ram, the Talmud (quoting R. Abbahu) answers: "God said: Blow before me the horn of a ram in order that I will remember the binding of Isaac the son of Abraham [who was replaced, at the last minute, by a ram] and I will account to you as though you bound yourselves" (b. R.H. 16a). Clearly, the Talmud views Abraham's willingness to follow God's command and take his son's life as meritorious. It is therefore offered in defense of Israel on the occasion of their judgment, as reason for reward. Quite obviously, the Talmudic authors here exhibit no misgivings concerning the command to end Isaac's life.

In a similar vein, the traditional morning prayer service, and, in a slightly different version, the Rosh Hashana liturgy, include the following formula:

> Recall on our behalf, Lord, Our God . . . the oath that you swore to Abraham our father on Mount Moriah [the site of the binding of Isaac], and the binding which he bound his son Isaac on the altar . . . Lord of the world! Just as Abraham our father overcame his love to do your will with a perfect heart, so too should your love overcome your anger with us and your mercy should triumph above your other qualities . . .

Abraham did just as he should have done, conquering his love to do God's will. Again, there are no signs of misgivings here, in the liturgy that was recited by at least Jewish males virtually every day of their adult lives.

How can we explain this difference between the modern and traditional receptions of this story? Though there are, in all probability, a variety of reasons for this difference, undoubtedly one of the most important is the difference in modern and pre-modern Jewish beliefs concerning death. If death is understood as a conscious and sentient state – the next stage in a life-cycle that includes life, death and renewed life – then the ending of *this* life cannot be seen as nearly so catastrophic. True, the pleasures of life-in-the-flesh may come to an end, but so too do its sufferings and burdens. And Isaac, who was described as "perfect," would surely have enjoyed reward after death. Thus, understanding death in this way, there is little or no reason to be troubled – surely not if it is God who invites Isaac, at Abraham's hand, to the next life.

In contrast, if death means annihilation, the end of all consciousness and feeling, then the cutting short of life cannot but be troubling except in the most extreme of circumstances (such as the cessation of intolerable pain). If death is nothingness, then death is certainly not reward. If this life is all there is, then this life is all that matters. How can God command that we bring an end to all that matters, particularly in the case of someone as innocent as Isaac? If death is extinction, then the God who commands premature death is a villain. If we do not believe in the life of death, then how can we not be troubled by the story of the binding of Isaac? Our understanding of death makes all the difference.

A second case concerning which our death-beliefs make a significant difference is in the matter of capital punishment, what we call "the death penalty." Discussions of capital punishment by contemporary Jewish theologians and ethicists have nearly all failed to account for changes in death-beliefs, and are, therefore, mostly misguided. Those claiming that "Judaism" supports capital punishment have referred to the many "he shall surely be put to death"s in the Torah as a demonstration of this conclusion. Surely, they have argued, the rabbis could not have denied this unambiguous expression found in their foundational canon. Moreover, they continue, the Mishnah and Talmud, in tractate Sanhedrin, spell out the procedures for capital punishment at length. Had the rabbis opposed the death penalty, they surely would not have spent so much time elaborating its details.

On the other hand, those who want to argue that the rabbis were opposed to capital punishment have referred, first, to the oft-quoted opinion, found at the end of chapter 1 of Mishnah Ta'anit, which declares, "A Sanhedrin which kills one person in seven years is called destructive." The Mishnah continues: "R. Eleazar b. Azariah says, once in seventy years. R. Tarfon and R. Aqiba say, 'If we had been on the Sanhedrin, no one would ever have been killed.'" By adding to this testimony the fact that Mishnah Sanhedrin, in its procedures for trying capital cases, makes it more and more difficult to reach a conviction, the proponents of this view seem to make a strong case. The rabbis do not deny the Torah outright, they say, but they interpret it in such a way as to make fulfillment of its command – "put him to death" – nearly impossible. This, in their opinion, is evidence of powerful rabbinic opposition to the death penalty.

But what both sides have failed to notice is that, in the commonly held rabbinic view, death is not death (not, that is, as we mean it) and execution by the court is not a penalty, at least not primarily so. As we saw in Mishnah Sanhedrin 6:2, Bavli Yoma 86a, and elsewhere, death in general, and execution in particular, is understood to atone for the one who dies, including the convicted criminal. For this reason, the condemned who does not know how to confess is taught to say, "May my death serve as atonement for all of my sins." There may be discussion of exactly *when* in the process of death atonement is effected – at death itself? after some of the pains of the grave? only after the flesh has decomposed? – but there is no doubt that it is effected by death at some point; for this reason, the remaining bones of the executed criminal may, in the end, be removed from the court-graves and reinterred in the individual's family grave.

Atonement is needed, of course, because there is life after death, both in the short and the long terms. So execution cleanses a person of his sins and assures that he will live peaceably in the life beyond. How could the rabbis have opposed such a thing, not a punishment but a gateway to reward! Indeed, in the rabbinic mind, there is no "death penalty" so there is no death penalty to oppose. What they were opposed to was the unwarranted trespass by humans (the human court) on the territory of God (matters of life and death). Therefore, unless they were absolutely sure that all procedures had been followed and that there was no remaining question that a person should be convicted, they preferred to leave death to the hand of God. Of course, it was better to err in the direction of safety in this matter – if a person was guilty, God would surely get her one way or another – so the rabbis worried little that they might let a guilty person go free. But they had no hesitation concerning the *theoretical* rightness of execution in cases where there was no question (scholars will continue to debate whether the rabbinic court ever had the power to execute in actual fact).

Of course, if we believe that death equals extinction, that it serves no purpose beyond an ecological one, then it will be far more difficult for us to justify capital punishment theologically – and certainly not in traditional Jewish terms. We might argue, on the one hand, that society needs to protect itself through the establishment of powerful deterrents to potential criminals, or, on the other hand, that official violence begets more violence. We might argue that God desires peaceful societies, conducted according to civilized norms, or that only God has the right to take life, whatever we believe about death. But we cannot claim that "Judaism," meaning traditional Judaism, supports one view or the other. Unless we see death as the next stage in life, and understand death as a cleansing transition, we are too distant from traditional Jewish beliefs to make any claims for them. Modern Jewish theology and ethics we may do, but we should be modest in our claims for "Judaism."

The third and probably most significant case that is framed by transformations in beliefs concerning death is the Holocaust. Writings about the Holocaust by serious theologians and popular writers alike have often argued for its uniqueness, for its unprecedented nature in Jewish history. This claim for uniqueness is crucial because it serves as an explanation for the theological crisis that the Holocaust allegedly precipitated. Because the Holocaust was an unparalleled catastrophe, the argument goes, Jews today must respond in unparalleled and unprecedented ways. Where was God? Why did God not intervene? Of course, these and similar questions have been asked before, in response to other historical crises. But earlier answers, addressing very different circumstances, cannot suffice. If more than half of European Jewry was destroyed, the explanation that they were punished for their sins simply cannot be defended.

But the weaknesses of this line of reasoning are easily uncovered. To begin with, arguments for the uniqueness of the Holocaust are difficult to make and probably insupportable. As Steven Katz has shown in his *The Holocaust in Historical Context* (1994), vol. 1, the Holocaust has been exceeded, in numerical terms, several times in the modern world, and even in Jewish history it is not certain that, proportionally speaking, the Holocaust is unprecedented.[1] For this reason, Katz is forced to argue for the uniqueness of the Holocaust based upon the following definition: "The Holocaust is phenomenologically unique by virtue of the fact that never before has a state set out, as a matter of intentional principle and actualized policy, to annihilate physically every man, woman, and child belonging to a specific people" (Katz 1994: 28). This may well be true. But this "objective" definition too easily becomes an ideological – even a theological – claim. Why does this particular intention make a difference? Why does it matter that this "intentional principle," expressed and supported by the state, was actualized in specific policies? Are wrongful deaths at the hands of imperial aggressors who care not about the lives of innocents and often murder them for reasons of convenience, anger, revenge or pure pleasure, any less criminal? Such imperial soldiers execute policy, acting on the express intention of the imperial authorities. Are deaths in such circumstances less problematic, less theologically challenging? I have my doubts. So what do we gain from so specific and exacting a definition? If we define far enough, any event can be shown to be unique or unprecedented. Katz, like other contemporary Jewish writers, wants uniqueness, because he, like other moderns, experiences the Holocaust as unique. But not, I think, for the reasons he claims.

For purposes of argument, let us grant that the Holocaust was, proportionally speaking, without precedent, and that Nazi policies were unique. It is still not clear why people living during or in the aftermath of the Nazi atrocities would *feel* this uniqueness. Of course, since it was they (or we)

146

who were experiencing the atrocities, they would be subjectively unique. But victims would not have the opportunity to sit and coldly consider, Are more Jews being killed now than in the past? Are Nazi policies different from the policies of Hadrian or Nebuchadnezzar? – no more than would victims of earlier atrocities. Did Jews pursued by Hadrian's armies, seeing the murdered and enslaved all around them, experience less of a crisis? Not for any objective reason. Did those threatened by the crusaders with death if they refused to convert feel that their challenge was less severe? Surely not.

Yet in all earlier circumstances, Jews responded with less of a sense of despair and total collapse than following the Holocaust. To be sure, the book of Lamentations shows the immense pain experienced by the Jews exiled to Babylon. But in this first, immediate response, we already see the value of what was already a traditional theological explanation: "the Lord has afflicted her for the multitude of her transgressions" (Lam. 1:5). Of course, this same explanation, variously elaborated, is repeated throughout Jeremiah, Ezekiel and Second Isaiah, all witnesses to the exile. Crucially, the same theology of punishment *and reward* provides a source of comfort and promise; if sin leads to exile, return to God's ways will leads to restoration. There is a redeemed life following this one, for these Jews a life of children and grandchildren in the rebuilt land of their forefathers.

In the face of the persecutions and losses of the war with Antiochus, the sense of immediate terror was again profound. But, as the last chapter of Daniel and the sixth chapter of 2 Maccabees both show, terror was soon joined by reassuring confidence, for, in their belief, death at the hands of tyrants is insignificant next to future life restored by God. As soon as it became clear that this life is not the full picture, the sufferings of mundane catastrophes, severe and brutal as they might be, could be assigned a more modest place in the figurings of divine justice.

The same would be true following subsequent historical tragedies suffered by the Jews of this new traditional Judaism. If this life is a corridor to the next, if future reward awaits the righteous, then despair cannot be absolute. This is not to suggest that there would be no protest or complaint; see my *Responses to Suffering in Classical Rabbinic Literature* (1995) for ample evidence of such responses. But the protest and complaint was addressed to a living God, a God somehow present in history, a God concerned with the fate of the person, the nation and the world. Precisely because this God was a living force, the protest and complaint mattered. And ultimately, in each case, protest yielded to justification, explanation, even understanding. Earlier theodicies were adapted to new situations. Modifications sometimes gave way to genuine innovations. One way or another, in case after case, religious equilibrium was restored. But not following the Holocaust.

Why not? Not because the Holocaust was objectively unique according to this or another academic definition. Not because those who could not find God after the Holocaust were more severely affected by its horrors than earlier

147

victims (in fact, many who responded by rejecting traditional theologies were not themselves victims at all, and many victims maintained their faith). Rather, it seems to me that the most significant factor which made the Holocaust subjectively unique was the prior loss of belief in death-as-life and life after death. Whatever the particularized responses following earlier catastrophes, one thing remained constant: the belief that there is life beyond death, that this life is not the only stage for the performance of the human–divine drama. But modernity engendered an extreme skepticism with respect to such beliefs. They were too irrational, too primitive. With no belief structure to make sense of mass death – no scheme for relativizing the horrors of this life by reference to a continuing life – modern Jews could not but respond with utter theological despair. To put it in somewhat more provocative terms: *The Holocaust did not precipitate a crisis of faith. A prior crisis of faith made the Holocaust the theological watershed it has become.*

Let me elaborate this claim further. Neil Gillman, in his book *The Death of Death* (1997), documents the rhetoric of religious leaders in modernity with respect to resurrection. He shows that modern Jewish rabbis and theologians, one after the other, rejected the literal claim of bodily resurrection in favor of the survival of the spiritual soul alone after death. Such a belief is consonant with modern Christian attitudes and thus represents Judaism in a far more rationalist mold. But the opinions Gillman records are only those of the religious leaders, individuals who were trying to rationalize Judaism for modernity. Unfortunately, they do not capture the popular belief, and it is that belief which is crucial for my argument.

The question is, what popular opinion served as the motivation for the reinterpretation of traditional Judaism suggested by the Jewish religious leadership? Clearly, most modern Jews did not believe – and could not believe – in the resurrection of the dead. But did they believe in the survival of the soul after death, and how powerful was that belief? Gillman, in private conversation, has shared with me his intuition that the audiences these rabbis were addressing did not, by and large, believe in any survival after death. At best, they had been taught to believe that the soul survived, but this was a rational, intellectual construct, not a heart-felt belief. Life-after-death had no genuine reality for these people. For them, as for so many of us, when life ended there was nothing else.

What the religious leadership was doing, in other words, was rationalizing Judaism to Jews who had a hard time believing traditional Jewish claims. The modern rabbis did not want to give up on Jewish tradition altogether, but they knew that resurrection didn't stand a chance of acceptance among those they addressed, and few of the rabbis believed the doctrine in any case. So they offered what they saw as a rational (or, at least, not contra-rational), modern revision of the traditional doctrine, allowing that the soul of a person survived his or her death. But this is not evidence of popular belief. Some may have believed deeply in the life of the soul after death, some may have spoken this notion without genuinely believing it. But most probably had serious doubts of the veracity of such a claim. This life was all we could demonstrate, all we could be sure of. Therefore, in Cartesian – that is, modern – terms, this life was all there was. Death was an irredeemable state, a nothingness that could never, therefore, ameliorate the injustices or horrors experienced in the here and now.

As I said, it was this modern state of belief that prevailed among most (Western) Jews when that most modern horror, the Holocaust, was perpetrated on the European part of their people. This was the first major tragedy in Jewish history when neither a belief in divinely supervised reward and punishment nor a belief in life after death was held by most Jews who experienced or witnessed the tragedy. Yet the Holocaust was death – six million strong. So utterly unprepared for a horror, an injustice, that ended in the oblivion of death, most modern Jews could make no sense of the Holocaust in theological terms. They therefore found themselves frozen without faith-options. They rejected the living, personal God they had already rejected, finding, in the Holocaust, confirmation of their earlier fears. Without the life-of-death, they could not draw upon the same sources of comfort and meaning as their ancestors. They and we, mostly stuck with death as final death, remained without genuine ways of making sense of the catastrophe of our generations.

The loss of the death-beliefs of our ancestors has changed our religious condition in radical ways. Personally speaking, what I have discovered is that I wish to be a death-agnostic, not knowing what is true of the state of death but refusing to reject traditional rabbinic beliefs without a hearing. Of course, the only place, for me, these beliefs can get a proper hearing will be upon my death. Unfortunately, I do not believe I will be able to report back.

NOTES

1 THE PRESENCE OF DEATH

1 This tradition, as recorded in the Mishnah, probably assumed its present form in the period after the publication of the Talmud. However, given its association with the expression in psalms, and in view of the classical rabbinic views quoted immediately below, it is reasonable to assume that the present opinions, if not the present formulation, were current during the Talmudic age.

2 For a description of Roman practice, see Toynbee 1971: 45–8.

3 An account of the transformation hinted at here may be found in Cohen 1987a.

4 Rubin 1977 and 1997. The problems with Rubin's work are several: (1) He puts his notion of Jewish beliefs before his examination of Jewish practices, assuming that the rabbis speak for and define the practices of all Jews. (2) He assumes that the attributions of rabbinic documents can be trusted, ignoring the documentary setting of individual teachings. (3) He strongly prefers "rational" explanations of what he finds, rarely mentioning more "mystical" possibilities and even then dismissing them quickly. Despite these flaws, there are significant strengths to Rubin's analysis of the rituals, and I often agree with his individual interpretations.

5 The most important studies are referenced in McCane 1992: 237–53. More complete is the bibliography in Rahmani 1994: 264–80.

6 The fact, noted by Lieberman and others (Lieberman 1950), that rabbinic sages and their disciples kept personal written notes, is perfectly consistent with our assumption of a basically oral context. Because of the difficulty of producing books and widespread illiteracy (education was not necessarily synonymous with actual reading), memorization and oral repetition were the most common forms of "textuality" in the ancient world. Thus, even if canonical texts were sometimes written – and even if they were first composed in writing – their authoritative versions (plural) were the lived versions, those spoken by recognized authorities.

7 Walter Ong reports that even in oral societies where verbatim repetition is a goal, success is quite limited. See Ong 1982: 62.

8 It seems to me that the reality described by Lieberman, wherein written notes and oral performances coexisted, is evidence for what I have here described. My critique of Lieberman's picture, as I have suggested above, would be directed against his assumption of the reliability of "oral publication." One need only compare the many differences between the versions of the Mishnah recorded in

the Palestinian and Babylonian Talmuds (see Schachter 1959) to appreciate how imprecise oral preservation and transmission inevitably is. (Undoubtedly, some of the differences may be attributed to errors committed in copying and the like. But many are evidence of the imprecision of oral recitation.) And if this is the case with the work that constitutes the canonical foundation of rabbinic tradition, how much more will it be so with other rabbinic teachings!

9 Reuven Firestone offers a magnificent case study of an oral tradition and its written records in *Journeys in Holy Lands: The Evolution of the Abraham–Ishmael Legends in Islamic Exegesis* (1990). See particularly pp. 15–18 and 153–5.

10 I am confident that, in light of his subsequent studies, Jaffee would view my present modifications of his older piece as a "friendly amendment."

11 Some readers will understand me here to be addressing the scholarly debate represented by Jacob Neusner, on the one hand, and many more traditional historians, on the other. For the specifics of the debate, see Kraemer 1995: 10–15. Here I offer important additional reasons for my preference of Neusner's approach.

12 I explain my dating of each of these rabbinic works in the openings of each chapter of my earlier book, *Responses to Suffering in Classical Rabbinic Literature* (1995).

13 Precisely such an approach is recommended by Eric Meyers (Meyers 1975: 28–42).

14 This is intended to serve as a critique of Eric Meyers' recommendations, referred to earlier.

15 Otherwise, we would have to date Maimonides' codification, the Mishneh Torah, to the early first century because it uses rabbinic Hebrew and describes practices which disappeared with the destruction of the Temple in 70 CE. This would obviously be absurd.

16 I have found Metcalf and Huntington's *Celebrations of Death* (1972) particularly instructive. This volume provides an excellent introduction to the range of anthropological interpretations of death-practices. A. Van Gennep's discussion of funerals in *The Rites of Passage* (1960), pp. 146–65, continues to be illuminating, as does the analysis of Robert Hertz in *Death and the Right Hand* (1960), pp. 31–86; many of my analyses of ancient Jewish practices follow Hertz's lead. See also Ariès 1991.

17 Despite fruitful reference to the sociological-anthropological literature, N. Rubin fails in this way, as I discussed in note 4 above.

2 JEWISH DEATH CUSTOMS BEFORE THE RABBIS

1 Of course, central to the tradition inherited by the rabbis and other Jews of their centuries is the Bible itself. However, the actual beliefs of the authors of biblical books have little relevance for this discussion, because later readers (more probably: listeners) would inevitably have interpreted what they read through the lens of their present beliefs, much as the rabbis would interpret the Deuteronomic promise that "your days and the days of your children be lengthened upon the land" (11:21) as referring to the World to Come. An excellent summary of both the biblical evidence and material evidence for popular beliefs during the same centuries can be found in Bloch-Smith 1992.

2 Copies of Tobit, in Hebrew and Aramaic, were found at Qumran, supporting the suggested date.

3 There is ample evidence of the popular custom of feeding the dead among Israelites and Jews during the centuries; see Bloch-Smith 1992: 122–6 and 141.

4 Ben Sira's "Hymn in Honor of Our Ancestors" (chapters 44–50), comes to conclusion with praises of the High Priest Simon, who served in the early second century BCE. Ben Sira's grandson translated his grandfather's wisdom book to Greek sometime after 132 (that is, after "the thirty-eighth year of the reign of Euergetes;" see the prologue), again suggesting a date of original composition in the early second century BCE.

5 See the discussion of H. May and J. Sanders, in Metzger and Murphy 1991: 169, of the apocryphal books.

6 Written between 168 and 164 BCE; see the discussion of Hartman and Di Lella 1977: 13–14.

7 In *c.*100 BCE; see Goldstein 1976: 62–3.

8 See below, p. 52.

9 Stern, assuming later rabbinic practice to be normative at all times and for all Jews, even lists these references in his index under the heading "sabbath confused with Day of Atonement"! See Stern 1976, vol. 3: 146. This same tendency has led scholars to translate an admittedly difficult term in Qumran's "Damascus Covenant" as saying "No one is to observe a voluntary fast on the sabbath" (xi, 4). Whatever the phrase does say, it does not say this. Such translation, based upon a speculative emendation, is motivated by the assumption that later rabbinic norms controlled earlier Jewish practice as well. This is poor scholarship. On pagan testimonies concerning Jews fasting on the sabbath, see also Feldman 1993: 161–4; and Schäfer 1997: 89–90.

10 I assume here that the Temple Scroll may be dated to the same period as other non-canonical Qumran scrolls. If this is the "book of Hagu" mentioned in the Damascus Scroll, then the Temple Scroll will be relatively earlier than other works found at Qumran. It is also not impossible that the Scroll is an earlier composition, preserved but not produced by the community at Qumran.

11 I am alluding here to scholarly debates over the nature of the Qumran library and its authorship. For a discussion of the different positions, see VanderKam 1994: ch. 3.

12 Thackeray 1926: 375–7.

13 For an example of one immense and elaborate burial cave structure, see Ritmeyer and Ritmeyer 1994: 22–35.

3 EARLY RABBINIC DEATH-PRACTICES

1 For a more detailed history of this period, see Alon 1980: 41–85. Alon's gullible reading of rabbinic texts causes him to misjudge the historical role of the rabbis, but his description of this period is otherwise complete and reasonable.

2 The best comprehensive description and analysis of the Mishnah is Neusner 1981. See also Zlotnick 1988.

3 It was evidently this Mishnaic omission which served as the impetus for the formulation of the "minor" tractate *Semaḥot*. See my discussion of the dating of this tractate in Chapter 1.

4 I put "in the academy" in quotations because I do not mean to make any claim concerning the actual institutional structure of rabbinic learning. Were there actual academies? Only disciple circles? I have no confident opinion on this question. For a discussion of these questions, see Cohen 1987a: 120–3.

5 Or, in the Yerushalmi's version, "in the future to come."

6 These and similar such "violent" symbols are, of course, widespread customs. See, e.g., Malinowski 1948: 49.

7 The view that close relatives of the deceased are somehow tainted by death and must therefore be removed from society is also widespread. See, e.g., Hertz 1960: 38.

8 See also Malinowski 1948: 48; Evans-Pritchard 1956: 144ff.; and Parker 1983: 35.

9 See previous note.

10 See my discussion, in the latter part of Chapter 2, of the anointing of Jesus on the third day following his death. The Gospel report and the Mishnah speak to a common phenomenon, and a common interpretation is therefore in order.

11 A similar belief is attested among the Kol of India who, according to Van Gennep's report, place corpses on the ground "so that the soul should more easily find its way to the home of the dead;" see Van Gennep 1960: 151.

12 Thus according to the version of this Mishnah quoted in y. Berakhot 3:1. In any case, Mishnah Ketubot 4:4 clearly assumes that flute-players and wailers are essential parts of the funeral; see below.

13 Roman religion also required that the dead be buried outside of cities. In fact, this regulation was codified in the Twelve Tables. See Toynbee 1971: 48.

14 Of course, the impurity of the dead is far from a uniquely Jewish belief. See Parker 1983: 35; Metcalf and Huntington 1972: 81–2. The deceased are a singularly powerful source of impurity in Zoroastrianism; see my discussion near the beginning of Ch. 7.

15 The exemption from prayer is mentioned explicitly in the Bavli's version of the Mishnah, as printed. Other versions omit it, suggesting that it is a later addition.

16 The same is true elsewhere. See Hertz 1960: 38; Metcalf and Huntington 1972: 82.

17 Because of this Talmudic tradition, Lieberman interprets "standing and sitting" as a ritual which takes places while leaving the grave; see Lieberman 1955: 533–4.

18 See Soferim 10:6, and M. Higger's comment in his edition (1937), p. 20.

19 Women were also hired to wail and play double-pipes (what I have translated from the Hebrew as "flutes") at Roman funerals; see Toynbee 1971: 45. The practice of hiring female specialists to sing laments continues to this day in Greek villages; see Metcalf and Huntington 1972: 47.

20 Metcalf and Huntington have an important discussion of emotional reactions to death. As they point out, it should not be taken for granted that death evokes a sad response, at least not officially. In some societies, mourning is appropriate, in some joy and even ecstasy is called for, and in some various combinations of sadness and joy are legislated; see Metcalf and Huntington 1972: ch. 2. To provide just one familiar example: it is common at Catholic funerals that those assembled be enjoined to be glad that the deceased has come to his or her peaceful rest with Jesus.

21 Metcalf and Huntington discuss the various functions of noise at funerals, observing, importantly, that loud noises were not nearly so common in pre-industrial society, making such noisy rituals much more noticeable; see Metcalf and Huntington 1972: 64–8.

22 I will have occasion to build further on the parallel between the rituals of the mourner and the perceived fate of the deceased below and in later chapters. Concerning this parallel, Hertz comments: "There is a complete parallelism between the rites which introduce the deceased . . . into the company of his ancestors, and those which return his family to the community of the living;" and further: "Mourning, at its origin, is the necessary participation of the living in the mortuary state of their relative, and lasts as long as the state itself." See Hertz 1960: 64 and 86.

23 See Toynbee 1971: 50–1.

24 The catalogue of objects found at Beth Shearim is typical; see Mazar 1973: 210–19, and Avigad 1973: 183–90 and 198–209.

25 There is a long history of secondary burial among the various peoples in Palestine. See Meyers 1971: 3–11.

26 Metcalf and Huntington's discussion of secondary burial is found in ch. 5 of *Celebrations of Death* (1972); the present quote is found on p. 97. Their interpretation largely follows that of R. Hertz in *Death and the Right Hand* (1960).

4 EARLY EXPANSIONS AND COMMENTARIES

1 For a discussion of questions concerning the dating of the Tosefta, see Kraemer 1995: 66 and nn. 1 and 2 there.

2 Malinowski rightly uses this latter practice to exemplify his observation that mortuary customs throughout the world are often astonishingly similar. See Malinowski 1948: 48.

3 See Metcalf and Huntington 1972: 47, 49 and 54–5. The Bara of Madagascar lay the deceased out in the women's huts before burial, in a manner reminiscent of the Toseftan practice described here; see p. 47.

4 Hertz 1960 reports that, in the practice of the native peoples of Borneo, the mourner is also separated by a ban from the rest of the community. In practice, this means that the mourner may not leave his village or pay visits to others; the deceased's closest relatives must stay at home and may not respond to questions from visitors (who are, in the first place, not supposed to visit in any case). Despite differences, both the conceptual and practical parallels with early rabbinic practice are obvious. See p. 38.

5 For the same or similar symbolic gestures in other societies, see Malinowski 1948: 49.

6 The Mishnah knows of the overturning of beds – but only as an individual opinion – in connection with the fast of the Ninth of Av, the commemoration of the destruction of the Jerusalem Temple. If this day is, among other things, an occasion for mourning the destruction, then the association of overturning beds and mourning is already established here. As I discuss following, the Mishnah also knows that the first meal for mourners is to be taken on overturned couches. Nevertheless, it is in the Tosefta for the first time that this is mentioned as a general mourning practice for the entire *shiva* period.

7 And see, again, Hertz 1960: 64, 86.

8 Such parallels between death rites and marriage rites are also noted elsewhere. See Hertz 1960: 80–1.

9 It is noteworthy that the common Roman practice – cremation – is seen by the rabbis of the Tosefta as the fate awaiting the wicked.

5 JEWISH DEATH-PRACTICES IN REALITY

1 A good general description of burial practices during this period can be found in McCane 1992: 41–55.

2 For a concise and reasoned discussion of the interpretation problem, see Rahmani 1994: 25–8.

3 I discuss the catacombs at Beth Shearim for two reasons: (1) because it is the largest Jewish burial site from these centuries, and (2) because of the unmistakable association of at least two of its caves with the contemporary rabbinic community. But Beth Shearim may be understood as illustrative; the burial customs in evidence here are repeated time and again at other sites from the same period. For a range of those sites, see Satran and Greenberg 1997.

4 This is the number which have already been excavated and reported. Isaiah Gafni, of Hebrew University, tells me that more caves are now being excavated, some in areas that were previously not known to contain such caves. Gafni reports that the new caves he has seen are similar to those excavated earlier.

5 An excellent example may be found in the caves in the Amaziah forest, south of Beth Guvrin.

6 Compare the photograph of this figure, found in Mazar 1973: pl. VIII, #3, with the heads depicted in Ariès 1981: illustration for p. 340 (found between pp. 428 and 429).

7 The conclusion that these burial places were visited regularly is supported by the nature of objects found in the catacombs as well. Despite rather complete robbing of the tombs, leaving a *relatively* small quantity of such objects, quantities of lamps, pottery, and the like were still discovered in the catacombs; see Mazar 1973: 210–19 and Avigad 1973: 183–90 and 198–209.

8 On the relationship between the practice of secondary burial – popular but not mandatory at Beth Shearim – and belief in resurrection, see Meyers 1971: 71–92.

9 A detailed report on this catacomb, numbered 20 by archaeologists, is found in Avigad 1973: 95–114. Detailed discussion of the sarcophagi is found on pp. 137–77.

10 See Toynbee 1971: pls. 44, 45, 83 and 85. Plate 28 shows an example of a marble ash-chest with the same feature. See also Ferri 1933: figs. 295, 492–5 and 500. Goodenough's collection of photographs includes an example of the top of a Roman tombstone which clearly represents the façade of a temple, gabled roof, acroteria and all; see Goodenough 1988: pl. 25.

11 See Boethius and Ward-Perkins 1970: pls. 13, 20, 107 (represented on coins) and 112. See also figs. 156, 159, 163 and 170.

12 My colleague Robert Stieglitz tells me that he has photographs in his collection showing Roman funerary monuments from Sicily (probably 1st–2nd cent.) built in the shape of altars with horns. Though ancient Israelite altars would not have

been a model available to 3rd-century Jews, such monuments may have been. If so, the present proposal is that much more plausible.

6 JEWISH DEATH-PRACTICES IN EARLY BYZANTINE PALESTINE

1 Later Jewish practice preserved the requirement that a person prepare for death. Particularly amusing, but still illustrative, is the testimony of Glückel of Hameln who, upon experiencing sea-sickness for the first time, thought she was dying. Accordingly, she immediately began to recite confession for her sins (*vidui*), provoking her husband's unsympathetic laughter; see Glückel 1977: 101–2. Custom in medieval Christian Europe similarly demanded that a person prepare for his or her death; see Ariès 1991: 5–18.

2 See the comments of Margulies 1972: 82.

3 The question recorded below in the same context, "If you are mourners, why have you eaten meat and drunk wine?" refers not to the mourning period but to the period before burial. The use of the term "mourner" is imprecise.

4 I have not found a report of archaeological support. However, such coincidental testimonies in the midrash have often found material support. For example, the Yerushalmi, at M.Q. 3:5, 82c, knows of Beit Shearim as a particularly popular burial place. Of course, archaeology has long since shown this to be the case, as we saw in the previous chapter.

5 Admittedly, the formulae of the marriage blessings are nowhere outlined in the Yerushalmi. But the version recorded in the Bavli claims to have been formulated early in the Talmudic period, and whatever the customary wording of the blessing as repeated in Palestinian circles, there can be no doubt that both communities inherited a tradition for these blessings from a common set of tannaitic masters. Moreover, I think it improbable that the redemptive promise of marriage was perceived in the Babylonian rabbinic tradition but not in the Palestinian.

6 Admittedly, the Gospel and the rabbinic record contradict one another concerning whether death is assured *on* the third day or *after* the third day. It seems to me, however, that the apparent contradiction is actually insignificant; they agree that the third day is the significant one, and for similar reasons. One could imagine that these two practices represent divergent interpretations of a common tradition which taught something like "death is not sure until the third day." Does this mean until the third day has arrived or until it is completed? The Talmud knows of this ambiguity in ancient Jewish expression and several times debates whether "until" means to include the last stated period or not.

7 Also at Sanhedrin 6:9, 23d and M.Q. 1:5, 80d.

8 M.Q. has "what they say in the line [of comforters when leaving the burial];" this seems to be a scribal error. Lieberman 1955 notes that some early versions have "house of the mourner" for "synagogue." He judges, however, that this is an emendation based upon later practice. See p. 49 n. 54.

9 On the growth of the synagogue, see Cohen 1987b: 160–1. On the increase in rabbinic involvement in the synagogue during the same period, see Levine 1992: 207–8.

10 We should recall that it was the custom in the ancient Mediterranean world,

including the society in which the rabbis lived, to drink wine diluted. At a minimum, one part water for one part wine was called for. Thus ten cups would have included a quantity of alcohol equivalent to or less than five of our cups – not an insignificant amount but far less than we might have thought at first.

11 Which is not to be confused with life in "the World to Come." In classical rabbinism, as in late Second Temple Judaism, "the World to Come" refers to the world following the messianic age and the resurrection of the dead. There is no technical term for the life of the soul after death but before resurrection.

7 LAW AS COMMENTARY

1 For detailed histories of the Jews of Babylonia, see Neusner 1972 (abbreviated from Neusner 1965–70); and Gafni 1990. On the dating of the success of the rabbis in "rabbinizing" other Jews, see Cohen 1987a: 221.

2 In Kraemer 1995, I argue that the Bavli came to closure sometime during the reign of the Persian king Khusrau, which began in 531 and lasted for forty-eight years; see pp. 152–3. For different reasons, Jack Lightstone arrives at precisely the same conclusion; see Lightstone 1994: 272–6.

3 For a detailed discussion of this part of the sugya, see Kraemer 1990: 133–7.

4 See Rabbinovicz 1867/1976, ad loc.

5 Or, in the printed text, "for mourners." See Rabbinovicz 1867/1976, ad loc.

6 To be absolutely correct, about the *not yet* deceased. In the Talmudic context, R. Ashi asks the eulogizers what they *will say* on the occasion of his death.

7 The translation of this last verse is that of M. Jastrow. See Jastrow 1992: 483, "haninah."

8 See *The Soncino Talmud, mo'ed*, v. 4, p. 187 n. 1.

9 See Jastrow 1992: 378.

10 This is the name found in the standard printed edition. Variants are found in manuscripts. The "actual" author of this teaching makes no difference in the current analysis.

11 The belief that the decomposition of the flesh causes pain is shared by other peoples as well; see, for example, Hertz 1960: 47.

12 See Hertz's discussion of the same belief held elsewhere, Hertz 1960: 46.

13 Van Gennep 1960 lists placement on or burial in (it is not clear which) a wicker mat as one of the "rites of separation" which are common at funerals among various peoples; see p. 164. It is not clear whether such a practice, now lost, is attested here.

14 This comment of the deceased explains the discovery in Jewish graves from this period of, among other household items, cosmetic spoons and other make-up utensils, perfume bottles, bracelets, earrings and other jewelry. See Mazar 1973: 210 and Avigad 1973: 215–16.

15 The phrase "after seven days," found in the printed editions, is a later addition.

16 Rationally inclined individuals have sought to deny the literal meaning of this text. The Soncino translation has "mourners," that is, those who are comforted. Maimonides paraphrases: "who has no mourners to be comforted" (see *Mishneh Torah*, Laws of Mourning 13:4). How, after all, could the deceased be comforted? The answer is obvious, as I shall discuss below, and there is no doubt that such rationalists have been blinded to the simple meaning of this text by their rationalism.

17 If, in the belief of a given people, the spirit survives death, then the belief that the spirit mourns the death can hardly be unexpected. For illustration of this connection, see Malinowski 1948: 155.

8 THE BAVLI INTERPRETS THE MOURNER

1 For the banning of the mourner from the rest of the community, see Hertz 1960: 38.

2 See Milgrom's discussion of "leprosy" as punishment, Milgrom 1991: 820–3.

3 See m. San. 2:1; m. Middot 2:2; t. San. 4:2 and b. San. 19a.

4 Rav expresses the same opinion. But, because Rav is considered to have tannaitic status (that is, his authority is deemed equivalent to that of the teachers of the Mishnaic period), he is permitted to contradict tannaitic traditions. Therefore, the gemara doesn't concern itself with resolving the contradiction with his opinion.

5 We may note that this appears to contradict the simple meaning of the Torah's narrative, according to which death seems not to be intended from the beginning but is punishment for the sin of eating from the forbidden tree. For discussion of the place of death in the divine calculus of reward and punishment, see Urbach 1979: 420–36.

9 POST-TALMUDIC DEVELOPMENTS IN JEWISH DEATH-PRACTICE

1 By "contemporary traditional," I mean of either Orthodox or non-Orthodox Jews who subscribe to what they believe to be "traditional" law in their practices relating to the dead. In fact, these practices are traditional from the perspective of recent modernity. They are, however, different in significant respects from the practices defined in Talmudic literature.

2 In this chapter, when I speak of "Talmudic," I intend the entire classical rabbinic literature, from the Mishnah through the Bavli. When I mean to distinguish Talmudic tradition from the earlier tradition, I shall make this distinction clear in context.

3 Wieseltier 1998 collects many of the sources relevant to such a history. However, his work is not – nor does it claim to be – a history of medieval Jewish death-practices.

4 The middle, responsive line of kaddish – *"yehay shmai rabba . . ."* – is known in the Talmud only in connection with synagogue ritual and other liturgy; see Ber. 3a; Ber. 57a; and Shab. 119b. Because only this line is quoted in the Talmud, it is impossible to know whether the text actually refers to what is later known as kaddish. On the history of the development of kaddish, see Elbogen 1993: 80–4 and Wieseltier 1998.

5 The custom of some later Jewish communities excludes the participation of women from the graveside ritual. I know of no such exclusion in any Talmudic or geonic writing.

6 See Gafni 1981.

10 A PERSONAL THEOLOGICAL POSTSCRIPT

1 Katz 1994: 65–100. Katz, with proper caution, avoids specific conclusions with respect to the proportion of Jews killed by the Romans during the Bar Kokhba revolt and subsequent persecutions. He "conjecture[s] that the death rate was lower than that experienced during the Holocaust," but he is not sure; neither am I. See pp. 80–1. In any case, it is clear that Jewish death rates in certain earlier catastrophes were not *so* different as to make the Holocaust obviously unique. See my comments below.

REFERENCES

Alon, G. (1980) *The Jews in Their Land in the Talmudic Age*, trans. G. Levi, Jerusalem: Magnes Press.

Ariès, P. (1981) *The Hour of Our Death*, New York: Alfred A. Knopf.

Avigad, N. (1957) "Excavations at Beth Shearim, 1955," *Israel Exploration Journal* 7/2.

—— (1973) *Beth She'arim*, vol. 3, New Brunswick, N.J.: Rutgers University Press.

Avi-Yonah, M. (ed.) (1975) *The Encyclopedia of Archaeological Excavation in the Holy Land*, London: Oxford University Press.

Avni, G., and Greenhut, Z. (1994) "Akeldama: Resting Place of the Rich and Famous," *Biblical Archaeology Review* 20/6 (November/December): 36–46.

Berger, P. (1967) *The Sacred Canopy: Elements of a Sociological Theory of Religion*, New York: Anchor Press, Doubleday.

Bloch-Smith, E. (1992) *Judahite Burial Practices and Beliefs about the Dead*, Sheffield: JSOT Press.

Boethius, A., and Ward-Perkins, J. B. (1970) *Etruscan and Roman Architecture*, Harmondsworth: Penguin.

Bowker, J. (1991) *The Meanings of Death*, Cambridge: Cambridge University Press.

Boyarin, D. (1994) *A Radical Jew: Paul and the Politics of Identity*, Berkeley and Los Angeles: University of California Press.

Cohen, S. J. D. (1987a) *From the Maccabees to the Mishnah*, Philadelphia: Westminster Press.

—— (1987b) "Pagan and Christian Evidence on the Ancient Synagogue," in L. Levine (ed.), *The Synagogue in Late Antiquity*, Philadelpia: American Schools of Oriental Research.

Elbogen, I. (1993) *Jewish Liturgy: A Comprehensive History*, trans. R. Scheindlin, Philadelphia: Jewish Publication Society.

Evans-Pritchard, E. E. (1956) *Nuer Religion*, New York and Oxford: Oxford University Press.

Feldman, L. (1993) *Jew and Gentile in the Ancient World*, Princeton, NJ: Princeton University Press.

Ferri, S. (1933) *Arte Romana Sul Danubio*, Milano: Popolo d'Italia.

Finkelstein, L. (1969) *Sifri Deuteronomy*, Berlin, 1939; reprint New York: Jewish Theological Seminary of America.

Firestone, R. (1990) *Journeys in Holy Lands: The Evolution of the Abraham–Ishmael Legends in Islamic Exegesis*, Albany: SUNY Press.

160

Gafni, I. (1981) "Reinterment in the Land of Israel: Notes on the Development of the Custom," in I. Levine (ed.), *The Jerusalem Cathedra*, vol. 1, Jerusalem: Izhak ben Zvi Institute.

—— (1990) *Yahadut bavel bitequfat hatalmud*, Jerusalem: Zalman Shazar Center.

Gillman, N. (1997) *The Death of Death*, Woodstock, Vt: Jewish Lights.

Glückel (1977) *The Memoirs of Glückel of Hameln*, trans. M. Lowenthal, New York: Schocken.

Goldstein, J. (1976) *I Maccabees*, The Anchor Bible 41, New York: Doubleday.

Goodenough, E. (1953) *Jewish Symbols in the Greco-Roman World*, vol. 1, New York: Pantheon.

—— (1988) *Jewish Symbols in the Greco-Roman World*, ed. and abridged by J. Neusner, Princeton, NJ: Princeton University Press.

Hartman, L., and Di Lella, A. (1977) *The Book of Daniel*, The Anchor Bible 23, Garden City, N.Y.: Doubleday.

Hertz, R. (1960) *Death and the Right Hand*, trans. Rodney and Claudia Needham, Glencoe, Ill.: Free Press.

Higger, M. (1937) *Soferim*, New York: Debe Rabbanan.

Horovitz, H. S. and Rabin, I. A. (1970) *Mekhilta de-Rabbi Ishmael*, Jerusalem: Wahrmann.

Horowitz, H. (1966) *Sifri debe Rab*, Jerusalem: Wahrmann.

Jaffee, M. (1992) "How Much 'Orality' in Oral Torah? New Perspectives on the Composition and Transmission of Early Rabbinic Tradition," in *Shofar* 10/2 (Winter).

Jastrow, M. (1992) (reprint) *A Dictionary of the Targumim, The Talmud Babli and Yerushalmi, and the Midrashic Literature*, New York: Judaica Press.

Katz, S. (1994) *The Holocaust in Historical Context*, vol. 1, New York: Oxford University Press.

Kloner, A. (1980) "The Necropolis of Jerusalem in the Second Temple Period," Ph.D. dissertation, Hebrew University.

Kraemer, D. (1990) *The Mind of the Talmud*, New York: Oxford University Press.

—— (1991) "The Formation of Rabbinic Canon: Authority and Boundaries," *Journal of Biblical Literature* 110/4: 613–30.

—— (1995) *Responses to Suffering in Classical Rabbinic Literature*, New York: Oxford University Press.

—— (1996) *Reading the Rabbis: The Talmud as Literature*, New York: Oxford University Press.

Levine, L. (1992) "The Sages and the Synagogue in Late Antiquity," in L. Levine (ed.), *The Galilee in Late Antiquity*, New York and Jerusalem: The Jewish Theological Seminary of America.

Lewin (= Levin), B. M. (1931), *Ozar hageonim, tractate Mashqin*, Jerusalem: Hebrew University Press Association.

—— (1938) *Ozar hageonim 8, tractate Ketubot*, Jerusalem: Mossad Harav Kook.

Lieberman, S. (1950) *Hellenism in Jewish Palestine*, New York: The Jewish Theological Seminary of America.

—— (1955) *Tosefta kifeshuta, mo'ed*, vol. 4, New York: The Jewish Theological Seminary of America.

—— (1965) "Some Aspects of Afterlife in Early Rabbininic Literature," in *Harry*

Austryn Wolfson Jubilee Volume, Jerusalem: Journal of the American Academy of Religion.

Lightstone, J. (1994) *The Rhetoric of the Babylonian Talmud, Its Social Meaning and Context*, Waterloo, Ont.: Wilfred Laurier University Press.

McCane, B. (1992) "Jews, Christians, and Burial in Roman Palestine," unpublished Ph.D. dissertation, Duke University.

Malinowski, B. (1948) *Magic, Science and Religion*, Garden City, N.Y.: Free Press.

Margulies, M. (1972) *Vayyiqra (Leviticus) Rabbah*, 5 vols., Jerusalem, 1953–1960; reprint Jerusalem: Wahrmann.

Mazar, B. (1973) *Beth She'arim*, vol. 1, New Brunswick, N.J.: Rutgers University Press.

Metcalf, P., and Huntington, R. (1972) *Celebrations of Death*, 2nd edn, rev., Cambridge: Cambridge University Press.

Metzger, B., and Murphy, R. (eds) (1991) *The New Oxford Annotated Bible with the Apocryphal/Deuterocanonical Books*, New York: Oxford University Press.

Meyers, E. (1971) *Jewish Ossuaries: Reburial and Rebirth*, Rome: Biblical Institute Press.

Meyers, E. (1975) "The Use of Archaeology in Understanding Rabbinic Materials," in Fishbane, M. and Flohr, P. (eds) *Texts and Responses*, Leiden: E.J. Brill.

Milgrom, J. (1991) *Leviticus 1–16, The Anchor Bible 3*, New York: Doubleday.

Moore, C. (1985) *Judith, The Anchor Bible 40*, Garden City, N.Y.: Doubleday.

Neusner, J. (1965–70) *A History of the Jews of Babylonia*, Leiden: Brill.

—— (1972) *There We Sat Down*, New York and Nashville: Abingdon Press.

—— (1981) *The Evidence of the Mishnah*, Chicago: University of Chicago Press.

—— (1983) *Judaism in Society: The Evidence of the Yerushalmi*, Chicago: University of Chicago Press.

Niditch, S. (1996) *Oral World and Written Word: Ancient Israelite Literature*, Louisville, Ky.: Westminster John Knox Press.

Ong, W. (1982) *Orality and Literacy: The Technologizing of the Word*, London and New York: Methuen.

Parker, R. (1983) *Miasma: Pollution and Purification in Early Greek Religion*, Oxford: Clarendon.

Paxton, F. (1990) *Christianizing Death*, Ithaca and London: Cornell University Press.

Rabbinovicz, R. (1867, repr. 1976) *Diqduqei soferim*, New York: M. P. Press.

Rahmani, L. Y. (1994) *A Catalogue of Jewish Ossuaries in the Collections of the State of Israel*, Jerusalem: The Israel Antiquities Authority and the Israel Academy of Sciences and Humanities.

Raphael, S. P. (1994) *Jewish Views of the Afterlife*, Northvale and London: Jason Aronson.

Ritmeyer, L., and Ritmeyer, K. (1994) "Akeldama, Potter's Field or High Priest's Tomb," *Biblical Archaeology Review* 20/6 (November/December): 22–35.

Rubin, N. (1977) "A Sociological Analysis of Jewish Mourning Patterns in the Mishnaic and Talmudic Periods" (Hebrew), unpublished Ph.D. dissertation, Bar-Ilan University.

—— (1997) *qez hahayim (The End of Life)*, Tel Aviv: Hakkibutz Hameuchad.

Satran, S., and Greenberg, R. (1997) "Burial Caves of the Roman and Byzantine Periods in Western Galilee," *'Atiqot* 33, Jerusalem: Israel Antiquities Authority.

Schachter, M. (1959) *Hamishnah bebavli uviyerushalmi*, Jerusalem: Mosad Harav Kook.

Schäfer, P. (1997) *Judeophobia: Attitudes toward the Jews in the Ancient World*, Cambridge, Mass.: Harvard University Press.

Shanks, H. (ed.) (1975) "Horned Altar for Animal Sacrifice Unearthed at Beer-Sheva," *Biblical Archaeology Review* 1/1 (March).

Stern, M. (1976) *Greek and Latin Authors on Jews and Judaism*, 3 vols., Jerusalem: Israel Academy of Sciences and Humanities.

Thackeray, H. St. J. (1926) *Josephus*, The Loeb Classical Library, London and New York: William Heinemann and G. P. Putnam's Sons.

Toynbee, J. M. C. (1971) *Death and Burial in the Roman World*, Ithaca: Cornell University Press.

Urbach, E. (1979) *The Sages: Their Opinions and Beliefs*, trans. Israel Abrahams, Jerusalem: Magnes Press.

van der Horst, P. W. (1991) *Ancient Jewish Epitaphs*, Kampen: Kok Pharos.

VanderKam, J. (1994) *The Dead Sea Scrolls Today*, Grand Rapids, Mich.: Eerdmans.

Van Gennep, A. (1960) *The Rites of Passage*, reprint, Chicago: University of Chicago Press.

Vermes, G. (1987) *The Dead Sea Scrolls in English*, 3rd edn, London: Penguin.

Wieseltier, L. (1998) *Kaddish*, New York: Knopf.

Zlotnick, D. (1966) *The Tractate "Mourning,"* New Haven and London: Yale University Press.

—— (1988) *The Iron Pillar – Mishnah*, Jerusalem: n. p.

INDEX